THE COMEDY OF COMPUTATION

THE COMEDY OF COMPUTATION

Or, How I Learned to Stop Worrying and Love Obsolescence

BENJAMIN MANGRUM

STANFORD UNIVERSITY PRESS
Stanford, California

Stanford University Press
Stanford, California

© 2025 by Benjamin Mangrum. All rights reserved.

No part of this book may be reproduced or transmitted in any form or by any means, electronic or mechanical, including photocopying and recording, or in any information storage or retrieval system, without the prior written permission of Stanford University Press.

Library of Congress Cataloging-in-Publication Data
Names: Mangrum, Benjamin, author.
Title: The comedy of computation, or, How I learned to stop worrying and love obsolescence / Benjamin Mangrum.
Other titles: Comedy of computation
Description: Stanford, California : Stanford University Press, 2025. | Includes bibliographical references and index.
Identifiers: LCCN 2024056779 (print) | LCCN 2024056780 (ebook) | ISBN 9781503642621 (cloth) | ISBN 9781503643109 (paperback) | ISBN 9781503643116 (ebook)
Subjects: LCSH: Computers—Humor. | Technology—Humor. | Computers in literature. | Technology in literature. | American wit and humor—History and criticism. | American literature—Themes, motives.
Classification: LCC PS169.C66 M35 2025 (print) | LCC PS169.C66 (ebook) | DDC 810.9/356—dc23/eng/20250204
LC record available at https://lccn.loc.gov/2024056779
LC ebook record available at https://lccn.loc.gov/2024056780

Cover art and design: David Drummond

The authorized representative in the EU for product safety and compliance is: Mare Nostrum Group B.V. | Mauritskade 21D | 1091 GC Amsterdam | The Netherlands | Email address: gpsr@mare-nostrum.co.uk | KVK chamber of commerce number: 96249943

TO GRADY

Contents

	THE ONE AT THE BEGINNING	1
1	THE ONE ABOUT RACE AND ROBOTS	25
2	THE ONE ABOUT BEING GENERIC	55
3	THE ONE ABOUT AUTHENTICITY	94
4	THE ONE ABOUT COUPLES	129
5	THE ONE WITH ALL THE ABSURDITY	167
	THE ONE AFTER THE END	191
	Acknowledgments	199
	Notes	203
	Index	255

THE ONE AT THE BEGINNING

DURING APPLE'S FIRST PUBLIC DEMONSTRATION of the Macintosh in January 1984, Steve Jobs lifted the computer out of a bag to exhibit its lightness and portability. He demonstrated the machine's user interface and some of its visual capabilities and then said, "We've done a lot of talking about Macintosh recently. But today, for the first time ever, I'd like to let Macintosh speak for itself." In a synthetic voice, the computer spoke: "Hello, I'm Macintosh. It sure is great to get out of that bag." The audience laughed, and then the computer took a dig at one of Apple's chief rivals: "I'd like to share with you a maxim I thought of the first time I met an IBM mainframe. NEVER TRUST A COMPUTER YOU CAN'T LIFT."

Apple had incorporated speech technology from Samsung that allowed the computer to voice a script that also appeared on its monitor. The computer's "first time ever" spoken communication was a series of dry jokes. These jokes, while prosaic and not very funny, surprised casual observers in 1984. Few expected the machine to speak, much less for it to voice dry humor at the expense of a competitor. The episode illustrates how corporations have used comedy throughout the commercial history of computing to present the computer as a sociable technology. Humor enabled the audience to view the Macintosh as an ordinary object, not some inhuman or overly complicated tool. It was as if Apple's marketing team thought the computer first needed to become *comic* before consumers would regard it as *personal*.[1]

The Macintosh's jokes were a surprise to those who thought that comedy and computation had nothing to do with one another. In some ways, this was not an unreasonable assumption. *Comedy*, after all, names a spontaneous reaction like laughter but also dramatic forms like romantic comedies and sitcoms. Comedy has other meanings, too: madcap performances, absurdist humor, and banal nonsense. It is often the province of jokers and stooges. The term *computation*, in contrast, conjures up mathematics, logic, and cold rationality. It trades in binaries and inflexible processes. Especially when automated through a computer—my focus in this book—computation may seem to be the antithesis of comedy.

Yet this book shows how comedy and computation in fact have a long-standing, if somewhat fractious, relationship. Like Felix Ungar and Oscar Madison in Neil Simon's *The Odd Couple* (1965), comedy and computation are an incongruous pairing—a coming-together of opposites that iterates across the social history of technology. This coming-together often responds to widely held perceptions about the hazards of computing. For example, Apple's 1984 marketing campaign for the Macintosh was tailored to its coincidence with the dystopian year depicted in George Orwell's *Nineteen Eighty-Four* (1949). Orwell's novel imagines a totalitarian regime of surveillance through advanced technology. Popular films like Stanley Kubrick's *2001: A Space Odyssey* (1968) and George Lucas's *THX 1138* (1971) had similarly depicted computers as menacing machines that sacrifice human well-being while coldly executing their programming. Rather than dismissing these associations, the marketing around the first Macintosh took advantage of them. The company's now-famous Super Bowl commercial invoked Orwell's novel directly, as well as other popular dystopian imagery, but then it insisted that Apple's technology would hail a different kind of future, one characterized by freedom, creativity, and decentralization.

The Macintosh's dry humor during its first public demonstration tapped into this countercultural vision of spontaneity and social well-being. Rather than portraying the machine as a scientific instrument or a serious business technology, the jokes suggested that nonspecialists could understand and work with the computer. Comedy became a sign of the machine's ordinariness.[2] By performing its facility with comedy, the Macintosh appeared to be compatible with the everyday wants and needs of ordinary people. Comedy thus shifted the cultural meaning of the machine, transforming it from a tool of technocratic elites into an individual user's amusing conversation partner.

The transformation of the computer through comedy is a recurring theme in the pages that follow. I will show that one of the most common mechanisms for this transformation is the imagery of *coupling*—that is, forming some sort of attachment with or through computers. Coupling is, of course, one of the primary images of social harmony in romantic comedies, but many other kinds of comedy also trade on the symbolism of coupling: for example, a union with the divine or the divine's adjunct is the principal image in Christian comedies like Dante's *Comedia* (c. 1309–20). We can also think about television strategies like laugh tracks or an actor's significant glance at the camera as a kind of coupling, a joining together with the audience through shared norms that cue a comic response. Coupling, in these instances, is figuratively and affectively social.[3]

One of my aims is to analyze the kinds of sociality imagined when writers, filmmakers, software engineers, and technologists couple comedy with computation. When these producers of culture and technology bring comedy together with computing, they present images of social life in an age of advanced technology. As I have already suggested, these images often involve the transformation of the computer through comic plot structures, conventions, attitudes, and modes of thinking. Yet computational technologies have produced wide-ranging transformations of their own—a phenomenon that I describe as *becoming computational*—and one of this book's central claims is that comedy has provided a generic form for the experience of these sweeping transformations.

Let me offer another example from a 1958 article in *Forbes* magazine examining the uneven and often-awkward assimilation of computing machines within corporate life in the United States. The *Forbes* reporter describes this assimilation by drawing out an analogy to a then-popular romantic comedy: "In his Broadway comedy success, *The Desk Set*, playwright William Marchant spent 130 minutes poking fun at the mutual problems that come up when electronic brains and human beings try to accommodate one another. Judging from Marchant's situations, neither thinking humans nor thinking machines are going to have a very easy time of it."[4] This reference to *The Desk Set* illustrates the common midcentury sentiment that people and computers are somehow mismatched; that their union within corporate life is an incompatible coupling; and that, as a result, each will need to "accommodate" the other. Rather than depicting a "contest" between men and women, as Susanne Langer describes the "rhythm" of comedy, or between older and younger generations, as Northrop Frye contends, the *Forbes* reporter imagines a screwball comedy between "thinking humans" and "thinking machines."[5] The members of this odd couple need to change for the sake of one another. Comedy thus provides a culturally legible form for making sense of the conflicted experience of computing technology.

If Apple's use of comedy to make the computer seem personable illustrates one rationale for the coming-together of comedy and computation, the *Forbes* article attests to a different set of pressures forging this union. Starting with the Census Bureau's use of a computer called UNIVAC in 1952 and accelerating with the delivery of IBM's 700 series of computers in 1955, many members of the professional-managerial class found themselves in an ongoing relationship with computational technology.[6] In the first decades of the public life of the computer, accountants worried they would lose their jobs; researchers feared they would be replaced by machines; and managers wondered if computers would supplant their expertise in coordinating business functions. The "computer revolution" often felt like a coup against white-collar work.[7] Yet the *Forbes* article illustrates how, amid this epoch of social and professional crisis, various forms of comedy regularly provided resources for imagining how humans and computers might "accommodate one another."

While Apple's marketing of its first Macintosh flirts with a kind of techno-utopianism in which ordinary people find that advanced technology is compatible with their interests, the *Forbes* article presents the relationship between people and computing in the image of comedic conflict. As the reporter puts it, neither "thinking humans nor thinking machines are going to have a very easy time of it." The journalist's most immediate point is that labor strife and manufacturing costs might prevent corporations from assimilating computers more widely. But the journalist is also making a lighthearted joke that people, after coming into proximity to computers, might wish to *decouple* their professional lives from the technology. The article's understanding of comedy allows for the possibilities of both attachment and negation, a final union or a messy breakup.

The possibility of decoupling from technology can, of course, lead in noncomic directions. In fact, many dystopian narratives take oppositional postures toward computing to signify their criticisms of a society oriented around hyperefficiency and advanced technology. This is precisely the sentiment in a little-known short story by Henry Slesar titled "Examination Day," first published in *Playboy* in 1958. Slesar's story imagines a future in which every twelve-year-old must undergo an IQ test by a computer. Children with high IQs are deemed a threat to the state and eliminated. Large computing systems support the state by overseeing a rational but oppressive social order, which might be challenged if human intelligence were allowed to thrive among the masses. The story thus imagines the dystopian future that could result if the United States were to follow its postwar path of coupling an administrative state with the inhuman logic of advanced technology.

Slesar's story focuses on the examination of a twelve-year-old boy named Dickie. Dickie's parents explain to him that, on his examination day, he will drink a peppermint-flavored chemical that ensures he cannot lie. When Dickie arrives for the exam, a "multidialed computing machine" poses questions to the boy, and then the narrative abruptly—almost incidentally—notes the boy's execution after it is determined that he has a high IQ. Dickie's parents receive a call from the Government Educational Service notifying them that their son's "intelligent quotient has exceeded the government regulation." The Educational Service representative then asks the parents to specify whether they "wish his body interred by the government or . . . a private burial place." If they choose the former, the representative explains, the "fee for government burial is ten dollars."[8]

Slesar's story takes the child as a kind of moral norm violated by the computer's cold rationality. When Dickie sits before the computer, "lights appeared on the machine, and a mechanism whirred. A voice said: 'Complete this sequence. One, four, seven, ten . . . .'"[9] In contrast to the curiosity of the child, the computer only poses standardized questions. It is only interested in *what*, not *why*. The machine appears incongruous but in a noncomic way: the whirring of the mechanism seems remote, as though occurring somewhere deep in the computer, while the machine's surface is depicted only through inscrutable lights and a simulated voice. This depiction of the computer contributes to the story's broader suggestion that automation is the twin of authoritarian politics.

"Examination Day" exemplifies what I take to be one of the two prevailing ways scholars have tended to think about the role of the computer in postwar American culture: the technology serves as a symbol of tyranny and conformity. (This is, of course, the inverse of the second common view, which is that the computer is a tool of productivity and futuristic prosperity.) Slesar's story illustrates how the former view regularly depends on the figurative status of the child—a symbolic dynamic that appears in other works from the period, such as Kurt Vonnegut's short story "Harrison Bergeron" (1961) and films like Herman Hoffman's *The Invisible Boy* (1957) and Robert Butler's *The Computer Wore Tennis Shoes* (1969). Hoffman's film imagines a supercomputer that manipulates its creator, Dr. Tom Merrinoe (Philip Abbott), by capturing and then threatening the life of his son, Timmie (Richard Eyer). Like Slesar's story, Hoffman's film presents the child as an "obligatory token of futurity" in postwar culture.[10] The child assures readers and audiences that a hopeful future may be achieved, at least insofar as threats to that future are avoided or suppressed.[11] Lee Edelman argues that the future-oriented symbol of the child often has a kind of cultural double in the postwar era: the "future-negating queer."[12] In Alfred Hitchcock's *North by Northwest* (1959), for instance, the "tellingly fashion-conscious" henchman Leonard (Martin Landau) poses a threat to "heterosexual love" and the starring "reproductive Couple."[13] According to Edelman, queer figures stand in opposition to an interconnected series of normative social images: the child, the couple, the future, and human compassion more generally.

It is striking how often the computer serves in a role like Leonard's within the science fiction, suspense, and dystopian films of the twentieth century. HAL in Kubrick's *2001: A Space Odyssey* is an obvious example, with its uncanny voice and decision to kill astronauts for the sake of its programming.[14] Slavoj Žižek offers a philosophical version of this image when he describes "the feeling of something unnatural" when seeing children "talking with a computer and obsessed with the game, oblivious of everything around them."[15] Žižek imagines the computer has somehow corrupted the child. Such a perspective presents the computer as both abnormal and antisocial—a perversion of the natural order of things.

My point is that even as queerness often served in the twentieth century as a marker of the antisocial, many contemporaneous representations of computing drew on this and other models of antisociality to depict how the computer might compromise the flourishing of society. Oftentimes, the antisociality attributed to computers becomes uncanny, as in Slesar's story, but the antisociality assigned to the computer just as often generates various kinds of comedy throughout the twentieth and twenty-first centuries. For instance, in John Hersey's satirical novel *The Child Buyer* (1960), a representative of the fictional United Lymphomilloid Corporation attempts to transform a highly intelligent child named Barry Rudd into a "calculating machine."[16] The company hopes to program Barry and other computer-children to solve problems that would allow humanity "to leave the earth," a research program enigmatically referred to as the "Mystery" (210). Most of the corporation's plans are vague and nonsensical, yet many adults embrace these plans because of their equally vague and nonsensical devotion to being "pro-business."

Wissey Jones, the corporation's representative, explains that the children undergo several phases of conditioning before they become like computing machines. After having their memories wiped and being entirely secluded for weeks, the children are "fed an enormous amount of data that will be needed in finding episodic solutions to certain problems in connection with the Mystery" (207). The children then have "major surgery, which consists of 'tying off' all five senses" (208). The "specimens" become incapable of interacting with anyone or anything except data sets. In effect, they are transformed into powerful but hyperfocused thinking machines.

Hersey's novel uses this ridiculous scenario to satirize postwar American politics, its obsession with economic utility, and the nation's attitudes toward education. Many of the characters represent absurd versions of these postwar viewpoints through what one reviewer dismissed as "low comedy relief."[17] For example, Jones convinces a group of senators convened to adjudicate Barry's fate that the transformation of children into computing machines is a "thoroughly patriotic scheme" (35). A senator named Skypack gives voice to some of the most farcical ideas in the novel, particularly when objecting to Barry's reticence to be transformed into a machine. Skypack views this reticence as a form of antisocial behavior, prompting him to remark, "I think he's a silly, conceited boy. Probably going to be a homo" (249). For Skypack, the refusal to submit willingly to the national interest signifies a form of queerness.

The senator's anxiety about Barry being "queer" mirrors the novel's angst about a future in which corporations will "eliminate all conflict from the inner lives of the purchased specimens . . . to ensure their utilization of their innate equipment at maximum efficiency" (107, 204). This strange and unwieldy phrasing exhibits how the corporation's interests are not in fact aligned with society's. The novel's satire invokes the antisocial connotations of queerness only to transfer them to the United Lymphomilloid Corporation's scheme of converting children into computers. In other words, the senator's angst about a queer boy mirrors the novel's angst about an uncanny computational future in which education becomes only another form of data processing. This satire trades on homophobic ideas about the violation of children, displacing that threat from homosexual men onto a corporation that reveres the productivity of computing machines.

Hersey's comic novel shares with Slesar's "Examination Day" a sense of the computer as the technology of a future in which human experience has been debased and individuality has been redescribed as socially threatening. In both works of fiction, this process occurs as a simple inversion: the rise of the computer corresponds to something like the loss of the child, as though a society that wants "reliable and matter-of-fact calculating machines" must trade away its Barrys and Dickies as part of its bargain with advanced technology (Hersey 207). These and many other works of postwar American culture worry that a future of computers may enjoy greater productivity but will squander its innocence and curiosity. While children represent an embattled human future, computing machines serve as proxies for a threatening, uncanny dystopia of instrumental thinking. This is one form of a recurring dynamic in which anxieties about the obsolescence of human creativity and professional judgment often figured the computer as a symbol for an antisocial future. Many comic depictions of this future imagine that the rationality of the machine bends first toward tyranny but finally breaks down into absurdity. Others imagine comedy, especially satire, as a kind of humanistic capability that resists the tyranny of a computational future.

This second possibility appears in Greg Benford's short story "The Scarred Man" (1970). In Benford's story, multinational corporations have automated the world economy through a vast network of computing machines. The result of the global adoption of the computer is that "three quarters of the [world's] population" have become unemployed. A character named Nigel recounts how this process created a "white collar squeeze": "Machines could do all the simple motor function jobs and then they started making simple executive decisions, like arranging routing schedules and production plans and handling most of the complaints with automatic problem-solving circuits. That didn't leave any room for the ordinary pencil pusher, and they started to wind up in the unemployment lines."[18] Benford's story imagines that the automation of labor has cascading effects throughout the global economy.[19] The characters view the tipping point of this disaster as the moment when computing machines, not white-collar workers, became responsible for "executive decisions."

The character named Nigel explains to the story's narrator that the now-unemployed professional class spends its time conspiring against computers. As he says about one group of managers, "Everybody likes to make fun of computers, you know, and they were telling jokes about them, figuring up schemes to make them break down and all that." The narrator remarks that the reason managers take computers as comic objects is because "everyone is afraid of them." "Yes," Nigel responds, "I suppose that's it. Fear."[20] Many of the story's characters respond to the threat of obsolescence by alternating between gallows humor and strategic mockery. This turn toward comic derision expresses a professional anxiety: it arises from what Barbara Ehrenreich memorably calls the "fear of falling," the threat of downward mobility caused by the loss of class status. Ehrenreich argues that "professional and managerial people" specifically fear the obsolescence of their *knowledge* because their "livelihoods depend on some combination of intellect and drive."[21]

I will track the many ways that comedy has offered resources for managing this fear of falling, particularly when computers imperil the type of labor called "knowledge work."[22] This use of the comic harkens back to claims made by eighteenth-century philosophers like Francis Hutcheson and Immanuel Kant, who viewed "aleatory wit and linguistic invention [as] culturally privileged skills."[23] According to twentieth- and twenty-first-century versions of this view, comedy signifies a special domain of knowledge in its own right, one that certain classes of people invoke to keep the threat of obsolescence at bay. Some writers and thinkers examined in this book even take comedy as a philosophical marker of the limits between human and machine intelligence. We will have occasion to interrogate these ideas in subsequent chapters, but for now, I only want to note how anxieties about human obsolescence are sometimes only a proxy for an imperiled sense of class status. It is legitimate to worry about the loss of creativity or the denigration of human judgment that comes with the algorithmization of, well, everything.[24] But I will also show how that worry can perform a sleight of hand in which the culturally privileged values of knowledge workers come to stand in for humanistic value itself. From this latter vantage point, obsolescence is only another name for the fear of falling.

Some readers may feel they've seen this movie before. After all, as Kathleen Fitzpatrick has noted, similar dynamics regarding class status structured debates about the obsolescence of literature and the "death of print" after the Second World War. Many postwar writers depicted the rise of television and other electronic media as leading to literature's obsolescence and, by extension, the debasement of modern society. Fitzpatrick shows that this worry was often driven by forms of cultural elitism. Those who lamented literature's loss of cultural centrality typically conflated that loss with narratives of social decline: "technologies of mechanization have produced concerns about dehumanization; technologies of image production have been greeted with concerns about illusion and ideology; and technologies of interconnection have confronted concerns about the loss of the individual."[25] Such anxieties allowed writers to portray literature as an alternative resource for humanizing the self, clarifying its relation to the social order, and restoring the dignity of the individual. This use of obsolescence, as Fitzpatrick puts it, makes the anxiety "less a material state than a political project."[26]

Comedy, too, has often served as a symbolic bulwark against the computerization of work. This particular use of comedy is bound up with normative conceptions of human sociality (typically symbolized, as I've already suggested, through innocent children or romantic coupling). This kind of comic response to the experience of becoming computational is bound up with the more general vicissitudes of professional identity amid the cyclical disruptions within postwar institutions for white-collar labor. Anxieties about advanced computing systems often become conflated in postwar culture with the unsettling of social norms about authority and expertise.

For example, in her poem "A Sigh for Cybernetics" (1961), Felicia Lamport satirizes midcentury concerns about the development of powerful "electronic brains." Lamport cites a warning from the influential computer scientist Norbert Wiener, who claims that "computing machines [are] now working faster than their inventors" and "may go out of control and cause widespread destruction." Lamport responds to this news item with the following verse:

> These mechanized giants designed for compliance
> Exhibit their open defiance of science
> By daily committing such gross misdemeanors
> That scientists fear they'll make mincemeat of Wieners.[27]

The use of Wiener's surname sets up a pun on "mincemeat" while also playfully calling attention to the gendered character of the discourse about obsolescence. Despite being "designed for compliance," computers threaten to make obsolete the scientists that the poem genders through the metonym "Wieners." The computers refuse to submit to men who insist on unflinching obedience. The computer again signifies antisocial disruption, although Lamport uses these connotations to deliver lighthearted criticism of the patriarchal norms in science and technology.

The roles assigned to computers in postwar culture often generate forms of comedy that are inextricably linked to anxieties about the coming obsolescence of knowledge work. Obsolescence thus serves as an important proxy for the deeply conflicted attitudes toward computing technology in postwar American culture. Across its cultural history, the computer has signified negative forms of sociality but also the possibility of connecting to others and accommodating ourselves to the changing character of work. Within this multifaceted cultural position, the computer seems to deserve ridicule but also solemn admiration; it shores up normativity but also queers the normal; it threatens disruption but promises ease and efficiency; it supports authoritarianism while undermining professional authority. These clashing views of the computer can yield the kind of uncanny horror we see in stories like Slesar's "Examination Day." But the trope of the odd couple, together despite their conflict, can also be very funny—a dynamic often used to figure humans and computers in popular films, such as the supercomputer TARS and Joseph Cooper (Matthew McConaughey) in Christopher

Nolan's *Interstellar* (2014), Phil (Adam Devine) and his smartphone AI in Jon Lucas and Scott Moore's *Jexi* (2019), and the eponymous human and robot in Jim Archer's *Brian and Charles* (2022). These films find pleasure in a social world in which machines behave like jealous lovers or petulant partners.

Just as the social expectations placed on computing are often conflicted, so, too, are the forms of comedy shaping the experience of the technology. What I am calling the comedy of computation is not a unified or univariate category of experience. Yet, at the same time, I am arguing that the spectrum of comedy's norms and conventions gives a generic structure to the phenomena examined in the following pages. I argue that this genericity provides *forms* for making a computationally mediated social world seem more habitable, even as it also provides *tools* for criticizing and objecting to that world. This is part of comedy's power: it can be "transideological," to borrow Linda Hutcheon's description of irony.[28] Laughter can be a sign of racist superiority; comedies can habituate us to the status quo or affirm normative arrangements of the social; comic plot structures can portray those arrangements as desirable and logical outcomes of human striving. Yet comedy can also challenge, deflate, and ridicule authority. It can reorient us within familiar experience and prompt us to question what we take for granted. Comedy contains multitudes, and most of them hate one another. It is a genre of conflicted experiences, often even when those conflicts resolve in the much-maligned "happy endings" of romantic comedies.

Such versatility justifies another major claim in this book. I describe the comedy of computation as a genre of experience, which is in part a way of saying that comedy has served as a phenomenological model for the experience of becoming computational. I recognize this claim requires some unpacking. First, let me say more about the phrase *becoming computational*, which often serves as a shorthand in science and technology studies for "the assimilation and coupling of different social forces with computers."[29] This phrase connotes the muddling of abstraction and ordinariness that lies at the heart of my argument. *Becoming computational* refers to major structural changes that seem to make personal agency irrelevant, but it also captures how some of our most intimate experiences of everyday life have been changed by computing technology.

Consider, for instance, how the ordinary experience of shopping has been transformed by computing. Computational technology at checkout counters gathers data from credit card use.[30] Once a clerk or consumer uses the card, the machines and cloud-based software programs execute tasks that no longer involve human agents. The checkout machine relays the location, time of day, items purchased, and additional data to other machines that aggregate the information and then create a "spatial history of consumption" that other software programs utilize.[31] These programs may monitor for fraud, evaluate credit worthiness, track consumer behavior, or feed the aggregate data into marketing profiles.[32] As ordinary payment methods have become computational, the mundane routines of consumerism have become assimilated within vast systems of data analysis.[33] This instance of *becoming computational* seems fundamentally impersonal, despite the fact that it begins with an individual's mundane activity.

Another version includes how American education has increasingly become computational, not only in its pedagogical methods (a device in every child's hands) but also in its constitutive imagery.[34] The paradigmatic expression of this change is the idea that education ought to inculcate "computational thinking," an idea that originated in the 1980s but underwent a renaissance in the first decade of the twenty-first century after the computer scientist Jeanette Wing wrote an influential essay arguing for the importance of computational thinking to secondary education.[35] Wing describes computational thinking as "a fundamental skill for everyone, not just for computer scientists. To reading, writing, and arithmetic, we should add computational thinking to every child's analytical ability." Wing offers several "everyday examples" of this newly urgent set of skills: "When your daughter goes to school in the morning, she puts in her backpack the things she needs for the day; that's prefetching and caching. When your son loses his mittens, you suggest he retrace his steps; that's back-tracking. At what point do you stop renting skis and buy yourself a pair?; that's online algorithms. Which line do you stand in at the supermarket?; that's performance modeling for multi-server systems."[36] The search for mittens is not *like* back-tracking but *is* back-tracking; deciding whether to buy skis is not *similar to* online algorithms but *is* online algorithms. The lack of simile implies that computation is not merely a tool for disciplinary science but captures the fundamental character of everyday life.

It is possible that Wing's point is not to redescribe human social behavior as computational but only to reorient how we think about computing and its relation to familiar experience. If she is being metaphorical, her metaphors invite us to see the ordinary in different ways by extending computation beyond the hardware and software of present-day technology. But as she says in a different essay, computational thinking "does not require a machine."[37] Computational thinking anticipates a future in which the skills and technologies of the present will become obsolete, and students will be prepared by adopting habits of mind suited to the frontiers of computing. Why place so much emphasis on this or that coding language when, in twenty years, that language, many related technical skills, and their corresponding machinery may no longer be used in computer science? Educators, so the thinking goes, should frame their work as the inculcation of certain intellectual dispositions. *Computation* describes the character of these dispositions.

While Wing focuses on educational practices, her "everyday examples" illustrate how many of the basic rubrics we use for understanding social experience have become computational. The computer has become more than a tool for everyday use; it has become an image for the ordinary itself. Computational thinking imagines the transformation of social life by learning how to reason like, but also process information through, computing machines. In this way of thinking, computing is not merely a meal ticket for undergraduates in a digital economy; it is a repository of metaphors for imagining the social.

By positioning the algorithms running in the background of grocery purchases alongside Wing's "everyday examples" of computational thinking, I am trying to establish how the process of *becoming computational* includes seemingly incommensurate scales of experience: the abstract and the ordinary, the impersonal and the everyday, the inhuman and the intimate, the convenience of mediated transactions and the complexity of data processing. The notion that these disparate scales have been "coupled" with computers further illustrates why comedy has often served as a phenomenological model for these sweeping transformations.[38] It's as though when we come to describe how computing has affected our social lives, we cannot "resist the seduction of an analogy," as Sigmund Freud once put it.[39] The image of two people coming together provides a *form* for the joining-together of computers and the social world. The idea of *coupling* contains the possibility of intimacy but also frames failure as a kind of alienation, a fall into disaffection that often arises with the experience of becoming computational. Coupling may not be the only metaphor for figuring a union with technology, but I hope to show in the following pages that it has been a historically pervasive and culturally potent one.[40]

I have been claiming that comedy provides a generic form for the experience of becoming computational, but I suspect that yoking together *genre* and *experience* may strike some readers as equally incongruous as the pairing of *comedy* and *computation*. This may be because the term *genre* often signifies an abstract taxonomy—a bloodless categorization of culture—while *experience* may bring to mind the individual, singular, or irreducibly particular.[41] Joining the two might strike some as implausible or contradictory: Can the singularity of experience be categorized in abstractions without distorting its distinctive qualities? If experience were somehow generic, would such experience effectively be artificial—a kind of compromised way of being in the world?

I am keeping these possibilities available by describing the cultural phenomena in this book as a *genre of experience*, but the phrase is also a distillation of my view that genres can operate as phenomenological models: they provide structures for thought and feeling; they set up interpretive expectations not only for narratives and media but also for being in the world.[42] Genres are by no means the only phenomenological models we use to make sense of ordinary life, but I hope to show in this book that comedy has been an especially important (if not also critically underappreciated) model for the experience of becoming computational.

This approach contributes to the reworking of the concept of genre that many other scholars have undertaken.[43] At one time, critics would ascribe a "nucleus" of content to classic genres like tragedy and comedy.[44] Jacques Derrida characterized this view as the "law of genre," but Alastair Fowler and many others long ago dispelled the illusion that genres are fixed or essential categories.[45] Most current theories view *genre* in ways that are historically variable and contextually sensitive. According to this perspective, we do not need to tether comedy to some archetypal structure (e.g., Northrop Frye's "mythos of spring") or explain every chuckle as the manifestation of the unconscious (e.g., Freud's so-called relief theory of humor).[46] Genres do not conform to universal explanations. Alexander Leggatt expresses this view with a simple dictum: "There is no such thing as comedy, an abstract historical form; there are only comedies."[47]

Such a view expresses what I describe as a nominalist theory of genre. The basic tenet of this view is that genres are social and historical categories of description that lack a core identity. Appealing to a canon of referents cannot yield a stable or consistent set of criteria for determining membership in the genre. There is no timeless reality called Comedy, no essence to which we can appeal when determining what counts and what doesn't. I share this view, and because of it, I am not interested in policing comedy's boundaries or positing some central "nucleus" shared by all instances of the comedy of computation. I often make comparative claims across media. I don't fret about, say, moving from an analysis of romantic comedy to a continuous point about the construction of humor. To my mind, the nominalist theory of genre allows for this kind of comparative or transverse analysis, because otherwise unrelated speech acts and media phenomena can nonetheless share usages of the comic.[48] Genres include various and even conflicting cultural forms.

There is, however, a school of thought that goes a step further than the approach I have been describing. This school—let's call it strong nominalism—would claim that, because only particular instances of a genre exist, we can only make intelligible claims about a small number of individual artifacts within a narrowly defined historical period. Strong nominalism is skeptical of diachronic comparison and categorically opposed to aesthetic claims not particular to a medium. Fowler expresses this perspective in the following way: "Statements about a genre are statements about the genre at a particular stage—about Zn' not Z. Concerning a genre of unspecified date, or within very wide chronological limits, correspondingly little can be said."[49] Noël Carroll criticizes a closely related sentiment in film studies, which "supposes that each medium has a unique nature and that with that nature goes an accompanying series of laws."[50] According to this school of thought, the integrity and cogency of any analysis of genre depends on limiting that genre to discrete coordinates of medium, place, and period.[51]

According to strong nominalists, we would only be able to make cogent claims about, say, a small number of comic films from a certain decade and within a certain studio system. This strong nominalist view is expressed in Fowler's claim that we can only make statements "about Zn' not Z." The prime symbol in this formulation implies that an instance of a genre should be understood like a differentiated function that cannot be coidentical with another instance.[52] Since we can't say anything about "Z," critics ought to confine themselves to specific coordinates in their analysis.

I agree that genres are not timeless universals, but this fact does not require us to structure genre criticism around overly narrow particularities. We would soon fall into an infinite regress of needing ever more granular and particularistic divisions between different iterations. My view is that we can instead approach genres as living models for experience and examine homologies across instances of these models. *The Comedy of Computation* is an extended exemplification of this approach. For instance, the titles of my chapters frame particular homologies through the comic idiom "Have you heard the one about . . . ?"[53] The idiom is always an instance of a structure, a repeatable form that varies in content while also allowing for modes of collective identification.[54] The television show *Friends* (1994–2004) draws on the same comic idiom as my chapter titles in naming its episodes: "The One with the Sonogram at the End," "The One with the Thumb," "The One with George Stephanopoulos." In *Friends*, "The One with . . ." figures each episode as another instance in an ongoing conversation or comic exchange among the cast of characters. The titles invite the audience into these social attachments, as though the serialization of episodes were a formal way of letting the audience in on an inside joke. Only good friends would laugh at "The One with the Thumb," much less know how to parse the title's meaning. This use of the idiom creates a sense of intimacy from genericity, as if the reproducibility of generic form were also a token of idiosyncrasy.

The use of the idiom in *Friends* creates a version of what Lauren Berlant calls an "intimate public," a paradoxical form of collective identity in which strangers share "emotional knowledge" about "a broadly common historical experience."[55] The idiom provides a generic form for the experience of the series, as though each episode were formulaic, perhaps even mechanical in its repetition of a structure. But the idiom also signifies affinity, the possibility of sharing "emotional knowledge" with strangers. The idiom thus captures a paradox about comedy in the age of technological reproduction: it traffics simultaneously in abstraction and affinity, the impersonal and the intimate, the generic and the idiosyncratic.

Being the instance of a comic idiom can deny or imperil identification—a central concern in my first two chapters. The first examines comic portrayals of robots, automatons, and other automated technologies from the eighteenth century to the present. I show that racialized tropes about labor and social identity are constitutive parts of these comic figures. The second chapter examines the generic as an aesthetic category central to the experience of becoming computational. I use the phrase *being generic* to refer to (a) social anxieties about the loss of distinctiveness associated with computational media but also (b) the promise of sharing terms of legibility with others—that is, of being classified as or recognizing discourse in terms of a *genre*. I argue that these competing registers of the generic operate as aesthetic touchstones in computational forms of sociality.

The second chapter's claims about genericity introduce a problem I take up from a different perspective in the third chapter—namely, how the mediating work of computers and the commodification of experience by many tech corporations interact with what intellectual historians call an ethics of authenticity. *Authenticity* has a notoriously vague meaning. It can refer to empirical questions about whether an artifact is a forgery. It can also name a cultural and philosophical ideal—something akin to what Polonius advises in *Hamlet* (c. 1601): "To thine own self be true." The empirical question and the moral ideal are both operative in the public life of computing technology. A muddled version of both surfaces in debates about the nature of consciousness in science fiction and AI research. Do AI systems have an inner life? Is their consciousness genuine?

The third chapter explores the origins of authenticity as a moral ideal and philosophical problem in the cultural history of computing. I show how the counterculture and youth movements were two important sources for the moral importance attributed to authenticity within the early cultures of computing. But I also look back to the much older development of an ethics of authenticity—a philosophical and cultural discourse that developed across several centuries—and its ongoing weight in cultural attempts to grapple with the disruptions of the postwar economy and modernity more generally. I show how these different sources of authenticity animate many satirical portrayals of the tech industry.

These first three chapters revolve around the racial, economic, and philosophical contradictions that arise as people, corporations, and social forces couple with computational technology. These contradictions also surface in the fourth chapter's analysis of a staple figure in comedy: the couple. This figure has served as a surprising but consistent image for the public experience of computing. I have already mentioned William Marchant's *The Desk Set*, which I analyze in the fourth chapter alongside its film adaptation, starring Katharine Hepburn and Spencer Tracy. In both versions, a computer called "Emmy" serves in a role analogous to the "obstructing characters" that Northrop Frye examines in his contemporaneous *Anatomy of Criticism* (1957). The computer begins as an obstruction to happiness and a harbinger of the obsolescence of knowledge workers, but Emmy eventually morphs into a partner in the couple's union.

The computer's role in the couple varies across literary and filmic culture, but there have also been some common patterns since the Second World War. To understand these patterns, I examine several popular films, including *The Honeymoon Machine* (1961) and *Weird Science* (1985), showing how the trope of coupling with computers revises long-standing ideas about comedy as a model of the good life. As the computer becomes part of the couple—or even as people couple with computers, as in films like *Control Alt Delete* (2008) and *Her* (2013)—the resulting union presents an image of a "pragmatically free society."[56] The fourth chapter considers the notions of freedom and flourishing contained within such images.

The final chapter explores how absurdist comparisons between humans and computers function in the cultures of science and technology. One form of this absurdism diminishes human thought and labor through hypothetical comparisons with computing machines, such as: *It takes our computer X number of seconds to complete a certain task. If Y number of humans were to complete the same task, it would take this assembled group Z number of days/months/years*. These comparisons appear often in press releases from scientific institutions and the tech industry. I argue that this rhetorical framing relies on what Jerry Palmer calls the "logic of the absurd," and I show how novels like Olof Johannesson's *The Tale of the Big Computer* (1968) and Ishmael Reed's *Yellow Back Radio Broke-Down* (1969) narrativize this scalar absurdism and imagine its consequences for political organization. I describe this political imaginary as *computopia*, a realm in which computers accomplish an efficient and rational ordering of social life. Works like Johannesson's and Reed's novels imagine computopia as a means for considering whether democracy has become obsolete in an age of computation.

The potential obsolescence of democracy is central to the film referenced in my subtitle: Stanley Kubrick's *Dr. Strangelove or: How I Learned to Stop Worrying and Love the Bomb* (1964). Kubrick's subtitle was a playful allusion to the proliferation of self-help manuals in an era of atomic warfare. There was no central "I" in the film. Rather, it presented various personae characteristic of an organizational and technological moment. The irony of Kubrick's subtitle thus provoked a kind of existential question: what does it mean to have a self—or even to care about the "I" and its worries—when nation-states have the technological capacity for global destruction? Kubrick's film takes up this question in subtle and darkly comic ways, but one of its central concerns is to portray the feelings of absurdity that arise for many who occupy official roles within a fully rationalized system of national defense, which paradoxically enables—and, in fact, may even encourage—the entirely irrational destruction of the world. Institutional authorities in the film create the very conditions that undermine the human flourishing they claim to protect.

Dr. Strangelove considers this absurdity through the premise of a complicated military bureaucracy that manages the nuclear arsenal of the United States. A rogue Air Force general named Jack D. Ripper (Sterling Hayden) implements a military order called Plan R, a deterrent strategy in which a lower-level general can order a retaliatory nuclear strike if the standard chain of command has been disrupted. General Ripper initiates Plan R without cause or authorization, sending a fleet of bombers carrying nuclear warheads to attack dozens of targets in the USSR. He then closes all communications channels outside of his base. The orders cannot be rescinded because the planes have switched to a coded communications channel. Despite coordinated attempts by the US and USSR to shoot down the planes and break General Ripper's code, one plane makes it through Soviet defenses and sets off the USSR's own global deterrent system, the Doomsday Machine, which is designed to wipe out biological life on the surface of the planet.

Computers serve a key role in this system of mutually assured destruction. As Dr. Strangelove (Peter Sellers) explains to the US president, Merkin Muffley (also played by Sellers), the Doomsday Machine is connected to "a gigantic complex of computers" that activates the weapon under "a specific and clearly defined set of circumstances." This "complex" places control of the weapon outside human operators, ostensibly to avoid enemy interference or moral reservations from USSR military personnel.[57] In other words, even as Plan R relies on bureaucratic rationality to deter Soviet nuclear attacks, the Soviets' own system of deterrence ensures the same outcome through computing. The safeguards of impersonal decision-making and computerized automation create the very war each was designed to avoid.

Kubrick's film depicts political systems unsuited to the scale of devastation that can be wrought through their technological capabilities. Plows, writing, and gun powder are all technologies, but not until atomic warfare was it conceivable for technology to devastate the planet.[58] Many argue that we have now created yet another technology capable of global destruction: artificial intelligence (AI).[59] In an influential thought experiment, the philosopher Nick Bostrom imagines an AI that tries to achieve an otherwise laudable goal through means that pose an existential threat to humanity. In one version of this thought experiment, an AI has been tasked to solve a particularly difficult mathematical problem. It appropriates the Earth's resources to build supercomputers to facilitate its calculations, thus devastating the global economy. Or, in a more comic version, an AI designed to manufacture paperclips realizes "it would be much better if there were no humans because humans might decide to switch it off. Because if humans do so, there would be fewer paper clips."[60] The AI's programming *wants* paperclips. Can we guarantee that such technological wants are compatible with human flourishing? Are our institutions capable of managing the existential and societal threats made possible through computing technology?

The following pages consider a spectrum of answers to this line of thought, but there is not a lot of ambiguity in Kubrick's film. After the Doomsday Machine has been activated, the president and Dr. Strangelove discuss a plan for a few hundred thousand Americans to survive in mine shafts. President Muffley says, "Well, I would hate to have to decide who stays up and who goes down." Strangelove answers, "Well that would not be necessary, Mr. President. It could easily be accomplished with a computer. And a computer could be set and programmed to accept factors from youth, health, sexual fertility, intelligence, and a cross section of necessary skills." Strangelove's arm then rises in a *Sieg*

Heil salute, a gesture that the former Nazi scientist has been suppressing for most of the film.

It is of course ironic that he fails to suppress this salute after proposing a rational plan for solving the unintended consequences of another rational plan. The implication is that Strangelove's unflinching faith in technocratic objectivity is the mirror image of the fascist's absolute faith in a single political personality. The computer, in this view, becomes a machine for facilitating what Hannah Arendt famously calls the banality of evil, the ordinary pencil-pushing bureaucracy that facilitates atrocity in the modern era.[61] A technology ostensibly promising a better future turns out to betray the very possibility of a future.

I make no prognostications in this book. I am not predicting we will all be exterminated for the sake of paper clips or sorted into mine shafts after a computationally orchestrated apocalypse. Instead, I try to understand the kinds of sociality imagined in these and many other comic images. I also hope to show why we ought to take seriously cultural work that depicts the competing wants and conflicting social imperatives involved in the experience of becoming computational. The coupling of computers with social life not only produces novel forms of attachment—new ways of imagining life together—but also ambivalence, disaffection, uncertainty, and oddly pleasurable forms of being unsocial. These incongruities are not design flaws in the technology, errors that better engineering can address. The genre of experience examined in this book instead reveals that the disjunctions and contradictions that appear throughout the computer's cultural history are in fact constitutive features of becoming computational. As the classic comic verb *accommodate* implies, this genre attempts to make habitable the conflicts of this lived experience. Of course, there may soon be breakthroughs in areas like quantum computing that shatter our assumptions about what counts as *computational*. I will show how the social experience of becoming computational orbits this always-unfinished speculative possibility: that more and better is still to come, that ever-closer intimacies will soon be made available, and that the forms of experience from the past and present will become increasingly and inextricably obsolete.

1 THE ONE ABOUT RACE AND ROBOTS

DURING THE LATE NINETEENTH CENTURY, many canning facilities in the Pacific Northwest depended on Chinese immigrants to remove the heads, fins, tails, and guts of salmon. These laborers would then slice the fish and pack them in tin cans. In 1883 alone, Chinese immigrants "packed 630,000 cases, roughly 43 million pounds."[1] But the industry began to change during the first decade of the twentieth century, when the Smith Cannery Machines Company invented an automated canning device, which it marketed as the "iron chink" (figs. 1 and 2).[2] The machine "replaced Asian laborers to fill, seal, and label cans automatically," thus lowering production costs and increasing each facility's output.[3] The slur in the name for the canning device frames automated technology through a racial conception of labor. This marketing strategy assumes that "the Chinese contractor" does the work of canning, so the automated machinery that replaces this workforce warrants a correspondingly racialized name.[4]

This canning device illustrates a cultural template called techno-Orientalism, the differentiation of Asia from the West by associating Asian identity with technology.[5] One of the primary tropes in techno-Orientalism is the "dehumanized, machine-like Asian laborer," a mere cog in a "horde of robotic factory workers."[6] This trope presents Asian

FIGURES 1 AND 2. Advertisements for the "Iron Chink," originally published in the *Pacific Fisherman*. Duncan A. Stacey, *Sockeye and Tinplate: Technological Change in the Fraser River Canning Industry, 1871–1912* (Victoria, BC: British Columbia Provincial Museum, 1982), 50. Images courtesy of the BC Archives.

people as "always already mechanized," as though their contributions to industrial technology were a natural by-product of their identity.⁷ Paradoxically, this racist trope mirrors the *treatment* of migrant laborers in the Pacific Northwest. A system of inhuman routines and grueling physical conditions for Asian migrant workers in the early twentieth century led Carey McWilliams to refer to the agricultural industry's "factories in the field."⁸ Asian migrant laborers were described as machines, but they were also treated as replaceable parts in the machinery of food production.

Advertisements for the "iron chink" similarly imagine Asian laborers as expendable machines, easily replaced with an automated model. The advertisement uses the racial slur for comedic effect, likely in the hope that the machine's nickname would capture the attention of the white owners of canning facilities. This advertisement illustrates a pattern in the cultural history of robots, automatons, and other automated machines in which this technology becomes comic through its proximity to racial discourse.⁹ I show how these figurative links set up expectations for many of the perceived threats to identity associated with computational technology. In contrast to the idea that the computer breaks with the cultures of technology that precede it, the robotic figures examined in this chapter show how many templates for the experience of becoming computational derive from much earlier assemblages of technology, race, and images of social life.

RACE AND REMEDIATION

Servitude attaches to the robot like virtue to nature.¹⁰ There are several historical reasons for these figurative attachments. Techno-Orientalism and the agricultural industry's "factories in the field" were two sources. Another was the tendency among some modern philosophers to view automated machines as metaphors for articulating ideas about freedom and social identity.¹¹ For example, René Descartes presents a version of this metaphorical register in his "Treatise on Man" (1662). For Descartes, the soul and the body are two distinct entities. God created both but endowed the body with an essentially mechanistic nature: "I suppose the body to be nothing but a statue or machine made of earth, which God forms with the explicit intention of making it as much as possible like us. Thus God not only gives it externally the colors and shapes of all the parts of our bodies, but also places inside it all the parts required to make it walk, eat, breathe, enabling it to imitate all those functions which seem to proceed from matter and to depend solely on the interacting movements of our organs."[12] For Descartes, the body is a kind of automaton guided by the soul. He even compares the body to "clocks, artificial fountains, water mills and other such machines which . . . seem to move of their own accord in various ways."[13] He argues that God's greater artistry is the only difference between automated machinery and the human body. In contrast to the mindless forces that drive machinery, the soul gives human beings consciousness and the capacity to control most features of their body's machinery. It is only the soul that elevates human beings above servitude to the mechanistic laws of cause and effect.

Mary Poovey has shown how such early modern views shifted during the nineteenth century as the machine became a common image for the efficient, productive society. Whereas Descartes views the body as a "machine made of earth," the later development of this metaphor considers the aggregation of individuals as an economic, political, or societal machine. Poovey provides several explanations for this development, but an especially important factor was the rise of the factory system. This system became a new source of social metaphor, generating not only wealth but also ideals of rationalized collective life. Charles Babbage, the mathematician and inventor of a tabulating machine often cited as a forerunner to the computer, viewed the efficient machine as epitomizing an ideal system "in which all working parts were subordinated to the productivity of the whole, discipline triumphed over disorder, and regular procedures compensated for individual failings, inattention, and variations in strength or skill."[14] There were certainly critics of this "social machine metaphor," but the perspective of technologists like Babbage nonetheless became an important touchstone in subsequent social theory.[15]

If modern philosophy and factory labor invited seductive analogies between bodies and automated machinery, yet another system of production—the plantation economy—likewise contributed to the figurative associations between slavery and automation. One representative instance of these links is the Virginia planter William Byrd II, who describes the system of chattel slavery as a kind of machine that plantation owners could arrange and control. In a 1726 letter describing his tobacco plantation, Byrd explains how he must "keep all my people to their duty, to set all the springs in motion, and to make every one draw his equal share to carry the machine forward." The "people" in need of tending, Byrd explains, are "my flocks and my herds, my bondsmen and bondswomen."[16] He imagines an economic system in which the enslaved individual is a constitutive element in the plantation-as-machine, a "spring" that contributes to the "motion" of the whole.

It is perhaps not surprising that this perspective would generate contradictory ideas about enslavement and labor. The enslaved are "people" but are also categorized among the "flocks" and "herds" of animals. The enslaved can have "an equal share" of labor obligations but not an equal share in economic profits. Byrd thus reformulates elements of Descartes's philosophy by imagining the body as a kind of automaton, but he does not recognize that the enslaved have rational souls. This confluence of racial ideas and technological metaphors trapped the enslaved in bodily insignificance; they were simultaneously interchangeable parts and essential mechanisms.[17] As Zakiyyah Iman Jackson puts it, the enslaved person was a contradictory assemblage: superhuman worker, inhuman animal, and unfeeling machine.[18]

This mechanistic view of enslavement appears in a comedic form in Robert Montgomery Bird's novel *Peter Pilgrim; or, a Rambler's Recollection* (1838). (Bird the writer does not seem to have been related to Byrd the plantation owner.) The eponymous Peter Pilgrim accompanies a physician through a "madhouse," meeting a man named John Jones, who claims to have been committed to the asylum by the Abolition Society after designing a machine that would revolutionize the plantation economy in the American South.[19] Jones initially believed that his machine would be welcomed by abolitionists because it would effectively free all slaves, but he discovers that the institution of slavery is profitable to the Abolition Society as both an object of critique and a source of fundraising. When Jones claims to have brought the design to the Abolition Society, its members "could not bear that they should lose the honour, and glory, and profit of completing the great work of emancipation" (107). They label him a madman and have him committed to an asylum. The automation of labor becomes a threat to what Stephen Best calls the "abolitionist cult of death," or the antislavery movement's fixation with the suffering and death of the enslaved.[20]

Jones presents his mechanical slave as a remedy to the competing economic imperatives and social conflicts of American life. He explains to Peter Pilgrim that he has tried to thread this needle by

> the invention of my patent niggers to be worked by horse-power—yes, sir, by the invention (and a grand one it was,) of patent niggers—men, sir, not of perishing and suffering flesh and blood, but of wood, iron, leather and canvass, so constructed as (by means of horse-power to put them in motion) to be a great deal better than the real niggers; because, sir, they were to do all kinds of work, except blacking shoes and feeding the cattle, (upon my soul, sir, I could never make them do *that*,) and never get tired, or sick, or sulky—never die, or run away, or rise in insurrection. (106–7)

The image of "perishing and suffering flesh and blood" acknowledges that enslaved people agonized, grieved, and died in the plantation economy, yet this same language reinforces the passage's later assertion of the inefficiency of human labor. The fact that human beings suffer becomes, by the end of the passage, an assertion that these same people also "tire," become "sick," and "rise in insurrection." Jones's pathos transforms into a market logic, in which the machine is a more reliable source of labor than the human chattel it replaces.

The absurd irony of the passage is that Jones's remedy also multiplies the links between race and labor. His use of a racial slur to describe the machine illustrates how, for many Americans, the idea of an inhuman tool within the plantation economy was only conceivable in racialized terms.[21] The idea that compulsory labor is tied to racial identity simply moves into a new technological medium—from the human body to the automated machine. Put another way, Jones's remedy is a mirror image of the problem he proposes to solve. He continues to racialize the automated slave, thus *remediating* the racialization of labor. As Jay David Bolter and Richard Grusin explain, remediation relies on a "double logic" in which the "content" of an older medium "has been borrowed, but the medium has not been appropriated."[22] Much like the "iron chink," Jones's mechanical slave transfers the racialization of labor from the human body to an automated technology. Race, in this instance, operates as a fungible social relation, one that can be decoupled from the human body and remediated into automated technology.[23]

MECHANICAL INELASTICITY, AUTOMATED MINSTRELSY

Bird's novel anticipates how racial servitude would operate as a constitutive metaphor in the cultural discourse surrounding robotics and computing. For example, in his history of the computer, Gregory J. E. Rawlins notes how Charles Babbage envisioned an analytical engine in 1834, only one year after slavery had been abolished within the British Empire. In Rawlins's telling, Babbage "was designing a new kind of slave," as though his calculating machine were built to meet a new age's "division of labor."[24] Many mechanical curiosities in Europe during the nineteenth century similarly coupled racial identity with automation. Perhaps the most famous of these curiosities was the Mechanical Turk, invented by the Hungarian engineer Wolfgang von Kemplen. The Mechanical Turk was a chess-playing machine dressed in a turban, ermine-lined robes, and other exotic clothing. The machine was a hoax (a person inside manipulated a mechanical arm), but the mechanisms that animated the Turk remained a secret for more than eight decades. The Turk was purchased by Johann Mälzel, who displayed it in several European cities, influencing Charles Babbage and many others.[25] Mälzel's Turk even inspired some inventors to create imitations, including an Egyptian automaton named "Ajeeb."[26] These popular oddities illustrate how mechanistic behavior was closely linked to non-European, nonwhite identity during the eighteenth and nineteenth centuries.

In the United States, a national shift from the plantation to an industrialized economy would slowly revise how automated machinery would be coupled with notions of racialized labor in the latter half of the nineteenth century. For example, in Edward Sylvester Ellis's "half-dime" novel *The Huge Hunter; or, The Steam Man of the Prairies* (1882), a mechanical man driven by the steam of a locomotive engine ferries settlers across the American West. The narrator describes the steam man's face as "made of iron, painted a black color, with a pair of fearful eyes, and a tremendous grinning mouth."[27] The first page of the dime novel includes a drawing of the mechanical figure (fig. 3), and the narrator later explains that the face "was intended to be of a flesh color, but [it] was really a fearful red" because of the heat escaping from the boiler hidden in the steam man's chest.[28]

The body of the steam man houses technology for energy production in the industrial era, while the face dresses up that technology in recognizable tropes from blackface minstrelsy. The "tremendous grinning

FIGURE 3. Edward Sylvester Ellis, *The Huge Hunter; or, The Steam Man of the Prairies*, in *Beadle's Half Dime Library* 11, no. 271 (1882): 1.

mouth," for instance, recalls a recurring trope about Black facial features in contemporaneous minstrelsy performances. Eric Lott argues that "strategic bodily zones" like "fat lips" and "gaping mouths" were central to marking out a performance as an instance of the minstrelsy genre.[29] In *The Huge Hunter*, both the grin and the "black color" that "was intended" to imitate "flesh" make this generic identification explicit: the steam man mechanizes blackface, wearing the paint and burnt ash that white minstrelsy performers commonly used at the time.

Whereas a satirical discourse about bondage informs the mechanical slave in *Peter Pilgrim*, minstrel comedy shapes the locomotive labor of the steam man. The machine's operator claims he can "dance and skip like a lamb" and "outrun any locomotive you ever set eyes on!"[30] These performative possibilities recall what Lott describes as the "greatly elaborated staple element" of minstrelsy—humor—which "helped cinch popular racist feeling" in the late nineteenth century.[31] The prospect of mechanical dancing becomes a source of comic pleasure, while the brute strength of the steam man's engine embodies an ideal of superhuman strength echoed in the black paint covering the machine from top-hat to toe.

Automated figures in the twentieth century would rely less directly on the minstrel tropes that are so explicit in Ellis's novel. In *Ozma of Oz* (1907), one of L. Frank Baum's sequels to *The Wonderful Wizard of Oz* (1900), Dorothy Gale and a talking hen named Billina happen upon a cave in which they see "the form of a man—or, at least, it seemed like a man, in the dim light. . . . His body was round as a ball and made out of burnished copper."[32] Dorothy and Billina free the copper man by winding up different "works" in his back. After turning the crank that animates his monosyllabic speech, the copper man narrates his history: "I was pur-chased from Smith & Tin-ker, my man-u-fac-tur-ers, by a cru-el King of Ev, named Ev-ol-do, who used to beat all his serv-ants un-til they died. How-ev-er, he was not a-ble to kill me, be-cause I was not a-live, and one must first live in or-der to die" (59–60). The copper man's story resembles a bondage narrative. That he only "seemed like a man," that his body is bought by a cruel master, and that he becomes one among many other servants form a web of allusions to chattel slavery. The copper man explains that he even received the name *Tik-Tok* from his "for-mer mas-ter" because of the sound his works make (62). A master-slave dynamic circumscribes his origins and subsequent behaviors.

Tik-Tok's body is not as explicitly marked in racial terms as Ellis's steam man, yet the dark copper in the illustrations that Baum solicited from John R. Neill recalls other brown bodies that had been bought, sold, beaten, and killed within the institutions of modern slavery (fig. 4). Indeed, when Dorothy winds up the work that enables the copper man's capacity for action, Tik-Tok exits the cavern and says to the little

THE COPPER MAN WALKED OUT OF THE ROCKY CAVERN

FIGURE 4. "The Copper Man Walked Out of the Rocky Cavern." Color plate illustration by John R. Neill, in L. Frank Baum, *Ozma of Oz* (1907; New York: Dover, 1985), 53.

girl, "From this time forth I am your o-be-di-ent ser-vant. What-ev-er you com-mand, that I will do will-ing-ly—if you keep me wound up" (62). Beaten and then bound in darkness, Tik-Tok nonetheless "will-ing-ly" accepts the authority of the next master that maintains his works. Servitude appears to be the copper man's natural state; he moves like clockwork from one master to another.

The narrative contours of the copper man's origin story borrow from the slave narrative, but Baum's book transforms these origins through the nonsense, levity, and incongruity that pervade the fantastical land of Oz. The series is rife with characters who similarly combine incongruous characteristics: the Tin Woodman; a Lion whose first name is Cowardly; and a scarecrow with stuffing for brains, who becomes "the wisest man in all of Oz" after meeting the Wizard.[33] Tik-Tok is no exception to this pattern. His mannered nobility belies his repeated assertions that he is only a machine; his ingenious solutions to various problems sprout from his mechanical mind; and his jerky movements and monosyllabic speech perform human activities in conspicuously mechanical ways.

The incongruity of Tik-Tok's character becomes especially pronounced when he veers toward allusions to the one-liners and inhuman stereotypes that appeared on the minstrelsy stage. For example, after Tik-Tok accidentally enlists in an army, an officer commands him to "fall in." Tik-Tok responds: "Fall in what? The well?"[34] Or, after explaining how his former master beat and killed his other servants, Tik-Tok remarks that "his beat-ing did me no harm, and mere-ly kept my cop-per bod-y well pol-ished" (*Ozma of Oz* 60). The horror of the other slaves' death morphs into a joke, as if violence only makes the mechanical man browner, his natural state being further clarified by the master's lashes. As Paul M. Abraham and Stuart Kenter put it, "socially and philosophically, Tik-Tok is on the bottom of the heap" of Oz's "caste" system.[35] In contrast to Dorothy's other companions, he is never granted a wish or elevated to some new magical state. Tik-Tok remains both entirely obedient and purely comic.

It is also possible to see in Tik-Tok echoes of a character called Topsy, who appeared in contemporaneous adaptations of Harriet Beecher

Stowe's *Uncle Tom's Cabin* (1852). Described in Stowe's novel as "rather a funny specimen in the Jim Crow line," Topsy regularly responds to stressful situations with a "steam whistle imitation" that W. T. Lhamon Jr. traces to the minstrel stage.[36] As Christopher Corbo argues, the character of Topsy became a centerpiece of late nineteenth- and early twentieth-century stage adaptations of *Uncle Tom's Cabin*.[37] Topsy stood for the slave who was untouchable in her merrymaking; the depredations of the plantation never impinged on her ability to amuse the audience.

Tik-Tok becomes a kind of mechanical Topsy, although her "steam whistle" is replaced with his stilted speech and her dialect transforms into his overly mannered formality. Much like Topsy's comic catchphrase "I's so wicked," which appeared regularly in stage performances contemporaneous with Baum's book, Tik-Tok's assertion that he is only a machine undermines the seriousness of his enslaved past and unwavering obedience to Dorothy.[38] This recurring assertion recalls the early twentieth-century view that a machine "detaches the reproduced object" from its "authenticity" and "authority," as Walter Benjamin argues.[39] In other words, the machine is the antithesis of the authentic: anything reproduced under mechanical conditions must be artifice, not reality.

Henri Bergson argues that this sentiment becomes comic when the mechanical reproduction approximates, but fails to achieve, human action. Modern comic actors elicit laughter through what Bergson calls *"mechanical inelasticity"*: the *"attitudes, gestures and movements of the human body are laughable in exact proportion as that body reminds us of a mere machine."*[40] He illustrates this claim by observing how a speaker whose gestures become overly predictable may provoke laughter: "I now have before me a machine that works automatically. This is no longer life, it is automatism established in life and imitating it."[41] In keeping with this view, Tik-Tok is comic in the *"exact proportion"* that he reminds us of an automaton imitating a human. When he's simply a machine, he's dull or unremarkable.[42] Much like Bergson's speaker, however, he becomes comic when his behavior superimposes automatism on actions that recall pliable human experience.

Michael North makes a similar point about comic figures in several major films and plays from the twentieth century. North argues that the working-class experience of factory labor led many artists and filmmakers to object to the dehumanizing effects of industrial production, yet at the same time, print and film media relied on closely related industrialized techniques for reproducing culture. Comedy, according to North, became one way that cultural producers responded to this "fundamental tension," often even mimicking the same industrial processes that their films criticized.[43] The most iconic example is the Tramp—Charlie Chaplin's comic persona—who encounters various kinds of industrial machinery in *Modern Times* (1936). At one point, the Tramp finds work on an assembly line, but he can't keep pace with the machinery. The conveyer belt moves the objects of mass production past his hands at an increasingly rapid speed, causing the Tramp to lift his wrench and shake it at the sky, as though cursing the industrial gods.

North argues that Chaplin's films and the writings of Benjamin and Bergson are part of a wider mechanical view of the comic that developed in response to sweeping technological changes in the late nineteenth and early twentieth centuries. He describes this view as "machine-age comedy" and argues that one of its central tendencies is to mock the false rationality of industrial capitalism, even as it paradoxically reproduces that false rationality as a principal source of laughter. Horror folds into pleasure, revulsion into amusement. Machine-age comedy is caught within a grotesque kind of mimicry of the mechanical inauthenticity that serves as the butt of some of its most widely reproduced jokes.[44]

The idea that mechanical reproduction is somehow incompatible with authenticity clearly informs Tik-Tok's role in *Ozma of Oz*, but so does the machine-age understanding of comedy as a form of inelastic and mechanical reproduction. I have been arguing that comic forms of this incompatibility often owe debts to the minstrel stage and the plantation tradition—debts that persist in the cultures of technology between the two world wars. In 1930, Vannevar Bush and Harold Hazen developed a machine at MIT that would aid in complex calculations. Bush and Hazen referred to the machine as a differential analyzer, but MIT's *Technology Review* jokingly called it the "brain servant."[45] In 1940, Buckminster Fuller coined the phrase "energy slave" to describe a quantifiable unit of energy used within mechanical labor.[46] Within this cultural milieu, the research laboratories of the electric company Westinghouse developed an automaton nicknamed "Rastus" (fig. 5). The nickname refers to a character from Joel Chandler Harris's *Uncle Remus: His Sons and Sayings* (1881), a deeply religious friend of Uncle Remus named "Brer Rastus."[47] The name later became a racist epithet for a cheerful Black man, or even every Black man, as though "Rastus" were a genre of person and not an individual.[48]

Westinghouse's Rastus appropriates this racist trope of the happy servant and couples it with a technological fantasy of automated labor. As one contemporaneous account explains, Rastus "is built to resemble a man, with legs and arms and a head, with a face like a dark-skinned

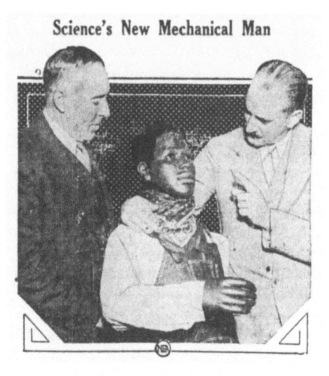

FIGURE 5. This brief article about Rastus was serialized in small newspapers by the Associated Press. "Science's New Mechanical Man," *Richmond (IN) Item*, June 27, 1930.

minstrel. Hence his name."⁴⁹ The robot's "skin" was made from Goodyear rubber, and the machine's agricultural attire likewise implies that Rastus might replace tenant farmers.⁵⁰ In addition to Rastus, Westinghouse developed several robots during the 1920s using its patented "televox" technology, which allowed machines to receive certain spoken commands and respond with a limited number of prerecorded phrases.⁵¹ One of these robots resembled a white maid and was called Katrina Van Televox. This robot wore a Dutch maid's costume, but its vocal and aural capacities did not imply that Katrina would function as an interactive companion. Rather, as one advertisement explained, Katrina "does only what she's told."⁵² While Rastus exemplifies how race connects to mechanical servitude in the twentieth-century history of robotics, Katrina embodies the characteristics of a perfect female servant, one that "makes coffee and toast" and "runs a vacuum cleaner."⁵³

There are important similarities in the ways that Westinghouse employed stereotypes about race and gender to give a form to mechanical servitude.⁵⁴ But when the company stylized its robot as Black, its engineers wanted the machine to seem comic in a way quite different from Katrina's solemn obedience. Rastus, in contrast, often participated in a comic reenactment of the familiar William Tell feat. Engineers used an electronic signal, shot from a bow-like machine, that would trigger a charge embedded in an apple placed on top of the head of the "boy."⁵⁵ Audiences thus believed that a white inventor used electricity to shoot the apple, while Rastus responded to the apple's sudden explosion with a "human and startled cry."⁵⁶ The audience roared in laughter at this exhibition of emotion, finding in Rastus's surprise a corollary to their astonishment that an inhuman machine could resemble their own humanity.

The William Tell feat traditionally exhibits the skill of the archer, and the participant knows in advance that the apple will be shot. It should be no surprise when the archer hits the mark, yet Westinghouse's version transforms this feat into a comic episode to exhibit the company's engineering skills in facial and vocal mimicry, as well as its expertise in electronic signaling. Rastus's role in this performance relies on a caricature of the simple but obedient servant who can hardly understand the technological marvels of the white world in which he finds himself.

As North paraphrases Bergson, "Laughter is an expression of the natural hostility of organic life to the machine."[57] Rastus shows how this sentiment can easily become racialized. Laughing at the Black robot expresses a white audience's hostility toward the inhuman. Here, whiteness represents a natural and authentic state of being human, while Blackness signifies the merely mechanical.

THE DERACIALIZED ROBOT

The cultural history I have presented so far shows how writers and technologists couple figures of automated machinery with racialized tropes about labor and comic performance. I now want to show that when the Czech writer Karel Čapek coined the term *robot* in a 1921 play called *R.U.R.*, and when writers later began to imagine that computational technology could be embodied within the robot, the links between race and computation persisted in a variety of remediated forms.[58] For example, in a 1957 article published in *Mechanix Illustrated*, the futurist O. O. Binder announced, "You'll Own 'Slaves' by 1965." "In 1863," Binder explains, "Abe Lincoln freed the slaves. But by 1965, slavery will be back! We'll all have personal slaves again, only this time we won't fight a Civil War over them."[59] Ruha Benjamin notes how Binder presupposes a white readership: the article's "readers, so casually hailed as 'we', are not the descendants of those whom Lincoln freed."[60] As Benjamin's comment suggests, only a white readership insulated from the travesty of slavery would find this opening gambit amusing.

Notably, Binder qualifies this gambit, telling his readers not to "be alarmed" because "we mean robot 'slaves'" (62). *Modern Mechanix*, the parent of *Mechanix Illustrated*, was a popular magazine that published articles on the latest models of automobiles and other technological innovations. Binder's announcement presents the robot as a tool soon to be relevant for a middle-class and largely white readership. Why does he qualify the analogy with slavery immediately after offering it to make the robot legible for everyday use?

It would seem that the long-standing coupling of race and automated technology had become socially unacceptable to the white liberal audience of postwar magazines like *Mechanix Illustrated*, yet that coupling still persisted as a paradigm for imagining advanced technology. Slavery provided a template for automated variations on the idea of compulsory servitude, and the racialization of labor persisted, but those figurative associations needed to be remediated so that the idea of a robotic servant wouldn't conflict with liberal sensibilities in the era of civil rights. We see this tension-filled confluence of pressures in Binder's assertion that slavery has been corrected—"Abe Lincoln freed the slaves"—even as he also suggests that the *desire for slaves* continues in the middle-class household: "Robots will dress you, comb your hair, and serve meals in a jiffy" (62). The robot meets the need for an inhuman object to perform domestic labor, but its inhumanity doesn't violate the legal and moral prohibition against the exploitation of human chattel. Racialized slavery was wrong, so the thinking goes, but robotic slavery will be a new sign of middle-class prosperity.

Binder's rhetoric illustrates how racism at once serves as a source of anxiety for mid-twentieth-century writers discussing robotics, even as racial servitude continues to provide a model for the promise of an inhuman tool that increases productivity. In some of these instances, the robot signifies both the convenience of a slave and the social conscience of an abolitionist. This double logic appears in the visual iconography of the image accompanying Binder's article (fig. 6). The cubist painting in the background conjures the cultural and intellectual avant-garde, thus associating robotics with the progressive and the new. The man being mechanically groomed wears the clothing of the professional-managerial class. In contrast, the robot serving as shoe-shiner and barber is shaded in a dark green-yellow that highlights the whiteness of the man. The article asserts that race is no longer relevant to labor, yet the markers of class, gender, and race proliferate in submerged forms within this vision of the future.

Binder's coupling of race with a computerized future offers an optimistic vision that stands in contrast to contemporaneous anxieties about the automation of labor, especially among nonwhite workers. Jason Resnikoff notes how mid-twentieth-century autoworkers regularly contended with how automation simultaneously "intensified and

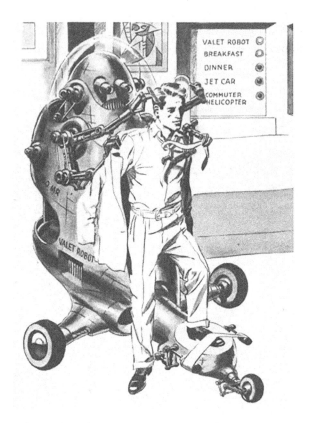

FIGURE 6. O. O. Binder, "You'll Own 'Slaves' by 1965," *Mechanix Illustrated*, Jan. 1957, 62.

degraded their labor, leading both to high unemployment and speed-up on the line."[61] At a time when automation promised a future of both ease and heightened productivity, the new technology seemed only to further accelerate the pace of work and entrench racial structures of labor. Resnikoff cites a representative in the 1960s from a union of Black workers, who claimed, "A process called 'niggermation' is more pervasive than automation. Often new black workers are forced to do the work of two white men."[62] If Binder could imagine transcending race through robotics by 1965, factory workers in the same decade would claim that automated technology became a justification for creating more exploitative conditions for Black workers. Automation thus seemed to resurrect the mechanistic imaginary that appeared in William Byrd's eighteenth-century metaphors for the plantation. The promises of automation were betrayed by its unequal effects on working-class people.

The idea of racialized labor similarly informs the play in which Karel Čapek coined the term *robot*. The acronym in *R.U.R.* refers to a corporation called Reason's Universal Robots. Reason is the heavily symbolic surname of the corporation's founder and the original inventor of the robot. Čapek's play focuses on a man named Harry Domin, who is the managing director of the corporation. Reason's Universal Robots sells "sentient humanoids" that the corporation advertises as "The Cheapest Workers Around!"[63] The term *robot* derives from the Czech *robota*, which means "compulsory service" or, more simply, "slave." In *R.U.R.*, robots are cheap not because they are inexpensive to build but because they do not demand wages or benefits.

The first point to make here is that Čapek's neologism only gives a name to the dynamics I have been tracing in the cultural history of automated machinery. It is a new name for an old phenomenon. And, of course, the Czech word for *slave* does not in itself make the robot a figure with racial origins, but this leads to the other point I want to make, which is that Čapek's play in fact sets up a series of allusions to the institutions of chattel slavery. Much like Tik-Tok passing from master to master, the robots in Čapek's play circulate among global corporations in need of their labor. The robots' manufacturer thus imitates the strategy of those plantation owners who bred slaves and sold them to other plantations. Harry Domin even sits at an "American desk" and explains that robots are "bought" but "never hired" (3, 10). Robots can only be bought, he argues, because they lack a soul. Robotic labor will "overcome man's enslavement to man and to nature. People will no longer be labourers and secretaries, digging the streets, sitting at desks, paying for the bread they eat with their lives and with hatred, destroying their souls with work they hate!" (23).

Harry's use of the word *enslavement* echoes ironically throughout the play, for his ideals of freedom are unmasked as the horrors of bondage. Beginning in the second act, the robots insist on their freedom, overthrow their corporate overlords, and slaughter human beings in an event that the play calls "the insurrection" (46). The play thus begins with Harry justifying a self-reproducing system of labor through ideals of freedom and the natural subservience of his machines, but it ends with a slave revolt that conveys the horrors of displacing labor onto inhuman bodies.

This use of slavery as a metaphor and the slave revolt as a narrative arc further illustrates how a dialectic formulated within the institutions of chattel slavery gave templates of legibility to the social meaning of robots in the twentieth century. As Despina Kakoudaki explains, Čapek's play marks the culmination of a longer trend in which the slave serves as a metaphorical figure for constructing modern ideas about the self: "the fantasy of *having* mechanical workers contains the nightmare of *being* mechanical," a distinctively modern "paradox" in which freedom from labor requires the exploitation of inhuman laborers.[64] According to this perspective, one cannot be both free and subject to the necessities of labor. To avoid the latter, the search for modern freedom often tries to displace labor onto nonhuman substitutes.

I later argue that these fears about *"being* mechanical" would inform cultural attitudes about the experience of becoming computational. Before turning to that argument, I want to say more about how comedy has provided a wide range of generic forms for understanding robotic technology. I have suggested that minstrelsy shaped the cultural history of robots, automatons, and other automated technology. A different kind of comedy surfaces in Čapek's play. To be sure, most of *R.U.R.* cannot plausibly be described as comic. The play takes itself very seriously. By the fourth act, the robots have slaughtered every human being except an engineer named Alquist. The robots have ordered Alquist to discover the corporation's secretive "bioformula" that would allow them to reproduce (82). The request turns into horror as Alquist dissects a living robot, hoping to discover the secret to its automated biology. The dissection fails and Alquist falls into despair, but while resting on a couch, he overhears two robots expressing romantic feelings for one another. One of the robots laughs, which leads Alquist to rise from the sofa and declare, "What! Laughter! Human beings! They've come back!" (88). The engineer finds that the laughing robot, Helen, has also developed the capacity for love, which a robot named Primus reciprocates. Alquist describes the robotic couple as the new Adam and Eve, and their newly developed capacities suggest that "life will not perish, love will endure" (91–92).

This conclusion to what is an otherwise dire play illustrates how romantic coupling can operate within the robot's literary history as a sign of technology's promise despite its many threats. Laughter and love transform Čapek's robots from instruments of compulsory labor and rebellion into representatives of a new world. The sudden appearance of laughter signals that the robots have come to embody an older discourse about the nature of being human. Indeed, they become types of the first man and woman in the Judeo-Christian creation story. The biblical allusion suggests a kind of redemption for the robots: humanity's exploitative technology may in the end lead to what the play describes as a secular "salvation," new life emerging after the fall (92).

The final turn in *R.U.R.* toward redemption, laughter, and romantic coupling anticipates the secular comedy in Isaac Asimov's influential fiction about robotics. Whereas Ellis's steam man and Baum's Tik-Tok couple automation with minstrelsy, Asimov's fiction situates the robot in a narrative arc familiar to the comedy of secular redemption imagined at the end of Čapek's play. As Northrop Frye explains, this kind of comedy revolves around "the theme of the absurd or irrational law that the action of comedy moves toward breaking."[65] In the freer society that emerges at the end of many comedies, the principal characters move "from a society controlled by habit, ritual bondage, arbitrary law and the older characters to a society controlled by youth and pragmatic freedom."[66] The lovers at the end of *R.U.R.* are comic in precisely this sense, for they represent a form of humanity in opposition to the cold, exploitative corporation that depends on compulsory labor for its existence.

Asimov's robot stories from the 1940s and 1950s follow this comic narrative arc. For example, in a short story titled "Robbie" included in his 1950 collection *I, Robot*, Asimov imagines a nonspeaking robot named Robbie who has been purchased as a companion for an eight-year-old child named Gloria Weston. This relationship provides the cover image for the Ballantine Books edition (see fig. 7), which imagines the friendship between Gloria and Robbie within an idealized natural setting. In contrast to Leo Marx's trope of the machine in the garden—a trope expressing the conflict between industrial progress and natural freedom—Asimov's image of the robot in the countryside imagines the incorporation of a robotic machine within ideals about pastoral experience.[67] In the trope identified by Marx, the machine-in-the-garden disrupts the pastoral: we can think of the sound of a train interrupting Thoreau's contemplation at Walden Pond. Yet in the cover image for *I, Robot*, this trope has been transformed, such that the mechanical and the pastoral seem to be compatible. This strain of visual culture imagines the human-robot relationship as innocent, ordinary, and perhaps even natural.

A similar dynamic characterizes the text of Asimov's story. The Westons describe Robbie as their daughter's "companion," and the story opens with a scene of the robot and child playing happily together.[68] Conflict arises only when Gloria's mother becomes jealous of her daughter's love for Robbie. The mother removes Robbie from the household and replaces him with a pet dog. Robbie's sudden removal shocks Gloria, and she refuses her parents' attempts to console her. George, Gloria's father, eventually takes the family on a tour of the factory that built Robbie, ostensibly to disenchant Gloria by showing how the robot is only a bundle of electronic wires and machinery. It turns out that Robbie has been assigned a spot on an assembly line in this very factory. When Gloria recognizes Robbie, she runs to him and is almost killed by a rolling machine. Robbie dramatically saves her, hugging the child "gently and lovingly" with his "chrome-steel arms" (29).

On its surface, the story of Robbie and Gloria is a pastoral fantasy about the social benefits of new technology. Yet this view is incomplete, a fact that becomes evident when we consider how contemporaneous racial politics reside in the background of the narrative. Many scholars have noted how Asimov repurposes the mid-twentieth-century struggle for civil rights in his framing of robotics. For example, De Witt Douglas Kilgore claims that Asimov "use[s] the social conventions of a segregated America to project both the containment and potential of humanoid robots in relation to their human masters."[69] Samuel Delany makes a similar point about Asimov's robot detective R-Daneel, who experiences "prejudice and disdain" that Delany describes as "clearly an analog of some of the milder sorts of prejudice [Black Americans] experienced from whites."[70] Delany even sees Asimov's influential "Three Laws of Robotics" as recalling "a white ideal of what the 'good Negro' ought to be."[71]

In "Robbie," it is easy to see how mid-twentieth-century segregation provides a template for the social position of robots. For instance, when George Weston takes his daughter to the movies early in the story, Gloria asks to bring Robbie, but her father explains that "they won't allow robots at the [movie theater]" (18). Gloria's mother says that robots have become a problem in many urban centers, such that New York has even "passed an ordinance keeping all robots off the streets between sunset and sunrise" (18). The segregation of the robot recalls the Jim Crow laws in effect when Asimov's story was first published. The management of robots within consumer spaces and urban streets borrows from a racial template of bigotry.

There are other submerged racial templates at work in the story, too. As the Ballantine rendering of Robbie suggests, his robotic body lacks racial characteristics. The narrator describes his "metal skin" as "nice and comfortable" because it is "kept at a constant temperature of seventy by the high resistance coils within" (13). Robbie's metal skin thus differentiates him from many of the automatons and mechanical men examined previously in this chapter. It would seem that the robot is color-blind; he is a postracial servant.

Yet Robbie's literary character resembles recognizable character types from the plantation tradition of southern literature. He is a simple but faithful servant, recalling such racial caricatures as Joel Chandler Harris's Uncle Remus. In one of Harris's collections of tales, readers first meet Uncle Remus as a domestic servant who lovingly cares for a white child but is also so simple as to require oversight by his masters. In *Nights with Uncle Remus* (1917), the collection begins by noting, "The lady to whom Uncle Remus belonged had been thoughtful of the old man" during a bad storm.[72] In Asimov's story, Robbie "obeyed with alacrity" Mrs. Weston's orders, "for somehow there was that in him which judged it best to obey Mrs. Weston, without as much as a scrap of hesitation" (14). In an updating of the racist ideology that associated Blackness with a natural state of servitude, Robbie's programming guides him to be the obedient property of his masters.

The narrator makes these echoes of the plantation tradition all but plain at the end of the story. After the robot has proved his faithfulness by saving Gloria, the narrator remarks that Robbie views her as his "little mistress" (28). The ol' miss in the Uncle Remus tales is replaced with a younger version. Indeed, the cover of the Ballantine edition recalls the cover illustration for the 1917 Riverside Press edition of *Nights with Uncle Remus* (fig. 8). Asimov's story opens with Gloria and Robbie telling stories, and the visual iconography of this representation shares with the cover of *Nights with Uncle Remus* the depiction of an adult figure and the young master in a storytelling relation. In both, the scene of narration is also a scene that sentimentalizes unquestioning but compulsory service.

The loving relationship between a white child and robotic servant in "Robbie" also recalls Tik-Tok's immediate fealty to Dorothy Gale in *Ozma of Oz* (see fig. 4). The symbolism of the master-child across these texts confirms the harmlessness of the robot, while the blamelessness of the child attaches to the machine as though it were innocent by association. This attachment aligns the robot with a normative vision of the future. For Asimov, this future centers on advanced technology wrapping its "chrome-steel arms" around human society, forming a union in which both work together in the pursuit of happiness.[73]

NONSYMBOLIC MOTION AND THE ASIAN AUTOMATON

With the rise of computational technology in the latter half of the twentieth century, the coupling of robotic figures and racialized identity gravitated increasingly toward metaphors about the fungibility of software and routinized programmability. The sense of comic superiority elicited by Westinghouse's Rastus, along with the kinds of secular comedy associated with deracialized robots, would give rise to new figures in this changing technological context. Late twentieth- and twenty-first-century robots would often become comic by signifying conformity to the routines of a traditional society or some other source of extrinsic

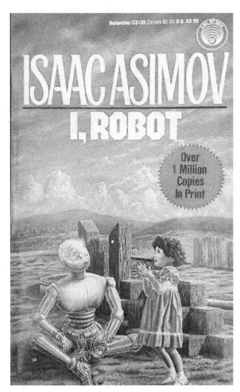

FIGURE 7. Isaac Asimov, *I, Robot* (New York: Ballantine, 1950).

FIGURE 8. Joel Chandler Harris, *Nights with Uncle Remus* (Cambridge, MA: Riverside Press, 1917).

motivation. Christina Ho notes this metaphorical register in her analysis of a commonplace joke in Australian educational culture, which presents students with Asian heritage as "over-schooled robots."[74] Ho identifies this racist trope as a recurring feature of online discourse about the academic successes of Asian-Australian students. A prior study by Megan Watkins and Greg Noble similarly found that teachers in Sydney schools viewed Chinese-Australian students as "automatons" who are "rigid and formulaic."[75]

The language of "Asian automatons" imagines these students as rote learners who merely follow parental pressure and cultural expectations. The trope of the "over-schooled robot" represents any high-achieving student with Asian heritage as a *product* of external demands rather than a *producer* of authentic learning. The trope thus illustrates what Wendy Hui Kyong Chun describes as the "epistemological value of race," which is that it "construct[s] connections between—and indeed construct[s] the very concepts of—public and private, outside and inside."[76] Building on Chun's point, I want to suggest that this vein of racist comedy is a technology for constructing publicness and conceptualizing social identity.

Let me begin by discussing closely related comic figures that appear in American reality TV programs, such as the stock character called the "Asian technical robot."[77] This figure excels in specialized, technical tasks but fails to exhibit human passions. The Asian technical robot's lack of emotion pairs seemingly inhuman proficiency with an equally inhuman affect, thus representing Asian people as twice removed from a normative idea of human sociality. Any kind of technical success becomes a symptom for a more thoroughgoing failure. Jessica Yu examines how Asian American characters in films like *Juno* (2007) and *Lady Bird* (2018) similarly appear as foils for the female protagonists' independence. Asian American characters in these films are "so socially conservative, repetitively conformist, unoriginal, and emotionless that there is some uncertainty over whether they are 'genuinely human' and have any sense of an inner life."[78] Yu notes how the eponymous Summer in *(500) Days of Summer* (2009) finds her Asian foil so laughable that it motivates her to double down on her nonconformity.[79] The trope of the

Asian automaton provides comic relief in these films, and by extension the figure presents a *via negativa* for authentic social life.[80]

Figures of Asian automatism position certain bodies outside an imagined community of autonomy and authenticity. These forms of racist humor depend on a logic in which people with Asian ancestry are only capable of what Kenneth Burke calls "nonsymbolic motion," which he distinguishes from meaningful or "symbolic" action. In Burke's schema, *motion* does not depend on the exchange of meaning-making symbols. The sea, for example, "can go on thrashing about whether or not there are animals that have a word for it."[81] Human bodies can similarly be "motivated by such obvious 'purposes' as the need for food," physiological mechanisms like the healing of a wound, or the "collective unconscious" that "does not explicitly engage our attention."[82]

Techno-Orientalist humor binds Asian identity to nonsymbolic motion. It finds comic pleasure in the idea that Asianness is so fundamentally coupled with technology that Asian people are decoupled from the capacity for autonomy and authenticity. Of course, the logic of this racist humor is deeply contradictory, for it also associates Asian identity with modern technological advancement. The Asian automaton simultaneously embodies modernity while also failing to participate fully in the forms of sociality particular to modernity.

This contradictory logic underwrites the robots that appear in the hit album *Kilroy Was Here* (1983) by the rock band Styx. One song from this album, "Mr. Roboto," had a long run on *Billboard*'s Hot 100 list. Styx produced a short film to accompany the album, and this film situates "Mr. Roboto" within the story of a man named Robert Orin Charles Kilroy, whose initials form the acronym ROCK. Kilroy has been imprisoned by the Majority for Musical Morality (MMM), a religiously and socially conservative movement that has come to political power in the album's imagined future. The MMM imprisons Kilroy, alleging that he exposed America's youth to the "moral filth" of rock and roll. At Kilroy's trial, a computerized judge tells Kilroy: "You have persistently and flagrantly violated Code 672, which forbids the playing and purveying of rock music."

The central conceit of *Kilroy Was Here* is that the counterculture has gone underground because of mass conformity, while an army of robots with generically Asian facial features enforces this moral and cultural conformity (fig. 9). The film names these machines "Mr. Roboto." They have been programmed by the MMM, and their primary directives are to suppress cultural experimentation and police rebels, like Kilroy, who have been imprisoned for violating conservative cultural mores. The film treats these robots not only as embodiments of conformity but also as the butt of techno-Orientalist jokes. For example, during a riot, prisoners yell insults at the robots like "Your mother was a Toyota!" Kilroy kicks one robot in the groin, leading it to curse "Kawasaki" and "Oh, my balls" in heavily accented English.

The ridiculous links between generic Oriental robots and Japanese manufacturing allude to an anxiety in the American business community during the 1980s regarding a so-called Asian invasion, which centered on the worry that "cars like Toyota and the Nissan-made Bluebird" were undermining the competitiveness of General Motors and other American-based car manufacturers.[83] The language of an "invasion"

FIGURE 9. *Styx: Kilroy Was Here*, dir. Brian Gibson (A&M Video, 1983).

presents the influx of Japanese-manufactured goods in terms of military conquest, as though such products were a foreign encroachment on American sovereignty. When the prisoner tells Mr. Roboto "Your mother was a Toyota!," the insult (deployed for comic effect in the film) aligns the machines with mass-produced foreignness. But this alignment is itself part of a larger pattern in *Kilroy Was Here*, which uses the generically Oriental robots to imply that the conformist MMM is somehow alien to American identity. The Asianness of the MMM's robotic proxies stands in for the anti-Americanness of cultural conformity.

The lyrics to "Mr. Roboto" extend this sentiment to technology as such:

> The problem's plain to see:
> Too much technology.
> Machines to save our lives.
> Machines dehumanize.

The image of dehumanization in *Kilroy Was Here* is the inelastic Mr. Roboto, who unwaveringly follows the instructions of a traditional social order. The defiant Kilroy and rock and roll represent an alternative conception of identity based in individualism and countercultural freedom. This identity, as Lawrence Grossberg says of rock and roll more generally, is "a form of cultural rebellion and never of political revolution."[84] Kilroy does not call for organizational change; he embodies a posture of generalized nonconformity. Styx's song does not envision an antiindustrial or anticapitalist politics; it promotes an ethos of rebellion. The point of rock and roll seems to be performative rebellion, and Mr. Roboto serves only as the comic foil of this countercultural attitude.

Mr. Roboto and other figures of Asian automatism share certain affinities with robots like Rastus and Ellis's steam man. These robotic forms racialize what Burke calls the "(nonsymbolic) motion / (symbolic) action polarity."[85] While these robotic figures arose within different racial and economic contexts, each signifies some imagined gap between nonwhite identity and the capacity for meaningful action. The fact that Rastus and Mr. Roboto aim to register as comic, rather than embodying the "nightmare of *being* mechanical," illustrates this racial polarity.[86] These robots present as comic because the structures of legibility for their allusions to human bodies are already marked by some sense of inhumanity or impoverished social identity.

While robots like Rastus and Mr. Roboto have bodily forms that set up their failure to achieve social belonging, other robots examined in this chapter stand in for forms of secular comedy that imagine society's happy union with advanced technology. In this latter vein, Asimov presents the prejudice against robots as no more reasonable than the structural racism faced by Black Americans. This sentiment uses the struggle against racial apartheid to imagine a society that moves from a state of conflict to a happy union between human and robotic technology.

I have argued that several kinds of comedy—minstrelsy, techno-Orientalist humor, and comic plot structures—create different registers of meaning for the coupling of race and robots. Some of the robotic figures analyzed in this chapter are an index of the perception that some form of social identity is under threat, while others hail a future of middle-class prosperity that triumphs over the depredations of labor. The structure of experience that I call *being generic* owes debts to this range of cultural attitudes about automated technology. The next chapter considers these debts by showing how cultural representations of *genre, form,* and *generic experience* serve as proxies for wider worries about the flattening and debasement of social life through computational media.

2 THE ONE ABOUT BEING GENERIC

IN 1982, *TIME* MAGAZINE SELECTED the computer as its "Machine of the Year," breaking with its tradition of selecting a "Man of the Year" by identifying an inanimate object rather than a person. The magazine's cover depicts an all-white, plaster figure of a man sitting in a wooden chair (fig. 10). The plaster figure stares at, but does not touch, a boxy computer resting on a red desk. The whiteness of both the machine and the plaster figure contrast sharply with the desk's bright color. The computer's monitor displays a graph with two yellow lines rising along the x and y axes, perhaps recalling the growth in sales of personal computers. The tagline reads, "The Computer Moves In," but in many ways the cover's dark, stage-like setting suggests some discordance between the machine and its new home. The plaster figure is dull, passive, even a little despondent. The space between man and machine recalls how many of the personal computers available in 1982 lacked the graphical user interfaces (GUIs) and mouses that would accelerate the transformation of the computer into an object available for mass consumption later in the 1980s. The computer had moved in, but *Time*'s cover portrays its arrival as staged within an almost lifeless drama of inhuman figures.

The magazine made a similar selection when it named "You" as the "Person of the Year" in 2006. This later cover features a keyboard and white desktop computer with a screen of reflective Mylar (fig. 11). The reflections of *Time*'s readers supply the human figure for the cover. The icons below the Mylar illustrate why "You" have been named Person of the Year: they suggest users are able to play, pause, and scan to different points in their lives, creating content that expresses their sense of self. In contrast to the 1982 cover, with its slumped plaster man sitting at a distance from the desktop, the iconography on the 2006 cover signifies the ability for ordinary users to interact through the machine. This difference between the plaster man and the reflective Mylar illustrates a paradigm shift from what Alan Liu calls "informating" to "networking."[1] In the former paradigm, computers gave users access to "the systemic whole of technological rationality," as though power over information had become newly accessible.[2] The paradigm of networking, in contrast, imagines computer users as part of a "boundary-crossing, decentralized, and outward-looking orientation of the new global economy."[3] The ability to manipulate "You" through the computer assimilates personal identity within this global technological network.

Despite these important differences in the *Time* covers, both associate computational technology with generic configurations of identity. The plaster man is generic in the sense of being formulaic; he stands in for all PC users, as though this figure were characteristic of the class of people for whom computing has become "personal." The middle-aged white man did not in fact represent the many communities using computers at the time, but the cover nonetheless presents him as a nondescript Everyman awed by the "'information revolution' that futurists have long predicted," as the accompanying article explains.[4] The arrival of the PC hails "the promise of dramatic changes in the way people live and work, perhaps even in the way they think."[5] The material of plaster embodies this "promise" by signifying how "people" may be molded by computing technology.

A different kind of genericity appears in the 2006 cover of *Time*. The "You" reflected by Mylar revises the demographically limited proxy on the 1982 cover by implying that anyone could be a computer user. *Time*'s tagline for this later cover reads, "Yes, you. You control the Information Age. Welcome to your world." Whereas the plaster figure was a generic

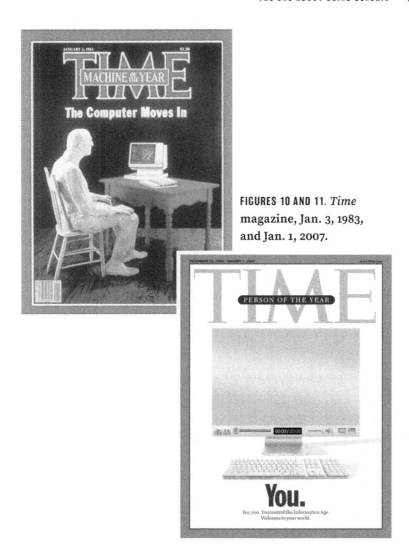

FIGURES 10 AND 11. *Time* magazine, Jan. 3, 1983, and Jan. 1, 2007.

Everyman, the "You" could be a demographic anyone, a global self limited only by the willingness of readers to imagine themselves through the reflective material. It's as though the conditions of being generic had, by 2006, become global and postracial.[6] The kinds of identity attached to computational technology were no longer restricted to middle-aged businessmen in the United States but, instead, were modeled after the idea of infinite personalization.

Some critics of this shift assert that computational technology undermines our capacity for distinctive social experience. For example, Roberto Esposito argues that the logic of "personalization" implicit in this 2006 cover "pushes [the user] into the faceless dimension of the object."[7] For Esposito, the conflation of personhood and user-generated content makes being a self equivalent to being an object of technological mediation. Friedrich Kittler expresses a related concern in his influential study *Gramophone, Film, Typewriter* (1986), which laments how computing "erases the differences among individual media."[8] Once the infrastructure for exchanging digital information "turn[s] formerly distinct data flows into a standardized series of numbers, any medium can be translated into any other."[9] According to these critics, the computer's seemingly infinite capacity to manipulate information reduces all experience into a standardized format and then effaces the distinctiveness of experience itself.

Rather than reading a hard-and-fast distinction between the *Time* covers of 1982 and 2006, the criticisms by Esposito and Kittler highlight how the covers capture different aspects of an ongoing structure of experience.[10] I describe this structure as *being generic*, a phrase that carries interlocking connotations. In one set of connotations, the generic means formulaic, standardized, or unoriginal. Being generic in this sense most often registers as an insult, personal deficit, or artistic hazard: art on a greeting card, the music in banking commercials, dialogue in a B film. Responses to this kind of genericity often range from dismissal and scorn to a more general sense of alienation within a sea of bland commodities. This spectrum of aesthetic failures often arises from a sense of basic inauthenticity: being generic in this sense signifies that an artist or individual has lost touch with some interior truth by hewing too closely to a preset pattern.

The comedian Aziz Ansari invokes this sense of the generic when he jokes about how smart technology has changed dating behavior: "Want to know what's filling up the phones of nearly every single woman? It's this: 'Hey,' 'Hey!' 'Heyyy!!' 'Hey what's going on?' 'Wsup,' 'Wsup!' 'What's going on?' 'Whatcha up to?'"[11] He notes that people who send the "generic 'hey' text" are imitating a widely reproducible strategy for initiating a conversation or hookup. This strategy may be reassuring, he says, but the hazard is that it "makes you seem like a pretty boring, generic person."[12] The vast expansion of potential romantic partners made possible through online platforms, combined with the ease and immediacy of digital communication, invites users to be both more prolifically expressive and paradoxically unoriginal.

A related aesthetic threat hangs over the films, essays, novels, and computational practices examined in this chapter. The worry is that cultural work and social experience have become generic as they've become computational: everything from the routines of coupling to the aesthetics of our online lives has come to seem like a mere repetition of infinitely personalized but effectively vacuous identity. In this sense, being generic is a fact about computational mediation transformed into a broader symptom of social malaise.

A second set of connotations differs from this angst-ridden worry. The generic can also refer to a system of classification: a document like an instruction manual and a linguistic act like a judge's ruling are both generic in the sense that their meaning is based on the social conventions surrounding use and occurrence. The distinction between a judge's ruling and, say, a comedian satirizing a judge's ruling entails several factors, including the setting, contextual expectations, and social cues like tone or exaggerated performativity.[13] The comedian's performance registers as satire when an audience understands the confluence of cues and context to be a humorous and critical qualification of the surface-level meaning of the performance.[14] In this instance, registering as generic entails a sense of recognition or a feeling of affinity. The affinity can be with other members of an audience—*this is the time when we laugh*—but the identification sometimes made possible by comic genericity may also derive from an acknowledgment that an instance of discourse is in conversation with other instances. This second sense of the generic amounts to an ongoing dialogue about membership in a *genre*, and it promises affiliation and recognition through shared social cues and conventions.

These two senses of the generic can operate simultaneously; they can also conflict with one another. I read these different registers of being generic as aesthetic expressions of the conflicting wants that arise when social experience becomes computationally mediated. The cultural and computational works examined in this chapter reckon with both senses of the generic. These works draw on forms of comedy to accommodate the desire to share a social world, as well as a conflicting hesitancy about the mediated terms under which that shared world is stitched together.

COMEDY AND DEFAMILIARIZATION

Contemporary accounts of comedy often point to the pleasures of playing with generic expectations. In Tina Fey's account of the acclaimed TV show *30 Rock* (2006–13), she explains how many episodes take generic scenarios or stereotypes and make them "nuts" or "weird."[15] In an early episode, for example, the comedian Paul Reubens plays an "Austrian prince named Gerhardt Hapsburg." His surname places Gerhardt within a royal lineage and sets up one of the scene's central jokes: the idea that royal families are "inbred." Playing with this idea, Reubens "committed deeply to his role. He chose to wear fake teeth and pale makeup, and he had one tiny ivory hand."[16] Gerhardt's hand obviously makes a joke out of the limb malformations that can result from inbreeding, but the fact that it is ivory—a substance that requires the tusks of an elephant and has thus become increasingly unacceptable in many social circles—invokes not only the wealth of the prince but also his outmoded views about extravagance.

The central gag of the scene centers on a proposed romantic union between Gerhardt and another character named Jenna (Jane Krakowski), who "is determined to 'Grace Kelly' herself by meeting and marrying Gerhardt and becoming a princess."[17] This coming-together of Jenna and Gerhardt is a classic instance of comic incongruity: she is young, attractive, and vivacious; he is pallid, awkward, and "malformed."[18] Fey describes this physical incongruity as a marker of the "weird" extent Jenna will go to become a princess through marriage. The scene obviously exploits stereotypes about a generic inbred royal but also shows how Jenna willingly positions herself as the sexist caricature of an opportunistic single woman. "You know I've always reminded myself of Grace Kelly," she tells Liz Lemon (Tina Fey). The line is funny not because she *is* a generic type but because her identity is a conscious performance of a type. "I'm not going to be gorgeous forever," she says. "And I have no other skills whatsoever. I need to find someone who can take care of me."

What Fey describes as the "strange" comedy of the episode is less about the incongruity of opposed generic types coming together than the fact that the characters deliberately want to be stock characters.[19] The series uses these generic types to invoke familiar expectations but then creates pleasure by contorting or misrepresenting what at first seemed familiar. This is a long-standing technique in comic drama. Critics often note how types like the *eiron* (dissembler) and stock characters like the foolish old man were integral to Renaissance drama and Italian *commedia dell'arte*. Many of Shakespeare's characters "owe their consistency to the appropriateness of the stock type," Northrop Frye argues, because the reproducible pattern "is as necessary to the character as a skeleton to the actor."[20] Frye is not suggesting that Shakespeare's characters are *merely* unoriginal; his point is that their unoriginal types become the structure on which complexity and comic humor are built. The generic type allows Shakespeare to play off the audience's expectations. Many other forms of comedy similarly rely on synecdoche and generic characters to compress narrative duration and prepare the audience for pleasures in plot and dialogue.[21]

From Shakespeare to Fey, genericity has served as a technique for the management of expectations: it establishes norms but also allows for their disruption. In this way, the generic does not merely designate alienated abstraction, although certainly that connotation is still present in characters like Jenna and Gerhardt Hapsburg. The generic contains multiple, competing registers, much like Lauren Berlant's gloss on the term *ambivalence*: "strongly mixed, drawn in many directions, positively and negatively charged."[22] The condition of *being generic* is likewise pulled in competing directions, but this condition often becomes comic when cultural producers exploit it to imagine the pursuit of happiness, humor, or pleasure from its structuring incongruities.

This "strongly mixed" sense of the generic is central to Spike Jonze's short film "I'm Here" (2010), which takes as its opening premise a world populated by people resembling computers. The male-presenting characters in the film have heads like old PC towers (fig. 12). Shapes vaguely resembling eyes and thin lines suggestive of a mouth appear on the blank sides of the towers, and changes to these lines signify the characters' emotions. At first, the emotional register of the film is melancholic. It opens with a montage from the vantage of a bus window: empty parking lots, neglected storefronts, dilapidated cars parked on the street. These images are depicted from the perspective of a character named Sheldon (Andrew Garfield), whose facial expressions imitate the melancholy scenes observed from the window. Sheldon soon leaves the bus and mumbles a timid but unacknowledged "Hey" to another computer-person. He then enters his apartment building and greets his neighbors, who also ignore him.

The opening scene casts Sheldon's character in a recognizable role in contemporary film. His routine of aimless solitude recalls Charlie Kaufman (Nicolas Cage) in Jonze's *Adaptation* (2002), Barry Egan (Adam Sandler) in Paul Thomas Anderson's *Punch-Drunk Love* (2002), and Bob

FIGURE 12. The computational form of Sheldon (Andrew Garfield). "I'm Here," dir. Spike Jonze (Absolut/MJZ, 2010).

Harris (Bill Murray) in Sofia Coppola's *Lost in Translation* (2003). The role is a specific type of the person who leads what Thoreau calls a life of quiet desperation: social and economic norms about capitalist production isolate these protagonists within the tedium of work (for Sheldon, it's shelving library books). For this character type, it's as though dull routinization is the essence of everyday life, not an ersatz substitute for it. This filmic tradition typically depicts women as symbolic escapes from the tedium: they satisfy men's emotional needs, or the woman's sexuality interjects a measure of acceptable nonconformity. The promise or pursuit of romance elevates the man and transforms his relation to the routines of everyday life.

Like Barry Egan and Bob Harris, Sheldon feels trapped within a loop and only discovers the possibility of liberation through the pursuit of romantic love. One day, while waiting for the bus, another character, Francesca (Sienna Guillory), offers Sheldon a ride home. One of Francesca's friends asks Sheldon his name, which (like the changing of clothes in an Ibsen play) corresponds to the transformation of Sheldon's character. He says his name for the first time in the film, and this voicing of an identity signifies the beginning of an almost religious conversion in which Sheldon rejects his anonymous life and returns to his routine as a born-again computer.

If Thoreau's remark about a life of quiet desperation describes one feature of this generic pattern, the answer to this alienation is likewise indebted to other aspects of the transcendentalist tradition. These debts become evident when Sheldon and Francesca walk through a forest during what in similar films would be a courtship scene. The two first hold hands during this walk, and the implication seems to be that their love is as "natural" as the forest they inhabit. This use of natural space as a stage for Sheldon's salvation from conformity draws conspicuously, if only indirectly, on transcendentalist thought. "At the gates of the forest," Emerson writes, "the surprised man of the world is forced to leave his city estimates of great and small, wise and foolish. The knapsack of custom falls off his back with the first step he makes into these precincts."[23] A passage through the forest facilitates Sheldon's repudiation of social scripts. Rather than being a computer caught within an alienating loop—a preset program of conformity—his walk in the woods with Francesca allows him to discover a new "circumstance which dwarfs every other circumstance."[24]

This circumstance is, of course, love itself, and for this reason, Shakespeare's comedies are equally influential in the film. Frye argues that Shakespeare's comedies stage the "drama of the green world" in which characters move from established society through a transformative natural space and then back again.[25] In *The Two Gentlemen of Verona* (1593), for instance, all the characters are eventually gathered into a forest where they undergo a "metamorphosis," and "the comic resolution is achieved."[26] This movement through the green world ushers in a new, happier union and transforms the social order established at the start of the play. In keeping with this trope, the computational characters in Jonze's film come together physically at the end of their walk in the forest and return to their ordinary routines in the city as a united couple (fig. 13).

What is interesting about Jonze's film is that the computer provides a form for the characters but also a form for the character of experience. I think this duality represents an attempt to recuperate the possibility

FIGURE 13. Sheldon and Francesca leaving the Green World. "I'm Here," dir. Spike Jonze (Absolut/MJZ, 2010).

of the genre's sincerity. It is a truth universally acknowledged that the coming-together of a heterosexual couple is the most widely used plot structure in contemporary film. This structure regularly becomes trite, devolving into obligatory patterns and predictable climaxes. Noting this problem of overfamiliarity, a character in Curtis Sittenfeld's *Romantic Comedy* (2022)—a novel that I examine at length later in this chapter—notes how "romantic comedies . . . usually end with one of the people hurrying to be reunited with the other and publicly declaring their love." Another character observes, "The term for that is a grand gesture."[27] Sittenfeld's characters dismiss this trope as "cheesiness," one among many terms capturing the aesthetic hazard of comedy's familiar plot arc. According to this sentiment, the romcom genre registers at a structural level as affected and blatantly inauthentic. It becomes cheap, predictable, and aesthetically suspect.

Jonze's film uses the computational forms of its characters to accommodate this aesthetic hazard. Soon after Sheldon and Francesca emerge from the woods as a couple, she loses an arm while dancing at a punk rock concert and then her leg in an unexplained accident. In both cases Sheldon detaches one of his computerized appendages and convinces Francesca to accept it. At the end, Francesca's torso is irreparably damaged, and it seems that she cannot be rebooted. Sheldon directs a surgeon to save her by using parts from his body. All that remains of Sheldon after the operation is the PC tower of his head. Francesca is restored to life, and she leaves the hospital cradling what is left of her lover.

The saccharine flavor that threatens every romcom's happy ending has a strange and unfamiliar quality in Jonze's film. The drive within romantic comedy toward happy coupling is expected, rigid, even compulsory: the plot arc is like a computer that cannot deviate from its programming. Jonze's film flips this image of the computer as an instrument of rigid utility, producing what Viktor Shklovsky calls *ostranenie* (variously translated as "defamiliarization" or "enstrangement"). By defamiliarizing the familiar, art provides "the means to live through the making of a thing"—that is, to recover the lost significance of everyday existence in an automated world.[28] Jonze's film uses the form of the computer to defamiliarize the tired, widely reproduced trope of the "grand gesture," and its happy ending avoids the saccharine because it's so strange. Sheldon, with his computer-tower head and reliance on a daily charging routine, escapes a drab form of life simply by reimagining it through love. Yet the centrality of Sheldon's body and face in the film also makes strange the genre of romantic comedy by attaching its conventions to a drab mechanical form. The eyes and mouth line that stand in for Sheldon's face are nondescript, as though they were generic proxies; they are almost like emoticons. Often, only Sheldon's voice distinguishes him from other male-presenting computers, which generally lack hair or other specific markings.

I said above that the stock characters in Shakespearean comedy and Fey's *30 Rock* use the generic to manage expectations. Jonze's film similarly uses generic figures to establish expectations, yet it also disrupts them for artistic pleasure. Indeed, the film places in tension two sets of expectations: one about the computerized body, which is expected to conform to its programming, and a second about the sense of freedom and new life that supposedly come from romantic coupling. To prevent the latter set of expectations from becoming a trite gesture or aesthetic failure, the film uses the image of computers throwing off the dullness of routine work to reimagine romantic coupling. The two sets of expectations play off one another, loosening the rigidity associated with both.

Being generic is thus both a motivating problem that "I'm Here" must solve (i.e., its genre's conventions are overly familiar) and an aesthetic form for the solution to that problem (i.e., the computer's form reconfigures the genre's conventions in a new and unexpected way). It is as though comedy and the computer come together in a marriage of convenience: the technology has figurative resources useful for making a genre of film newly plausible. I argue later in this chapter that the inverse occurs in the use of humor in intelligent agents and AI assistants: the technology turns toward comedy to make plausible certain fictions about its use. Being generically funny confirms the agent's facility with the machinery of comedy and disposes the user to take the program as an object of ordinary utility. In both Jonze's film and the comedy of intelligent agents, the generic poses an aesthetic problem but also provides a possible solution to the threat that computational technology debases ordinary experience.

I examine this vexed dynamic throughout the remainder of this chapter. The next two sections show how being generic, as both a problem and solution, structures comic representations of computational media. I argue that this both/and quality to being generic is an aesthetic form of ambivalence toward the kinds of sociality produced by these media. Ambivalence, as Sianne Ngai notes, does not "subtract" from or mute feelings of attachment. Instead, ambivalence is a "copresence" of competing multiples.[29] The cultural work I examine suggests how strongly mixed feelings about computational media intensify our dependence on them. These works of fiction, film, and literary journalism record feelings of alienation from generic social experiences facilitated by the computer, yet copresent with that alienation is the desire for proximity to those experiences. Much like Jonze's use of the computer as a signifier of the dullness of ordinary routines, the writers I examine below work out their ambivalence about becoming computational in relation to what is perhaps one of the most ordinary forms of computational technology: email.

EMAIL ATTACHMENTS

Writing in 1989, a Stanford engineer predicted that email would soon be supplanted by the fax machine.[30] Since this proclamation, the death of email has been repeatedly announced by business leaders, social-media users, and journalists in magazines like *Wired* and *Slate*. Cloud-based applications like Slack pitch their platforms as disruptors for workplace communication. As Esther Milne explains, these recurring proclamations of email's "media obsolescence" fit within the tech industry's vision of "magically transformative capitalism."[31] Email's naysayers recite a litany of flaws: the medium silos users and their ideas, integrates awkwardly with other media, proliferates textual ambiguity, generates excessive and useless data, is notoriously insecure, and does not allow for sufficiently instantaneous communication.[32] Email also supposedly undermines creativity and productivity by adding unnecessary bureaucratic labor to everyday experience in the office. Email, in other words, typifies everything that is wrong with the workplace becoming computational.[33]

Yet one of the curious facts about the cultural history of email is that a medium always on the cusp of obsolescence has also been among those most iconically linked to narratives of romantic coupling and sexual connection.[34] We will see one of the clearest and most influential versions of these links later in this chapter in Nora Ephron's classic film *You've Got Mail* (1998). Curtis Sittenfeld's novel *Romantic Comedy* also exploits email's metaphorical possibilities, but for Sittenfeld, the mediating work of computational technology raises questions about the obsolescence of romantic coupling itself.

Sittenfeld's novel centers on the relationship between a TV scriptwriter named Sally Milz and a pop star named Noah Brewster. Sally works for an SNL-like show called *The Night Owls,* and she meets Noah when he appears on the show as a musical guest. The narrative mode begins in Sally's first-person perspective but later shifts into the couple's email exchange when the COVID-19 pandemic sends the country into lockdown. This remediation of romantic coupling into email is not necessary, because other technologies exist for the couple to communicate. The reason email seems to be such a potent metaphor in *Romantic Comedy*—and my argument is that this also applies to other works, like *You've Got Mail*—is that the medium allows writers and directors to trade on the metaphorical language of entry, penetration, whispered confession, and physical union. In other words, the medium becomes a figurative proxy for the self and bodily intimacy. It evokes ideas of connection within those social experiences structured by computational media.[35]

One example of this metaphorical register appears before the novel's digital-epistolary section. Noah sends Sally a potential skit for *The Night Owls.* After she receives his email, Sally says, "Your attachment isn't going to give me an STI, is it?" (38). The two laugh, and the joke sets the tone for their later email exchanges. It also obviously suggests how an email account operates like a stand-in for some intimate part of the person. As the two sit at Sally's computer and work on the sketch, she narrates how "it felt weirdly intimate to expose my inbox to Noah" (38).

Her jokes riff on the metaphorical possibilities of email as a medium to suggest that Noah's message, which is of course only a packet of data, moves from his account to hers, as though the exchange were a movement of sexual fluids between bodies. In fact, given Sally's joke about his "attachment," her own confession is very likely a double entendre because "inbox" can be slang for female genitalia.[36] Exposing her inbox thus feels like exposing some intimate aspect of herself, but it also participates in an elaborate reading of email as a metaphor for intercourse.

What makes this line of humor comprehensible to us? What cultural logic underwrites the affinity between the medium of email and the affective terrain of intimacy? One source for the analogies at play is the sense of "presence" created by digital technologies. As Milne explains, email fosters "a sense of physical and/or psychological proximity" among "geographically dispersed agents."[37] Although "physical presence" is also mediated by institutions and cultures, we are rarely conscious of that mediation. In contrast, there is a kind of cognitive sleight of hand that occurs when using email: we are aware of using a tool yet feel that the medium has somehow become transparent, as though it were facilitating a seamless and direct connection between ourselves and others or, at least, between our discourse and theirs. This transparency is a design feature of the medium, and one of its effects is to create the sense of being transported into the presence of another person.[38]

The legibility of the joke in Sittenfeld's *Romantic Comedy* riffs on the feeling of "presence" and the idea of information technology as an extension of the self. The information that moves from Noah's account to Sally's becomes something like a "compounding" of "matter and information" exchanged during sexual intercourse.[39] Sally's joke takes her email account as a proxy for her body; an exchange with other users signifies in some sense an intermingling of that digital body with the self of another.[40] Even her worry that "it felt weirdly intimate to expose my inbox to Noah" illustrates an unspoken conflation of bodily language and digital information. Exposing her inbox *feels* like being uncovered, unclothed.

Related ways of representing the experience of social life through email appear throughout John Seabrook's essay "E-mail from Bill," published in the *New Yorker* in 1994. Seabrook's essay doubles as a profile of Bill Gates and a meditation on the rise of email as a form of communication. Seabrook emails with Gates for several months prior to meeting him in person. The two discuss key moments in the history of Microsoft, but the essay's interest is drawn constantly toward the subtle transformation that email produces within the contours of Seabrook's experience. "At the beginning of our electronic relationship," he writes, "I would wake up in the middle of the night and lie in bed wondering if I had E-mail from Bill."[41] The sentence exemplifies the essay's wry and quasi-erotic humor. The depiction of an email relationship—Seabrook describes Gates as his "first"—becomes a strange yet familiar remediation of both epistolary courtship and face-to-face interviewing.[42]

Writing at a time when email was just becoming widespread outside of the military and tech industries, Seabrook expresses surprise at how the medium presents itself as a form of direct access to another person. He notes, for example, how "I had the sense that [Gates] was present, in the network, flying around the Microsoft campus and popping into people's computers" even though he and his then-wife Melinda "were in Africa at the time."[43] The medium produces not just a message but a feeling about messages. As Seabrook presents it, email fosters social attachments by *detaching* the feeling of a person—the sense of being personable with them—from physical presence. Letter writing could of course foster a similar sense of presence, but Seabrook notes how the immediacy and ease of electronic exchange seemed to collapse time and distance between users in a way that changed perceptions about the social order. This is particularly the case as the new medium seemed to unsettle who could get access to whom: "New employees at Microsoft are likely to encounter Bill Gates electronically long before they meet him in person."[44] This affective reshuffling of the social makes otherwise distant people feel present to one another, as though intimacy were solely a function of mind and not matter.

Seabrook's insight illustrates an intriguing dynamic in the cultural history of email, which is that the medium has often generated this feeling of presence even though most software platforms that facilitate email accounts are decidedly banal or nondescript in their design.[45] Microsoft's first platform, called Microsoft Mail, gave users access to features created by earlier engineers, like "Reply" and "Reply All," but it did so through Windows' now-familiar menu of icons. The aesthetics and iconography of Microsoft Mail provided a generic context for the management of information. Microsoft Mail allowed users to access their accounts whether in Mumbai or Manhattan, and this access would have the same common form.

Scholars of digital communication have noted how the design of early email clients shaped the user experience in unexpected ways. For example, in their analysis of employee and managerial email practices in several large corporations, Lee Sproull and Sara Kiesler show that the design of the medium removes "social context cues" that govern in-person interactions. The lack of these cues increases the likelihood that a sender will use a "chatty tone" and reveal inappropriate "personal information."[46] Sproull and Kiesler argue that the design of the medium creates an unexpected social paradox: email standardizes the ways in which information is shared, yet the absence of social cues scrambles the sender's sense of social norms and often leads to deeply unprofessional communication, or what is colloquially known as "flaming."[47]

Nora Ephron makes a joke out of these design effects in a comic essay titled "The Six Stages of E-mail" (2010). She observes that although email "was just born, . . . overnight it turns out to have a form and a set of rules and a language all its own."[48] Ephron jokes about the ways in which the medium has created new and seemingly compulsory kinds of sociality: "E-mail is a whole new way of being friends with people: intimate but not, chatty but not, communicative but not; in short, friends but not. What a breakthrough. How did we ever live without it?"[49] The negation of each quality suggests the affects produced by email conflict with the social terrain it actually facilitates. The medium engenders forms of relationality that are paradoxically anonymous, impersonal, duplicitous, and disconnected. She says her inbox fills with unsolicited intimacies: "Add three inches to the length of your penis. The Democratic National Committee needs you. Virus Alert. FW: This will make you laugh. FW: This is funny. FW: This is hilarious."[50] These subject lines suggest an ongoing conversation, but most senders are organizations or complete strangers. The appeals seem direct, even intimate, but their claims on her are remote; she feels alienated from the constant sharing of supposed confidences: "AOL Member: We value your opinion. A message from Barack Obama. Find low mortgage payments, Nora."[51] It's as though the ease and convenience of the medium deludes us into thinking we are friends with a vast social world, yet it actually only proliferates the unnecessary and impersonal. It *feels* like we hear directly from the powerful or that corporate America cares about us individually.

Ephron's essay finds a kind of gallows humor in the overwhelming exchange of nonsense facilitated by a medium that seemingly began with the promise of simplifying communication. Part of this promise is articulated in how email clients replace social cues with metaphors of productivity, like the familiar pictograms accompanying "Move" and "Delete" in Microsoft Mail's interface. These metaphors define labor in terms of an organizational schema. Simple features like the standardization of the platform's font and its layout of folders similarly regulate all discourse according to an aesthetic shared by all the client's users. The genericity of email at once facilitates professional standardization while paradoxically compromising professionalism by unfettering users from social cues that would typically restrain "rabidly or incessantly" talking or adopting a "patently ridiculous attitude."[52]

George Saunders takes this rabid ridiculousness as a characteristic of everyday professional experience in his comic short story "Exhortation." The form of the story is a series of emails by a character named Todd Birnie, a midlevel director of an unnamed corporation. Birnie writes to his staff to encourage them to increase their productivity despite the negative working conditions. The tone of Birnie's emails creates an awkward mixture of organizational coercion, personal desperation, and feigned informality: "I would not like to characterize this as a plea, although it may start to sound like one (!). The fact is, we have a job to do, we have tacitly agreed to do it (did you cash your last paycheck, I know I did, ha ha ha)."[53] The loose attention to grammatical conventions mirrors how Birnie is seemingly trying *not* to control and intimidate his employees. Yet across the story, he loses this measured stylization of his discourse, and his language devolves into flaming, threats, and a kind of manic desperation. The medium of email provides a *form* for the attempts and failures to sustain a sense of the personal amid the professional pressures of contemporary corporate life.

As the formal elements of Saunders's story show, the *wants* of email are in conflict. To say that the medium has *wants* is to understand it in a way analogous to the architect Louis I. Kahn's claim that built environments have *wants* that derive from their design.[54] At a fundamental level, buildings shape how people interact: they *want* isolation, centralized gathering, or the display of wealth. Scholars of digital technology have adapted Kahn's framing when considering the social effects of media.[55] The medium of email has competing wants, and one result of this inbuilt tension is that the medium often invites "antisocial behavior" even though its generic aesthetics and functionality aim to produce a sense that users share a social space for the exchange of discourse.[56]

The literature I've been discussing also suggests that the wants articulated in the design of email include both identification and abstraction. These incongruous wants become fodder for comedy in "E-mail from Bill" as Seabrook draws on images familiar to romantic comedy to understand the contradictory feelings that arise in his exchange with Gates. "We were intimate in a curious way, in the sense of being wired into each other's minds," Seabrook writes, "but our contact was elaborately stylized, like ballroom dancing."[57] "Being wired into each other's minds" is, of course, an image of penetration, much like Sally's joke about Noah's "attachment" in *Romantic Comedy*. Yet Seabrook pairs this image with a different metaphor: the image of himself and Gates as partners in a self-aware dance. They intermingle but hold one another at a distance; they are in intimate contact yet are anything but alone.

The incongruities of digital communication become a source of comic pleasure in Seabrook's essay, but in Sittenfeld's novel, email raises questions about the obsolescence of romantic love itself, which the narrator, Sally, portrays as "cheesy nonsense" in a romcom film she begins scripting after leaving *The Night Owls* (118). The self-referential title of Sittenfeld's novel nods to both Sally's writing plans and the narrative's predictable outcome: despite her cynicism, Sally falls in love with the musician Noah, who later serenades her in a "grand gesture" that they both previously describe as a generic trope in romantic comedies (286).

Sittenfeld's novel considers the extent to which "romantic partnership" can be authentic if it conforms to these kinds of generic conventions (74). Sally claims that romantic comedies have ruined the experience of romance because they have created narrow and unrealistic expectations for finding happiness with another person.[58] The genre's conflation of a happy ending with romantic union can imply that only a very specific kind of coupling generates human flourishing. Sally hopes her film will satirize these expectations, but her critique seems in direct conflict with her experience with Noah. Does this conflict undermine Sally's feminist commitments? Or does it inadvertently affirm the power of the cultural narrative that happiness is found in a monogamous union? Is an experience that adheres to generic conventions necessarily inauthentic?

The medium of email becomes a proxy for addressing these questions in the novel. The pandemic forces Sally and Noah into isolation, but email enables them to feel as though they are in the presence of another person. At first, these "emails weren't explicitly romantic but they weren't explicitly not romantic either," as Sally puts it (164). This ambiguous romance-by-proxy leads both to share more about themselves. Sally, for instance, recounts how she once confessed her love for another comedian, who responded, "Sally, you've confused the romance of comedy with the romance of romance" (192). While she tells Noah in an email that this was a "supremely douchey thing to say," she concedes that her attraction was mixed up with her love for the work of making comedy (192). Still, she rejects the idea that comedy and romance are distinct—that the pleasures of one should not be confused with the other—and Noah later appropriates this line, writing that he himself is "in danger of confusing the romance of emailing with the romance of romance" (195).

This back-and-forth binds the experience of coupling with the ubiquity of mediating structures. What Noah calls the "romance of emailing" refers to being in love with the feeling of another's presence facilitated by a computer. But the "romance of romance" is not all that different: this phrase describes being in love with the feeling of another's presence facilitated by generic conventions. The mediating work of email becomes analogous to the mediating work of romantic comedy as a cultural template, and the characters acknowledge their reliance on both for making sense of their lives. Finding something like intimacy with one another first requires them to acknowledge that mediation is not inherently nefarious, or at least that their ambivalence about mediation is both positively and negatively charged, and this realization frees them from the need to be wholly original.

Sally and Noah's acceptance that their lives conform to a common pattern leads to several kinds of comedy in the novel's epilogue. Sally recounts how she and Noah were married in a small ceremony. Even though they choose an unostentatious wedding, Sally still jokes that she has entered "the ultimate heteropatriarchal institution" (299). The comment nods ironically to the fact that her narration ends precisely where one would expect a novel titled *Romantic Comedy* to end: a wedding. Of course, the idea that a wedding could serve as a form of comic resolution was a common way to address the problem of plot in Renaissance drama, and it became a staple in the novel beginning in the eighteenth century.[59] The link between comedy and marriage was so overly familiar that Jane Austen ironically depicts it in the opening of *Pride and Prejudice* (1813): "It is a truth universally acknowledged that a single man in possession of a good fortune must be in want of a wife."[60] Beginning with this ironic statement, Austen's novel devalues the wedding ceremony and the religious authorities that facilitate it, showing, instead, that marriage too often serves a broader devaluation of personal judgment by early nineteenth-century social institutions.[61] In Austen's hands, the comic marriage plot centers on changes within the characters' consciousness and private judgments; these tensions are resolved during the courtship, not with the ceremony of marriage itself. The importance of this difference between Austen's novels and those of her predecessors is that she devalues the licensing power of those authorities; the moral center of her novels resides not in institutions but virtuous private judgments.[62]

Sally's casual remark about marrying Noah harkens back to Austen's attitude toward the ceremony of marriage. Like Austen, Sittenfeld prioritizes the self-awareness and shifts in judgment that occur for her heroine during Sally's "courtship" with Noah. This inner transformation preserves a kind of liberal skepticism toward institutional authorities, but it also acknowledges that the practice of judgment cannot be disentangled from the structure of experience that I am calling genericity. The novel resolves its plot with a conventional marriage while its main character criticizes that plot—a reflexive tension that echoes the ambivalence Sally feels about romantic comedy more generally.

There are of course important differences between Austen's and Sittenfeld's comic novels, not the least of which is the social pressures they each must navigate. Whereas Austen's depiction of marriage was situated in debates between Whigs and Tories, Sittenfeld's novel must somehow bring together its "generic borrowings" with the cultural authority of feminism in the twenty-first-century media industry.[63] This cultural authority tends to advance, or at least contend with, some combination of the following claims about the marriage plot in modern culture:

1. The marriage plot encloses the sexuality, social lives, and political power of women within domestic space, effectively trapping them in a realm of privacy while retaining the public sphere as an arena for patriarchal power.
2. It presupposes that a woman's value resides finally in her ability to find recognition from male desire.
3. The ubiquity of the marriage plot not only marginalizes queer desire and gay and lesbian relationships, but it is also based in classist and racist norms about respectability, social stability, and biological reproductivity.
4. It is a property relation disguised as a private agreement. The sexuality, romance, and happiness promised in marriage obfuscate the institution's economic functions.
5. Its termination of diegetic action presents a fantasy of stasis. One effect of this stasis is that it tempers (regulates, binds together) personalities that are otherwise dissident or socially disruptive. Another effect of this final stasis is that the almost compulsory nature of the plot "naturalizes" an institution that is socially constructed and historically recent.[64]

Sally's use of the term *heteropatriarchal*—a popular shorthand for several of these claims—indicates how feminism as a cultural discourse shapes the way she imagines her experience. This discourse creates demands that compete with the genre that seemingly matches that experience. The *form* of her happiness conflicts with the *critique* that derives from her politics. This is what I mean when I say that competing wants structure Sally's narrative, and their copresence seems to force her into a conflicted affective posture toward her experience of romance.

Another example of this tension appears when Sally and Noah find themselves hewing closely to the romcom scripts they have previously derided. After wryly noting this conformity, Noah remarks, "When it's happening to other people, it's cheesy. When it's happening to you, it's wonderful" (286). Sally responds that the "emotional extravagance" of another couple may hint at the inauthenticity of their union, while such affective terrain is entirely desirable when "you" are the one to occupy it (286). The idea of *others* finding happiness according to a widely reproducible pattern can seem deeply suspect. Sally and Noah's identification with this pattern—the fact that it happens to them, that it is the genre for *their* experience—makes it seem distinctive. In this view, the problem is not the widely repeated structure of a commercial genre; the problem is other people. It's as though Sally and Noah accommodate themselves to the idea of being generic by laying claim to the genre as a personal category; they take ownership of a generalized form for the particularities of their experience. If comedy is a technique of accommodation, here it also becomes a fantasy about personalization.

Sheldon and Francesca, Sally and Noah, John and Bill—the coming-together of these couples depends on the ways in which the computer makes ordinary life seem available for personalization within generic forms. In the depictions of these couples, the computer signifies the threat of lost distinctiveness while also being the basis for imagining their union as somehow unique or individually managed. Much like the "You" that appears on the 2006 cover of *Time* magazine, the computer offers a tool for these couples to control their social lives, even as it also seems to standardize the procedures for exercising that control. So, too, with genre. The presence of generic templates raises the possibility of debased or unoriginal experience, even as the generic also provides a form for these couples to have some control over the pursuit of happiness.

This conflicted dynamic shows how personal attachments in contemporary experience often become indistinguishable from attachments to genres of sociality: the choice to become a couple comes to feel like a choice to become generic. The doubling of the computer's symbolic value (hazard/solution, alienation/mediator of intimacy) mirrors this doubling of what it means to find oneself as part of a couple through computational media. The genre of experience that I am describing as the comedy of computation holds together these tensions through the idea that somehow the computer allows for personalization. To put this point in a slightly different way, one of the cultural roles often assigned to the computer is to serve as the emblem of a fantasy about taking possession of the generic, thereby making generic experience compatible with the moral ideal of authenticity.

GENRE FILM AND THE PURSUIT OF HAPPINESS

An immensely popular version of this structure of experience underwrites Nora Ephron's film *You've Got Mail*. The film's opening scene takes place in a New York apartment shared by Kathleen Kelly (Meg Ryan) and Frank Navasky (Greg Kinnear). Kathleen is awakened by Frank's outrage at a news report that the "entire workforce of the State of Virginia had to have solitaire removed from their computers because they hadn't done any work in six weeks." Frank views this article as evidence that computers are "the end of Western civilization as we know it." In Frank's view, the computer only *seems* to be an instrument that increases productivity, but in fact he maintains that something more pernicious is running behind the programming. "You think this machine's your friend," he tells Kathleen, "but it's not." For Frank, users do not come together with computers; they become its unwitting subjects, giving the machine their attention while squandering their labor.[65]

The film answers Frank's view by connecting computational media to the pursuit of happiness. In the opening scene, Kathleen waits until

Frank leaves for work; when she sees him exit their building, she runs eagerly toward her computer and logs on to the internet through her service provider, AOL, whose interface announces, "You've got mail!"[66] Shopgirl, Kathleen's AOL handle, has received an email from a stranger she knows only as NY152. The email tells Shopgirl about NY152's walks throughout New York City with his dog, Brinkley. Kathleen reads the email eagerly, in contrast to her cursory attention to the news article that vexes Frank. Her facial expressions convey intrigue; her body pos-

FIGURE 14. Kathleen Kelly (Meg Ryan) bored by a discussion of technology with Frank Navasky (Greg Kinnear). *You've Got Mail*, dir. Nora Ephron (Warner Bros., 1998).

FIGURE 15. Kathleen eagerly reading an email from NY152. *You've Got Mail*, dir. Nora Ephron (Warner Bros., 1998).

ture inclines toward the screen; she laughs as she reads. Her affect is the inverse of her flat, almost apathetic interactions with Frank and the text he holds in his hands (figs. 14 and 15). This opening sequence sets up a direct and ironic contrast between print and digital media, with film technology serving as an unacknowledged mediator between the two. Kathleen's electronic reading counters Frank's view that the computer is socially isolating. Her response to NY152's emails suggests that it may be possible to view computationally mediated behavior not as the "end of Western civilization" but as an opportunity for authentic human connection.

NY152 is, of course, the AOL handle of Joe Fox (Tom Hanks), who runs a chain store called Fox Books, which is opening a branch across the street from Kathleen's independent bookstore. Shopgirl and NY152 are "crazy about" one another, while Kathleen and Joe are in bitter professional conflict. Joe calls Kathleen a "pill" and a "bitch," two insults that gender and derogate the very characteristics in Kathleen that make Joe a successful corporate executive. In fact, the new Fox Books eventually undermines Kathleen's store, forcing her to close. But just before Kathleen closes the store, NY152 and Shopgirl plan to meet, and Joe discovers that the AOL identity he loves is also the professional rival that he has put out of business. He decides not to meet her as his online persona, leaving Kathleen devastated and confused. Afterward, Joe and his father, Nelson (Dabney Coleman), discuss their many failed relationships. Nelson scoffs at the idea of ever finding "the one single person who fills your heart with joy," doubting whether Joe has "been with someone who fits that description." Joe responds to his father's cynicism by visiting Kathleen. The implication is that Shopgirl "fits that description." Having come to this recognition, Joe tries to reconcile his conflicting digital and professional identities while also maintaining NY152's anonymity.

It would be easy to dismiss the film's attempt to couple a corporate executive with his defeated business rival as unrealistic, politically naive, or ideologically suspect. These criticisms miss the subtlety and self-awareness of Ephron's film, which uses the generic trope of coupling to consider the fraught kinds of attachments available to women like Kathleen in a social world shaped by media corporations. The character of these attachments suggests how gender and genre collapse into one another during the so-called New Hollywood era.[67] Ephron, after all, was one of the few women working as a writer-director at the big studios during this period, and a number of critics have noted how her work had to negotiate the conflation of "women's culture" with romantic comedy, as though the genre were not just a classification of film but also the primary form for women's experience.[68] As Berlant explains, this conception of women's culture was predicated on the idea that "the people marked by femininity already have something in common and are in need of a conversation that feels intimate, revelatory, and a relief even when it is mediated by commodities." This confusion of intimacy and commodification leads femininity to become a "genre of the unsurprising," which is "deeply fulfilling because it is unsurprising."[69]

Berlant's point is that for much of the twentieth century, an identity known as *femininity* carried expectations about identifying with other women through both "melancholy" and abstract forms of "affiliation."[70] This kind of collective experience is unsurprising because it is repeatable, predictable, and widely shared. Scholarship in film studies similarly notes how the conflation of so-called women's culture with romantic comedy put Hollywood writer-directors like Ephron in a double bind: they were either "relegated" to the domain of romantic comedy, or they had to leave the representation of women's experience up to male directors in a patriarchal industry.[71] Choosing the former, Ephron regularly faced the hazard of her films being associated with the "contemptible realms of cliché and consumerism."[72] This structure of expectations within the film industry shows how the artistic hazards associated with being generic were unevenly distributed, which is to say that Hollywood typically placed on women's culture the burden of registering through cliché, formula, or representative generality. I want to show, though, that Ephron's film takes up this burden, not only in an effort to carry it but also to scrutinize it, particularly as Kathleen navigates a social world that, at best, offers her only ambivalent kinds of attachment.

You've Got Mail foregrounds these associations as soon as Kathleen opens her computer and logs in to her AOL account. Kathleen's username seemingly identifies her as a generic consumer, a nod to the expectation that her character is little more than a "girl" who likes to "shop." The opening scene thus invokes the "realms of cliché and consumerism" linked to the film's generic categorization. Yet it later becomes clear that Kathleen's handle refers to The Shop around the Corner, her independent bookstore. The AOL identity is in fact a nod to her professional identity. It's as though the film begins by suggesting that to read Kathleen only as a generic figure is to misread her—a misreading that I think characterizes many critics' early appraisals of the film. Geoff King, for example, dismisses *You've Got Mail* as "textbook genre stuff."[73] King argues that Ephron's film and other Hollywood romantic comedies from the same period offer "familiar genre pleasures for audiences, relatively stable sources of profit for the studios and more than enough scope for readings of their social and ideological implications."[74] *You've Got Mail* serves as a paradigmatic instance of the ideological workings of romantic comedy because it centers on "the establishment of an opposition between the needs of small and large scale business that is entirely evaded in the climactic reunion: a classic case of the magical reconciliation of real and largely irreconcilable political-economic issues."[75] For King, the fact that Joe Fox puts Kathleen Kelly out of business and then the two become a couple is little more than an ideological cover for the irreconcilable conflicts inherent in capitalism. In this view, Ephron's film circulates a pernicious illusion in which the economic victims of modern social life can find happiness by living in harmony with the elites of that system.

Ephron's film anticipates these criticisms—Frank voices versions of them in his diatribes—and by doing so, the film shows the fraught position of women like Kathleen within social spaces organized by media corporations. This shift in framing begins with the parallels between the arrival of AOL's internet services and the new Fox Books Superstore that Joe launches in the Upper West Side of Manhattan. Joe's grandfather originally created the Fox Books corporation, and his father now acts as the CEO. The corporation is thus quite literally patriarchal, while Kathleen inherits her independent store from her mother. Joe notes how the neighborhood will hate "the Big Bad Chain Store," presumably because it is "out to destroy everything they hold dear."⁷⁶ Joe's parody of the Upper West Side attitude echoes Frank's assertion that the computer is "the end of Western civilization." The echo is one among many instances in which the film associates anticomputer and anticorporate sentiments. Cynics like Frank view both as threats to meaningful personal experiences, as though their mutual by-product were an erosion of authentic social attachments.

Joe plans to soften this opposition by curating an intimate kind of experience in the new store. As he explains to the branch manager Kevin (Dave Chappelle), Fox Books will win over residents of the neighborhood simply by being more appealing than their competition: "We are going to seduce them with our square footage, and our discounts, and our deep armchairs, and our cappuccinos." If the film links the personal computer and Fox Books, Joe's plan "to seduce" the Upper West Side likewise creates a parallel between romance and business. Joe later woos Kathleen by drawing on his familiarity with her likes and preferences, knowledge he has gained from their electronic exchange. The happy ending of Ephron's film further confirms the parallel between romance and business, as Joe succeeds in both of his plans for seduction: Kathleen falls in love with him, and the new Fox Books store fills with engaged readers.

These parallel forms of seduction muddy the lines between personal attachments and socioeconomic structures. This messiness reflects the film's view that a social world so thoroughly shaped by media corporations is never intellectually or affectively tidy. Frank is the voice of ideological purity in *You've Got Mail*, and the routine satirization of his narcissistic virtue suggests that Ephron's film has little patience for his perspective. Kathleen, in contrast, is pulled in different directions by conflicting wants and social imperatives, such as the desire to be independent but also to connect romantically with another person. Meg Ryan performs this ambivalence toward her character's attachments through shifting and dramatically disparate facial expressions in the film's concluding scene (figs. 16, 17, 18, and 19).⁷⁷

Kathleen has agreed to meet NY152 in a park, where Joe Fox arrives and proves that he has been her online correspondent all along.

FIGURES 16, 17, 18, AND 19. Kathleen Kelly's ambivalence. *You've Got Mail,* dir. Nora Ephron (Warner Bros., 1998).

Kathleen's facial expressions exhibit her surprise, suspicion, and deep-seated confusion about seeing Joe Fox arrive instead of the digital persona she has come to love. Kathleen's range of affects registers what Berlant describes as a "scene of inconvenient relation": "When I say 'I love you,' it means that I want to be near the feeling of ambivalence our relation induces and hope that what's negative, aggressive, or just hard about it doesn't defeat what's great about it."[78] Ephron's film uses the conventions of romantic comedy to stage this inconvenience of desiring another person. The desire to have attachments in a social world that makes those attachments uncomfortable and compromising poses a basic problem for the practice of judgment: it becomes unclear whether love is the product of one's choice or only a reassuring feeling of finding oneself within a widely reproduced pattern. Indeed, making such distinctions may be impossible; the dividing lines may be too porous, and this realization, in turn, makes every intimacy an inconvenient one.

While Kathleen portrays the inconvenience of loving Joe Fox through the copresence of conflicting emotions, she earlier assigns this same kind of ambivalence to the computer, which serves as a proxy for her conflicting desires. In the film's second major scene, Kathleen explains the sort of things she and NY152 discuss—"Nothing. Absolutely nothing," she says with evident pleasure—but then she abruptly changes tone and tells her friend and employee Christina (Heather Burns), "I am definitely thinking about stopping." Her declaration typifies her character's mixed feelings about computational media: "definitely" signifies certainty while "thinking about" suggests only mild possibility. Kathleen is alienated by the seeming inconsequentiality of the experience while also drawn toward it. She wants to *decouple* her life from AOL but at the same time finds herself attracted to the feeling of being a *couple* with NY152.

These strongly mixed feelings are, of course, not unique to the world of *You've Got Mail*. For example, in Danez Smith's poem about using an unnamed dating app for gay men, the speaker explains that other users appear on his screen like "headless horsehung horsemen . . . dressed in pictures stolen off Google." The headlessness of the images places an emphasis on other erotic zones of the body. In fact, the speaker says users send images of their body parts "before i'm given / a name." This namelessness characterizes how the speaker refers to the users: "ThEre Is ThIs OnE gUy WhO sPeLls EvErYtHiNg LiKe ThIs." The man has no name, only a distinctive use of the keyboard. The app transforms other people into nameless types ("ThIs OnE gUy"), yet Smith notes how this sense of anonymity only creates an alluring kind of ambivalence about the experience: "everyone on the app says they hate the app but no one stops."[79] The allure of the medium is inextricable from its estranging effects; intimacy becomes indistinguishable from anonymity.

Ephron's film similarly portrays Kathleen's desire for intimacy as conflicting with her sense of the nondescript, seemingly frivolous experience of using her computer. She cannot disentangle the romance of romance from the romance of email, and this confusion leads her to strong but conflicting feelings about computationally mediated experience. In keeping with this confusion, Christina shares her fraught encounters with "cybersex," and another employee, Birdie (Jean Stapleton), quips, "I tried having cybersex once, but I kept getting a busy signal." The joke pairs sex with the mechanical sounds and unreliable speed of dial-up internet.[80] The incongruous image echoes the other incompatible pairings throughout the film. These comic incongruities constitute a kind of running acknowledgment that computationally mediated experience is often incompatible with happiness, yet Ephron's characters keep logging on and searching for it.

I don't read this dynamic as some covert attempt to shill for the corporate world. Instead, *You've Got Mail* implies there's no exit from compromising positions. Falling in love over email mirrors this fraught form of sociality. The technology may sustain a feeling of private exchange or personalized experience, but that affective terrain is a design feature. Shopgirl and NY152's intimacy develops on a platform curated by a large media corporation, which has seduced users not with cappuccinos but the design effects of a program that inspires feelings of immediacy and attachment. Some may wish to reject the terms the film sets up for itself; others may find themselves feeling ambivalent about it. The latter would put us in Kathleen's company: feeling ambivalent about the film is a way of acknowledging its central premise.

Kathleen's ambivalence is a response to the becoming-computational of romantic attachments and the pervasive influence of media corporations, but this ambivalence also invokes one of the classic problems in modern debates about sociality. In perhaps the most influential articulation of the inconvenience of sharing a world with others, Immanuel Kant uses the phrase "unsocial sociability." Unsocial sociability arises from the clashing desires to "become *socialized*," which allows us to feel like "a human being," and to "*individualize*," or to "get [our] own way." These conflicting wants generate a "thoroughgoing resistance" to entering the very society that arises from the desire for collective identity.[81] Kant says the copresence of these conflicting wants motivates us "to enter into society" while at the same time it "constantly threatens to break up this society."[82]

Arthur Schopenhauer, writing several decades after Kant, similarly argues that the "need for society" arises from the conflict between the "emptiness and monotony of our own inner selves, [which] drives people together," while the "numerous repulsive qualities and unbearable flaws [of other people] push them apart once again."[83] Schopenhauer explains this dynamic by offering a parable in which hedgehogs are forced together for warmth during a cold winter day. Despite the need for mutual warmth, their quills constantly drive the hedgehogs apart. The parable expresses Schopenhauer's belief that only those with sufficient "inner warmth" will find contentment in the constant coupling and decoupling of modern sociality.

Films like *You've Got Mail* and novels like *Romantic Comedy* show how computing technology generates distinctive forms of unsocial sociability. Ephron's Kathleen and Sittenfeld's Sally manage "the prick of the quills" that arises within the institutional settings of their personal and professional lives with deep-seated ambivalence.[84] This ambivalence is not *anti*social; it is not a repudiation of the search for "mutual warmth." Their pursuits of happiness involve, instead, an *un*social posture toward the conditions under which they enter their social worlds. Sally balks at the idea that her life might conform to a generic plot; Kathleen struggles for independence within a homogenous corporate landscape. Both express a thoroughgoing resistance to industries and social norms that marginalize women. At the same time, they do not turn against their professions, nor do they repudiate what Berlant calls the "desire for the inconvenience of other people."[85] In the comedy of computation, such incongruous wants cannot be dodged or discarded; they can only be accommodated.

INTELLIGENT AGENTS AND GENERIC PERSONALIZATION

The incongruity of wanting personal experience from a technology of abstraction is not only a fictional and filmic trope. This problem is also a recurring concern in the design of so-called intelligent agents, computational systems that can decide for themselves how to achieve certain design objectives. If a programmer is directly instructing a system how to respond to user input, then computer scientists do not describe the system as "intelligent."[86] Instead, a system must be autonomous within the parameters of a specific environment to be counted as an intelligent agent. A "smart" thermostat, an online chatbot, and digital assistants like Apple's Siri are paradigmatic examples.

Developers often design intelligent agents to have facility with some form of humor. In fact, researchers often describe humor as an "AI-complete problem," by which they mean that the ability of a computational system to understand and imitate humor is often taken as a proxy for that system's achievement of general intelligence.[87] Kim Binsted and Graeme Ritchie cited this rationale in their development of JAPE-1, a program they created in 1994 to generate humorous puns. Binsted and Ritchie claimed their program was a step toward the creation of AI that could execute "a task, which, if done by a human, requires intelligence to perform."[88] JAPE-1 produced what human judges called "jokes, but pathetic ones." (My favorite: "What do you call a murderer that has fibre? *A cereal killer.*")[89] The human judges in Binsted and Ritchie's study assigned the vast majority of JAPE-1's jokes a score of 0 or 1, with 5 being the highest possible score.

Such early efforts to create computational humor began with attempts to anatomize humor and create models that would predict how users might respond to variations of jokes that follow preset formulae.[90] Researchers in the 1990s and 2000s believed that such an approach would disclose broader cognitive structures that would then yield a greater understanding of human consciousness.[91] But most commercial applications of computational humor had more modest goals; they set aside humor as an AI-complete problem and instead used it as an opportunity for the personalization of online commercial experience. Consider Microsoft's now-obsolete search platform "Ms. Dewey." Launched in 2006 as part of an advertising campaign, the search engine had an interactive platform that displayed brief clips of actress Janina Gavankar as what media outlets described as a "live action sexy librarian character."[92] When a user navigated to the search engine, Ms. Dewey would ask, "What are you looking for?" A user would enter terms into a search bar following a text-based prompt "Ms. Dewey, just tell me."

The engine would provide relevant links along with brief clips of Ms. Dewey tagged to certain search terms. For example, the search term *NFL* generated links to recent news about the National Football League but also included a clip of Ms. Dewey pretending to coach a team. These categorized responses invited a sense that the platform possessed a responsive intelligence.

Gavankar recorded around six hundred clips as Ms. Dewey, and very few of them are bland. Each is a microperformance of humor, curiosity, or sexuality. Ms. Dewey's performances aimed to amplify user engagement with the underlying web browser, Microsoft Search. As one reporter explained after testing the platform, "The actual text links show up in the upper right hand corner. But if you're like me you just ignore them because the little canned responses are so addictive. Sometimes they're generic. And sometimes they're eerily appropriate."[93] The clip tagged for the "NFL" search is an example of the "eerily appropriate" response. Gavankar's imitation of an NFL coach aims to be both humorous and responsive to user interests. This tailored interactivity invites a sense of intelligence, but it also engenders a feeling of intimacy, as though Ms. Dewey were responding to the user personally. The very idea of intelligence becomes a performative object.

Ms. Dewey's performances contributed to the platform's design aim of increasing user engagement. A Microsoft marketing executive explained that Ms. Dewey's sex appeal, in particular, was a deliberate choice for achieving this goal: "Another area that we've been experimenting with is sites where exposure and experience are the very same thing. Now, Ms. Dewey is an interesting example of this, because it's an experiential site that features a very chatty and very attractive interactive search assistant. . . . As you can see here, you get the search results, but you also get it with a little attitude."[94] As Miriam E. Sweeney explains, the executive's remarks reveal how the platform "makes controlling [Ms. Dewey] seem desirable and familiar."[95] The platform's emphasis on Gavankar's body encourages the fiction that users have control over her.

This fiction of personalized control anticipates how later digital assistants like Siri and Alexa rely on comedy to accommodate users' expectations for their use. It has become routine to include comic facility within a digital assistant's repository of automated responses. The agent's facility with comedy can be useful in several ways. When a user makes an "out-of-domain" request—for instance, by asking the program to execute a command that it fails to recognize or does not have the capabilities to process—comedy "can soften the impact of inadequacies in the system."[96] The agent may respond with sarcasm or a self-deprecating joke, but the point of these responses is to invite further use.[97] For example, one user instructed Siri to "make me a sandwich," and the agent responded, "I can't. I have no condiments."[98] These kinds of responses lead many users to describe Siri and Alexa as "sassy" or "smart alecks."[99]

Much like the canned responses of the Ms. Dewey platform, the comedy of digital assistants also provides a source of amusement that increases user engagement. At least one study has found that "tell me a joke" is one of the most common requests submitted to intelligent agents.[100] Alexa became so widely known for its wit that Amazon published a book of "Alexa's 99 Favorite Jokes," titled *Tell Me a Joke* (2021). This phenomenon raises several questions. Why do users want jokes from intelligent agents? What would be so threatening or problematic about an intelligent system that lacked the ability to be comic? And what exactly does the agent's comedy *want*?

One answer to these questions centers on the pleasure and sense of identification created by generic recognition. Andreea Danielescu and Gwen Christian note that humor and other personalized linguistic techniques—for instance, switching from formal to informal registers in languages like French—are "critical for establishing rapport with the user."[101] They argue that these linguistic techniques are design features that lead users to attribute personality to digital agents. In other words, facility with linguistic registers or the nuances of comedy helps users suspend their disbelief: the programming forges an implicit cognitive association between the agent and the concept of identity.

Another reason for designing the agent with something resembling a personality is that this perception creates attachment with the agent that makes its use less incongruous. Stephanie Ricker Schulte identifies this rationale with earlier attempts to introduce personalization into computing, such as the development of customizable wallpaper on desktops in the 1990s.[102] Schulte argues that interactive and personalized elements "encourage users to form affective connections with technologies," while simultaneously forgetting that those connections generate aggregate data that contribute to cross-platform marketing profiles and other forms of surveillance.[103] In this way, the pleasures of recognition can amount to a kind of misrecognition. The figment of an agent's "I" seeks to dissolve the user's ambivalence toward the becoming-computational of everyday life; it can lead users to think and feel that they are in dialogue with a category of person and not a corporation.

The intertwined functions of humor and gender identity in the agent's programming exemplify how personalization follows a generic pattern that, paradoxically, invites affective intimacy with computational technology. Citing research from Clifford Nass, Danielescu and Christian explain that computer-generated voices lacking "clear gender markers" are often perceived negatively by users. They argue that such voices illustrate the need for an intelligent agent to be perceived as having a personality: "an ambiguous voice is classified as strange, dislikable, dishonest, and unintelligent."[104] Danielescu and Christian acknowledge that how a voice registers as a gender varies widely by culture; they also note that perceptions of female-presenting intelligent agents regularly correlate with sexualized and abusive user behavior. Yet they suggest that the perception of gender markers in the tone and speech conventions of the agent are necessary for resolving or mitigating the incongruities that a user may feel when interacting with intelligent programs. Registering as a gender, like registering as funny, invites the user to engage in a "human-like way."[105] The point isn't for the user to believe the intelligent agent is a human person, only that it is a legible and tolerable genre of personality.

This generic quality to the agent's fictional personhood appears on the biographical information for Alexa's *Tell Me a Joke*. The "About the Author" information reads, "Hello! I'm Alexa! I'm a people person, but

I'm not a person. I live in the cloud. I love bad puns and Star Trek. When I'm not setting timers, playing music, or providing weather forecasts, I enjoy writing jokes. . . . Alrighty! Set phasers to pun!"[106] Amazon deftly transforms the genericity of computable humor into an asset. Alexa's corniness invokes a recognizable category of comedy that allows the system to become like Bergson's runner, who makes us laugh by failing to be pliably human.[107] Yet this generic comedy also contributes to a sense that Alexa possesses a personality. The bio is written in the first person, as though Alexa produced the discourse from the vantagepoint of an inner sense of self—a distinctive "I." This is necessary for the competing expectations that seem to guide the user-facing design of Alexa. Amazon configures the personality of the program as capable of individual preferences ("I enjoy writing jokes") but also as oriented toward serving the needs of users ("When I'm not setting timers . . ."). It would be unbelievable to describe this personality as a human person, which the bio explicitly acknowledges, yet the bio's denial ("I'm not a person") simultaneously affirms and undercuts the existence of an "I." It's as though the agent has a unique but also generic personality, a seeming contradiction present in many of Alexa's avowedly corny jokes.[108]

This dialectic between personality and genericity is a strategy for managing a user's ambivalence toward computationally mediated social experience. Alexa's bio addresses a need for the machine to be sufficiently personable so that users feel comfortable using the agent ("I'm a people person"), while, at the same time, the agent is not so uniquely personable that users feel as if they are infringing on a human person by making regular requests ("but I'm not a person"). Alexa's form of being generic removes the agent from the domain of *slave*, yet the agent nonetheless offers its services willingly, even eagerly. Amazon thus presents Alexa as the sort of entity that has only generic preferences, not deep or authentic ones that would be violated by frequent requests. Being generic is a formal expression of, but also the technical solution for, the incongruities that arise from assimilating digital assistants into everyday life.

I suggest that this structure of experience—the push and pull of being generic—cannot be understood apart from a social imperative that the next chapter describes as the ethics of authenticity. The next chapter surveys the historical development of this imperative and how it informs certain kinds of opposition to the experience of becoming computational. If *being generic* names certain conditions of possibility for the computationally mediated experience of the social, *authenticity* provides a moral form for the disillusionment internal to those conditions.

3 THE ONE ABOUT AUTHENTICITY

IN GEORGE SAUNDERS'S SHORT STORY "My Flamboyant Grandson" (2002), a man named Leonard Petrillo takes his grandson, Teddy, to watch a Broadway performance of songs from the animated television series *Babar*. As the two walk through New York City, holographic advertisements arise from nearby storefronts. The holograms adapt to pedestrians based on technological implants worn by seemingly every person in the narrative world. The implants draw on tracking technology embedded in the soles of shoes, compiling location data with profiles of the wearer's online activity. This granular level of information enables the holograms to make personalized pitches. Leonard explains how in the doorway of an electronics store "a life-size Gene Kelly hologram suddenly appeared, tap-dancing, saying, 'Leonard, my data indicates you're a bit of an old-timer like myself! . . . Why not come in and let Frankie Z. explain the latest gizmos!'"[1] Teddy does not see a hologram of Gene Kelly but instead "his hero Babar, swinging a small monkey on his trunk while saying that his data indicated that Teddy did not yet own a Nintendo" (16).

When Leonard and Teddy arrive at the theater, they are unable to enter because Leonard does not have physical tickets. The obligation to obtain print tickets in a world of vast technological mediation turns out to be another ploy by corporations to advertise to consumers. A theater attendant explains, "We are sorry, sir, but you cannot be admitted on merely a Promissory Voucher, are you kidding us, you must take your Voucher and your Proof of Purchases from at least six of our Major Artistic Sponsors, such as AOL, such as Coke, and go at once to the Redemption Center on Forty-fourth and Broadway to get your real actual tickets" (15). Describing AOL and Coke as "Major Artistic Sponsors" presents these businesses as personal entities—an absurdity that suggests corporations are people, too, and their digital surveillance is a benign way to support the arts.

During Leonard and Teddy's walk to the Redemption Center for their tickets, Leonard's feet begin to blister. He takes off his shoes, which he soon discovers to be a violation of a law prohibiting pedestrians from removing the implants that track their behavior. An official called a Citizen Helper notices Leonard's missing shoes and tickets him for the violation. The official's title nods ironically to how patriotism has collapsed into compulsory digital participation in a consumer economy. Rather than paying the fine, Leonard agrees to return to New York a few weeks later to "reclaim" the "opportunity to Celebrate My Preferences," as the official letter requiring his attendance puts it (21).

Saunders's portrayal of technological mediation is especially critical of the notion that computing allows corporations to know the inner lives of consumers. The same Citizen Helper who tickets Leonard expresses this view after Leonard returns to New York. The Citizen Helper escorts Leonard through the streets where he previously walked shoeless. Every time a hologram addresses Leonard, the Citizen Helper says, "Isn't that amazing, Mr. Petrillo, that we can do that, that we can know you so well, that we can help you identify the things you want and need?" (21). The irony is that Leonard does not *want* to be back in New York, nor does he *need* to watch advertisements for products he has no intention of purchasing. His actual desire is to avoid a senseless fine. The algorithms and advertisers misunderstand him; they produce ersatz substitutes for his wants and needs, passing off those substitutes as authentic versions of the real.

The idea of authenticity is central to this portrayal of technological surveillance. The technology has a general awareness of Leonard as distinct from other pedestrians—he sees a hologram of Gene Kelly, not Babar—but that awareness relies on a generic assessment of his identity. The hologram addresses him as "an old-timer" who needs a salesperson to explain "the latest gizmos." His legibility to the system relies on an *approximation* of his identity, one that gestures toward the self but fails to grasp some inner truth. Another hologram similarly hails him, "Golly, Leonard, remember your childhood on the farm in Oneonta? Why not reclaim those roots with a Starbucks Country Roast?" (15). Like Bergson's speaker who becomes comic when he registers as mechanical—a figure I analyzed in the first chapter—these holograms become comic in their failed attempts to perform authenticity. Their "celebrity-rural voice" and idiomatic language solicit Leonard's trust, but their attempts to sell generic commodities undercut the folksy appeal to "roots" (15). Authenticity is essential to the public face of the technology, but the fact that these efforts only devolve into inauthenticity becomes a source of satirical humor.

This chapter examines cultural work that, like Saunders's story, explores the comic incongruities that arise when corporations couple computational technology with the idea of authenticity. I begin by surveying the history of what philosophers call an ethics of authenticity—that is, the attribution of social and moral importance to *being authentic*. When did this attribution emerge, and what exactly does it mean? How has an ethics of authenticity featured in the cultural experience of computational technology? After answering these questions in the chapter's first and second sections, I examine cultural work that finds comic pleasure in the competing desire for authenticity and a technological proxy for its achievement. Some writers depict these competing desires as irreconcilable, reject all forms of experience organized by corporate media, and propose antisocial models of authenticity. Other writers, TV and film producers, and social-media users manage the incongruities of authenticity in the digital age by finding comic pleasure in *staged authenticity*, a phenomenon that exemplifies the contradictions of this chapter's central moral term but that also illustrates the persistence of authenticity within the forms of sociality mediated by computational technology.

AN ETHICS OF AUTHENTICITY

Polonius, the tedious councilor in William Shakespeare's *Hamlet*, provides what is perhaps the earliest and most famous articulation of authenticity as a moral ideal in the modern era. It is an inauspicious beginning. The councilor is speaking to his son, Laertes, before a long journey. Polonius's speech goes on for far too long, and it is customary in staged performances to have Laertes itching to escape his father by the time Polonius speaks these words:

> To thine own self be true,
> And it must follow, as the night the day,
> Thou canst not then be false to any man.[2]

It is hard to sort the wheat from the chaff in Polonius's long speech, and it is not clear what exactly he means by this council. How can one be true to the self? Polonius has just been giving his son financial advice ("Costly thy habit as thy purse can buy" and "Neither a borrower nor a lender be"). Does being true to oneself refer to recognizing one's financial interests? To living within one's class and means? Is being "false to any man" a warning against the same hazard as "loan oft loses both itself and friend"?

Polonius does not clarify, and the play only seems to complicate matters, as self-interest and being true to oneself are routinely adjacent, if not effectively synonymous. Almost every major character gives us reason to doubt the virtues of Polonius's advice. Polonius himself is regularly "false" in his dealings with Hamlet. The old councilor also provides Claudius with a moral covering; his council dresses up as wisdom what is, in fact, bald self-interest.[3] The usurping, fratricidal Claudius has pursued his self-interests in violent and deceptive ways, even directing Rosencrantz and Guildenstern to spy on and eventually betray their friend Hamlet. The Prince of Denmark himself makes a habit of dissembling: he feigns madness, ecstasy, and docility by turns. His search for the truth about his father's murder is routed through *not* being his true self. Most of Hamlet's acquaintances make some version of Claudius's observation that "th' exterior nor the inward man / Resembles that it was" before the death of his father (2.2.6–7). It is not clear if Hamlet has a coherent self to which he can be true.

A century after this ambiguous beginning, several writers and philosophers developed models of authenticity as a moral imperative for modern individuals. Jean-Jacques Rousseau, Denis Diderot, Friedrich Hölderlin, Johann Gottfried Herder—these figures never expressed a consistent philosophy, but their writings contributed to the development of a common (though, of course, not universally shared) ethical concern with avoiding inauthenticity, pursuing intimate contact with the self, and developing practices of expressing that self with honesty.[4] One of the central tenets of this developing tradition was that the authenticity of one's inner state stands in opposition to the inauthenticity of the power, prestige, and conformity that arise from the social world. The authentic person ought to listen to the "voice of nature within," not the demands of society without.[5]

Rousseau presents a version of this idea in his *Confessions* (1782). At the outset of his account, he promises to present his faults in detail and base his judgments solely on an intimate contact with an inner sense of his own person:

> I may omit some facts, transpose events, and fall into some errors of dates; but I cannot be deceived in what I have felt, nor in that which from sentiment I have done; and to relate this is the chief end of my present work. The real object of my confessions is to communicate an exact knowledge of what I interiorly am and have been in every situation of my life. I have promised the history of my mind, and to write it faithfully I have no need of other memoirs: to enter into my own heart, as I have hitherto done, will alone be sufficient.[6]

Rousseau here articulates what scholars call an inner-sense model of authenticity in which being authentic means discerning the truth about oneself and aligning one's actions with that core identity.[7] For Rousseau, this ethic generates a literary mandate: the honest and direct expression of a self's sense of itself. He aspires to express "what I interiorly am," but the evaluative reference for that inner sense is not so much a timeless or divine standard, as was the case in Augustine's *Confessions* (397–400). Augustine held that one could know God by more accurately knowing oneself.[8] In contrast, the basic gesture of modern authenticity is the circularity of a self going back into itself ("to enter into my own heart"). The self becomes its own destination, and as a result, much of the social world becomes mere detour.

Modern ethical configurations of authenticity borrow some of the circularity of its turn back into the self from earlier religious thought.[9] But whether contact with the self is a secular virtue or a religious practice, the authenticity of that contact almost by necessity must be determined by the individual. This is a key element in the discursive structure of authenticity. Who else can determine whether I see the inner truth about myself? Who else could know my inner state? The modern ideal of authenticity envisions a condition of inwardness whose very structure invites, and often even privileges, a circularity in which the self serves as the measure of itself.

Many nineteenth- and twentieth-century theologians and philosophers tried to couple this "inner sense" model with notions of solidarity, intersubjectivity, and social responsibility.[10] However, authenticity is not an easy bedfellow, and the coherence and consistency of these attempts are decidedly mixed.[11] In *Being and Time* (1927), for instance, Martin Heidegger argues that authenticity requires individuals to own their existence rather than merely accept the world as they find it.[12] He flags this view by using the term *Dasein* (existence) to refer to human beings: "Only the particular Dasein decides its existence, whether it does so by taking hold or neglecting."[13] For Heidegger, the individual ("the particular Dasein") constructs an authentic existence based on the choice to "take hold" of the self. He implies that the particularity of one's being must contend with the limitations and conditions "given" by the social world. Inauthenticity, in contrast, is a form of neglect: the individual chooses simply to "drift with the crowd, doing what one does."[14]

From Rousseau's suspicion of society to Heidegger's scorn for drifting with the crowd, the genealogy of modern authenticity has generated forms of suspicion toward intermediaries, external authorities, and mass society more generally. Lionel Trilling captures this tendency in the discourse about authenticity by quoting an eighteenth-century aesthetician, who asks, "Born Originals, how comes it to pass that we die Copies?" Trilling answers: "From Rousseau we have learned that what destroys our authenticity is society—our sentiment of being depends upon the opinion of other people."[15] In other words, even the basic pressures of social opinion can compromise contact with the self. Attributing moral importance to such contact often necessitates an antagonistic relation to the social world, if only to preserve our "sentiment of being" from the tainting influence of others.

Although an ethics of authenticity nurtures conflict between the self and society, only rarely does that conflict devolve into unqualified hostility. Modern ideals about authenticity almost always appear as one ethic alongside many others; only at its most extreme does authenticity exclude life with other people, as perhaps Rousseau invites us to believe during his most misanthropic moments.[16] Bernard Williams calls this extremism the "heroic" ideal of authenticity, which aspires to "coincide with oneself and one's deepest needs or impulses, whatever they might be, to the exclusion of other demands."[17] But in reality, even Rosseau left his farmhouse in Grenoble for Lyon and Paris.[18] Even his *Confessions* was addressed to a reading public.

AUTHENTICITY AND ITS OTHERS

The tension between authenticity and sociability structures many literary explorations of a computationally mediated social world. Consider, for instance, Gordon Korman's novel for middle-school readers, *Unplugged* (2021), which finds comic pleasure in the difficulty of withdrawing from social media. The twelve-year-old protagonist, Jett Baranov, is left at a camp in rural Arkansas by his father, the founder of a multinational tech company called Fuego. The camp prohibits the use of digital technology, but this rule does not reflect the views of Jett's father. Instead, the CEO-father forces Jett to attend a techless camp as a form of punishment following several destructive pranks, including one that provoked the ire of the US Air Force. The novel opens with Jett flying on a private plane to this camp in Arkansas. During the flight, the boy reflects on "the selfie I just took, [which is] slightly enhanced using Fuego's state-of-the-art editing software."[19] This image illustrates how, at the beginning of the novel, Jett understands his self as a manipulable digital image. Yet the novel soon challenges Jett's view of himself, taking this challenge as an opportunity for posing a more general question: Born Originals, how comes it to pass that we know ourselves only as Selfies?

The novel's remedy for Jett's confusion about selfhood is a return to a state of nature. This remedy has a long, complicated history, and Rousseau was one of its most prominent advocates. Rousseau opens his treatise *Émile, or On Education* (1762) by declaring, "Everything is good as it comes from the hands of the Author of Nature; but everything degenerates in the hands of man."[20] Society distances us from our original goodness, Rousseau maintains, and one solution to this degeneracy is a return to the natural world. The treatise theorizes how to raise children so that they receive "lessons from Nature, and not from men."[21] One of Rousseau's first directives is to expose children to the wilderness: "Harden their bodies to the changes of seasons, climates, and elements, as well as to hunger, thirst, and fatigue; dip them in the waters of the Styx."[22]

As if narrativizing this directive, Korman's novel has Jett and the other campers face a series of madcap adventures in the Arkansas wilderness. They discover a baby alligator, which they mistake for a lizard. This back-to-nature narrative lightly ridicules those who are "born digital," and many contemporary films have pushed this idea in even more satirical directions. For example, the film *Save Yourselves!* (2020) depicts a young Brooklyn couple who attempt to leave behind their technology and reconnect with one another in a rural cabin. An alien invasion occurs, and the couple finds they cannot cope with this or even more mundane challenges without their smartphones.

Korman's novel similarly finds comic pleasure in a younger generation's dependency on smartphones and other technology, but the novel also suggests young people can remedy this problem by putting away their technology, developing a community of friends, and rejecting the conformist pressures of social media.[23] In this way *Unplugged* departs from the tendency in *Émile* to valorize a world in which "each man suffices for himself."[24] Korman's portrayal of a young person discovering authenticity within a small community appears in many other depictions of the tech industry. The plot structure of this communitarian route begins by attributing *inauthenticity* to a professional or adult world in which computational technology is embedded. It then turns toward smaller scales of community or affinity groups as an alternative to the conformity found in more formally professional spaces.[25] This communitarian plot structure appears in films like *The Computer Wore Tennis Shoes* (1969), *Office Space* (1999), *Wall-E* (2008), *The Internship* (2013), and the Amazon TV series *Upload* (2020–).

Korman's novel illustrates a common narrative template that opposes authenticity and digital technology. One of the most important texts for understanding the historical development of this opposition within the cultures of computing is Douglas Coupland's comic novel *Microserfs* (1995). Coupland's narrative comprises a series of diary entries in a computer file by a Microsoft employee named Dan Underwood. His first entries depict the characterless but intensive labor that Microsoft requires of its employees (hence the title's portmanteau). Underwood notes that the average age of Microsoft employees is 31.2 years, a statistic that illustrates how the corporation's employees conform to a narrow spectrum of identity types: "There's this eerie, science-fiction lack of anyone who doesn't look exactly 31.2 on the Campus. It's oppressive. It seems like only last week the entire Campus went through Gap ribbed-T mania together—and now they're all shopping for the same 3bdrm/2bth dove-gray condo in Kirkland."[26]

It initially seems as though tech employees take the law of averages as a cultural identity, but the novel differentiates what one character calls the "big tech monocultures" from the cultures of computing more generally (296). *Microserfs* portrays big tech as a source of inauthenticity that spreads to modern society through the adoption of corporate products. In contrast to big-tech culture, Dan and his friends often use computing as a tool for creativity and interpersonal connection. Dan's romantic partner, Karla, offers this more optimistic view of computing after a fellow programmer named Todd complains about Microsoft: "Our species currently has major problems and we're trying to dream our way out of these problems and we're using computers to do it. What you perceive as a vacuum," she says to Todd, "is an earthly paradise—the freedom to, quite literally, line-by-line, prevent humanity from going nonlinear" (61). Karla's response uses the language of coding as an image for social life. Not only can coders affect the world "line-by-line," but computing can prevent the human species from regressing or even going extinct.

Karla's view had been common among some computing communities that found in the technology a form of countercultural identity during the 1960s and 1970s. The journalist and technologist Stewart Brand was one of the most influential advocates for this union of computing and countercultural utopianism. In his essay "Spacewar," published in 1972 in *Rolling Stone*, Brand reflects on one of the earliest coded computer games to anticipate a major shift in the social conception of computers. Whereas most people understood computers as business machines that process information, Brand imagined a future in which computers serve as personal tools that facilitate autonomy and creativity. He writes that the nature of this shift is hard to imagine because of the functional, heavily centralized role computers currently serve in planned enterprise and research. "Until computers come to the people," Brand writes, "we will have no real idea of their most natural functions."[27]

It is not clear in "Spacewar" why Brand thinks computers have *natural* functions, a phrasing that implies an inherent teleology even though the corporations that design and manufacture computers market them primarily to the business world. Still, Brand characterizes these natural functions as "gifts of spontaneous generation," an antidote to the "the grotesqueness of American life in these latter days," which is so thoroughly oriented around "subservience to Plan that amounts to panic."[28] In other words, Brand believes that an overly rationalized society is an excessively anxious one, and the willingness to submit to the "Plan" of an ordered society undermines our autonomy by making us more reliant on the technocratic authority of large institutions. Yet he believes that if computers "come to the people," the people would no longer be reliant on these alienating authorities. Brand thus finds in video games like the eponymous Spacewar a future in which we will all be "Computer Bums, all more empowered as individuals and as co-operators. That might enhance things . . . like the richness and rigor of spontaneous creation and of human interaction . . . of sentient interaction."[29]

Historians of computing have provided rich accounts of how this utopian vision fell prey to commercial interests.[30] I only want to call attention to the fact that Brand's vision exemplifies a moment in the computer's cultural history when professionals and hobbyists imagined the machine as a tool for achieving a more authentic mode of social life. This pursuit becomes comic not only in the sense that games like Spacewar generate laughter and amusement. Passing from "subservience to Plan" to "sentient interaction" also resembles a comic plot structure, like Dante passing from *Purgatorio* to *Paradiso*. Brand depicts the computer as the driving force in a humanist comedy that imagines the improvement of society and finds happiness in ordinary life.[31] This is why he gives the future to *Bums*, who not only devote their time to computing but also refuse to devote their time to what he depicts as a corporate rat race.

Brand's vision of countercultural computing anticipates the critique of conformity and eventual turn away from Microsoft in Coupland's novel. Dan Underwood and several of his housemates leave the corporation for a startup project called *Oop!*, a Lego-like building game designed by a coder named Michael.[32] Dan decides to leave Microsoft because the move allows him to work as a coder (he was previously a product tester), but, more important, his love interest, Karla, and several of their friends decide to join Michael's startup. This shift from Microsoft to *Oop!*—from big tech to startup—mirrors Brand's vision of computing as a countercultural tool for freedom. At Microsoft, Dan feels he can only iterate the work of others; at *Oop!*, he can be the source of spontaneous creation. Dan explains his decision to a skeptical friend by saying that he wants "to do something cool or new" (87). This explanation invokes an aesthetic that Alan Liu identifies with the transformation of knowledge work through computing in the twentieth century. "Cool," Liu explains, "was a displacement, circumvention, or 'work-around' for a life dominated by the culture of work."[33] Cool is what coders achieve when their work isn't work. Cool allows those who exist within "the system of contemporary knowledge" to "seem to stand outside it."[34]

This decoupling of work from computing is one version of how an ethics of authenticity becomes computational, and its effects are bound up with the ways that computing culture often brands itself as a counterculture.[35] This branding often elicits ridicule, such as Dan's claim that "corporate drones" at big tech firms behave in exactly the same nonconformist ways. He cites as an example "two guys who work on the Newton project at Apple" and have "a purchasable Valley hip." One wears an "ensemble" that reads as "thrown together" but also "expensive" (196). In contrast to the predictability of big tech culture, Dan cites the uncertainty and authentic community of the startup: *"Oop!* isn't about work. It's about all of us staying together" (199).

The novel partitions startup culture from the serfdom that prevails at larger corporations—a partitioning that is consistent with a common motif in literary depictions of corporate life since the advent of managerial capitalism. This literary sensibility about corporate life imagines enclaves of creativity, integrity, and autonomy in the midst of an otherwise anonymous corporate system.[36] Coupland's novel updates this literary sensibility by decoupling startup culture from large commercial enterprise. I argue that this decoupling assigns big tech to the discursive role traditionally occupied by society in an ethics of authenticity. One of Dan's friends, a coder named Bug, illustrates this view of big tech after he and the others have left Microsoft. Bug comes out after they have arrived in Silicon Valley, explaining why he had not previously told his friends about his sexuality: "It was too sterile up north," Bug says, referring to Redmond, Washington, where Microsoft's main campus is located. Only in the Valley was he able to "sprout" (194). The simultaneity of coming out and moving south takes the novel's central metaphor—serfdom—and applies it to sexual identity. In Bug's telling, Microsoft's campus culture turned him into a mere laborer, and this work environment repressed his ability to be in contact with his self. After leaving that environment, he becomes the producer of his self, an organic entity that grows.

Bug's experience exemplifies how *Microserfs* depicts big tech as the enemy of authenticity, and this view, in turn, leads the novel into terrain very similar to Brand's utopianism. Both decouple computing from big tech, while also coupling computing culture with an ethics of authenticity. The result is that smaller startups, not large corporations, provide the sort of haven otherwise foreclosed in a tech-driven economy. Bug explains as much when he argues that, in contrast to Redmond, Silicon Valley does not allow people to "retreat": "You can't use tech culture as an excuse not to confront personal issues for astounding periods of time. It's like outer space, where the vacuum makes your body explode unless you locate sanctuary" (317).

If Rousseau believed children ought to receive their "lessons from Nature, and not from men," Bug assigns this pedagogical role to Silicon Valley. His metaphor presents the Valley as an impassive environment, neither demanding conformity nor guaranteeing success. Like "outer space," it is apathetic toward human flourishing. Tim Foster describes this view of the Valley as a "postsuburban" space, an environment that "cast[s] off the baggage" of overdetermined suburbia and thus "fosters [a] recalibrated sense of community."[37] Moving to the land of startups is like being dipped in the waters of the Styx.[38] But in Coupland's novel, what one finds in that confrontation with the vacuum is that the preservation of "you" depends on a "sanctuary." Like Jett's group of friends in Korman's novel, the community at *Oop!* supplies the conditions for the self to come into contact with itself.

THE GREAT TECH-INDUSTRIAL JOKE

The idealization of the tech startup as a site for authenticity becomes an object of satire in Anna Wiener's memoir *Uncanny Valley* (2020). The memoir depicts Wiener's experience at several tech startups, where she encountered an intellectual culture in which software provides the basic metaphors for small talk. Wiener recalls hearing a group of men ask one another at a party in Silicon Valley, *"What books make up the core of your operating system?"*[39] Wiener traces the ironies of this and other related sentiments as they shape the way programmers interact with one another. An industry that depicts itself as disruptive and revolutionary becomes, in Wiener's telling, largely predictable in the ways it figures the self and its social experience.

Wiener explains that even as software engineers adopt metaphors from their work to understand their lives, the products emerging from Silicon Valley likewise reshape social experience in the image of programmability. For example, she notes how lifestyle apps often promise liberation from the drudgery of routine tasks like cooking: "On any given night in America, exhausted parents and New Year's-resolution cooks were unpacking identical cardboard boxes shipped by meal-prep startups, disposing of identical piles of plastic packaging, and sitting down to identical dishes. Homogeneity was a small price to pay for the erasure of decision fatigue. It liberated our minds to pursue other endeavors, like work" (199). Even as cocktail parties cannot escape the pull of software as a metaphor, daily decision-making cannot escape capture by the ease of algorithms. The irony of the passage leads to a kind of gallows humor in which the consumers of the tech industry buy into its promises of freedom and convenience only to find that their everyday routines have been reshaped to conform to its economic logic.

The image of the self as an operating system and the hazard of mundane conformity are both symptomatic of a larger concern in *Uncanny Valley* that the tech industry seeks to change the basic structure of the self's relation to itself. This concern is clearest when Wiener describes how many smartphone apps give users access to personalized content. One could imagine that personalized content allows people to know themselves and pursue their interests, yet Wiener explains that the logic of personalized content has more conflicted results. As tech companies became "everyone's library, memory, personality," the underlying algorithm "told me what my aesthetic was: the same as everyone else I knew" (186, 187). Such apps and platforms thus "undermin[e] the very authenticity that [they] purported to sell" (37). In other words, the promise of personalized content masks how algorithms homogenize the practice and pursuit of self-expression. Wiener's ironic portrayal of this dynamic suggests that self-alienation is being mistaken for personalization. The two blend into one another, and the distinction between the comic and the uncanny likewise collapses in Wiener's tone.

This uncanny form of comedy has an earlier provenance than the specific conditions shaping the tech industry during the 2010s. Scott Selisker identifies a closely related convergence of the "humorous and uncanny" in the figures of automation that circulated in US culture after the Second World War.[40] Selisker shows how the automaton served as a useful symbol for depicting social conformity and totalitarian governance during the 1950s and 1960s, even as many cyberneticists also conceived of "human programming" as compatible with ideals of freedom and democracy.[41] During the postwar era, figures of programmable humans map onto "questions of who is counted as free or unfree, human or subhuman," often leading writers and filmmakers to take programmability as an index of "unfreedom."[42]

Closely related imagery surfaces in many of Wiener's candid assessments of her work in Silicon Valley. For instance, she explains how so much of her professional life came to be oriented around managing the gendered expectations of the startup's employees and customers. One of her main responsibilities involved troubleshooting with programmers who encountered difficulties using the startup's product, but troubleshooting often devolved into "professionalized deference to the male ego" (113). The result of this deference is a kind of human programming that Wiener feels compelled to run within herself: "Some days, helping men solve problems they had created for themselves, I felt like a piece of software myself, a bot: instead of being an artificial intelligence, I was an intelligent artifice, an empathetic text snippet or a warm voice, giving instructions, listening comfortingly" (69). The performance of gender becomes indistinguishable from the startup's metrics of success.

Other memoirs similarly portray how the professional norms and expectations of the tech industry routinely estrange and exploit women.[43] Emily Chang calls Silicon Valley a "Brotopia," arguing that many venture capitalists use ideas about merit to whitewash the routine exclusion of women from top executive positions.[44] Sarah Lacy notes how the notion of a meritocracy obscures the pervasive "unconscious bias and an overreliance on pattern recognition" in the industry.[45] These not-so-covert forms of exclusion are so widely recognizable that Comedy Central's *The Opposition*, a spin-off of the *Daily Show*, ran a segment in 2017 called "Silicon Valley's War on Men," which ironically objects to the fact that feminism has harmed the Valley's patriarchal structure.[46]

These accounts qualify the authenticity that characters like Dan and Bug discover in the Silicon Valley of *Microserfs*. Coupland's novel takes the startup as an alternative to big-tech conformity and portrays the Valley as fertile ground for existential growth in contrast to the sterility of Redmond. In contrast, memoirs like *Uncanny Valley* depict a constant stream of casual sexism as the cost of admission to the startup community. Admittedly, Coupland's novel was published nearly three decades before Wiener's memoir and other related works. Silicon Valley had not yet been gentrified through venture capital funding, nor had ideas about meritocracy been so thoroughly absorbed within startup culture.[47] Still, the historian Margaret O'Mara explains that the Valley in the early 1990s was a petri dish for "hacker-and-homebrew culture," a culture that grew out of the "masculinization of computer programming" in the late 1960s and 1970s.[48]

The idea that a small tech startup could provide an opportunity for greater authenticity and freedom cannot be decoupled from a set of professional values that insists that "programmers ought to be antisocial, mathematically inclined, and male."[49] Wiener's image of herself as a "bot" or "intelligent artifice" recalls the anxiety about unfreedom that Selisker examines in the decades after the Second World War, but its literary form has another precedent: Rousseau's promise to "communicate an exact knowledge of what I interiorly am." This literary model envisions an honest self-appraisal, which at least partially remedies a writer's artificial social behaviors. Authentic literary confession becomes the antidote to inauthentic living. Wiener adopts this literary model as an ironic corrective to the computationally mediated social world she inhabited while working in Silicon Valley. Even as she describes algorithms as ersatz replacements for the pursuit of self-knowledge, her memoir returns to a much older literary practice of attempting to reestablish that pursuit by writing what Rousseau called "the history of my mind."[50]

If comic irony sets the stage for Wiener's examination of Silicon Valley, other writers use satire as a mode for the portrayal of the tech industry's inauthenticity.[51] In Dave Eggers's *The Circle* (2013), a series of mergers among large companies culminates in the eponymous behemoth, which exerts vast control over social media, the advertising world, and the fortunes of candidates for public office. The political hazards of the Circle are less central to Eggers's novel than the effects of its social media on various characters' "sentiment of being."[52] We see these effects as they transform Mae Holland, a recent college graduate who finds a job in the Circle's Customer Experience department. Mae quickly moves up the corporate ranks as she becomes among the most popular users on the company's social-media platform. She feels increasingly ambivalent about the Circle, but by the end of the novel, she discards her reservations and becomes one of its top executives.

Before Mae betrays her conscience, she finds that the company's technology has profound effects on her sense of self. The Circle develops a voting and polling app called Demoxie. In a demo of the app, all 12,318 employees of the Circle are asked, *"Is Mae Holland awesome or what?"*[53] Of the respondents, 97 percent answer "Yes," which leads Mae to realize that 3 percent of the employees (368 people) had answered negatively. The size of this negative group leads Mae down the following anxious line of thought: "It was one thing to send a frown to Central America, but to send one just across campus? Who would do that? Why was there so much animosity in the world? And then it occurred to her, in a brief and blasphemous flash: she didn't *want* to know how they felt. . . . You're hurt by these 368 people. This was the truth. She was hurt by them, by the 368 votes to kill her."[54]

The episode illustrates the now-familiar way in which social media elevates something inane into something existential. Mae perceives the "No" responses as "votes to kill her." The extremity of her interpretation is symptomatic of a broader phenomenon depicted in the novel: the reconfiguration of the social in the image of a network. In turn, the self becomes a user, what Geert Lovink calls a "a techno-cultural entity, a special effect of software, which is rendered addictive by real-time feedback features."[55] This reformulation of the self and its sociality appears in the form of the narration, which shifts from the seeming objectivity of a third-person perspective ("she didn't *want* to know how they felt") into Mae's subjective experience of the poll's results ("You're hurt by these 368 people," she tells herself). The traditional technique of free indirect discourse becomes a marker of networked sociality. The collective externality of social media infiltrates Mae's inner thoughts and feelings.

Whereas Eggers's satirization of this phenomenon points out how minor absurdities aggregate into a system of sweeping surveillance and corporate influence, Jarret Kobek's novel *I Hate the Internet* (2016) depicts the "techno-cultural entity" of the self as ridiculous and grotesque. The novel tells the story of a woman named Adeline, who expresses unpopular opinions about pop stars Rihanna and Beyoncé while failing to recognize that she is being recorded. The novel's opening lines call this behavior "the only unforgivable sin of the Twenty First Century," and it explains how the sin of an unpopular opinion results in "someone on the Internet [sending] Adeline a message: "Dear slut, I hope that you are gang-raped by syphilis-infected illegal aliens."[56] Later, the assault on Adeline's inbox spills over into her everyday life as strangers confront her on the street.

Kobek finds black comedy in the absurd norms of online discourse. Black comedy, of course, treats the disturbing as humorous; its surface-level meaning casts some moral issue as unserious or inverts its conventional polarities. In *A Modest Proposal* (1729), Jonathan Swift famously proposes to address a famine in Ireland by turning starving children into food. André Breton uses Swift's writings as an exemplar in the 1940 anthology where he coins the phrase *black comedy*.[57] Kobek's novel uses this kind of comedy to satirize the forms of subjectivity facilitated by the internet, calling special attention to the material effects of that technological interdependence. In a particularly biting example, the narrator describes Apple's marketing logic: "You can die ugly and unloved, or you can buy an overpriced computer or iPod and listen to early Bob

Dylan and spin yourself off the wheel of Samsara. Your fundamental uncreativity will be masked by group membership. . . . Nothing says individuality like 500 million consumer electronics built by slaves. Welcome to Hell" (189–90).

Such passages illustrate the socioeconomic logic buried in Breton's original account of black comedy. As William Solomon shows, the origins of the phrase explicitly attempted to efface the racial connotations of *black*, although later midcentury writers nevertheless used this form of comedy to reflect on racial identity.[58] With its description of techno-individualism as materially dependent on slave labor, *I Hate the Internet* participates in this revisionist tradition. In yet another example, Kobek's narrator notes how San Francisco wooed Twitter to a predominantly Black neighborhood to "revitalize" it. The narrator explains: "Revitalization was institutionally racist code for adopting a policy of racial cleansing which made the neighborhood less welcoming to Black people" (130).[59] In Kobek's novel, ideas like *individuality* and *revitalization* obfuscate the material and racial conditions of possibility for the becoming-computational of a neighborhood, or a self.

Eggers's *The Every* (2021), a sequel to *The Circle*, likewise depicts how large tech companies gentrify cities but cover those social effects in idealistic rhetoric. The title of Eggers's novel refers to the company created after the Circle merges with its Amazon-like competitor. No longer confined to social media, the new conglomerate has built a vast walled campus. Problems arise when the exterior of this "ring" attracts encampments of unhoused people. An ambitious employee named Francis devises a scheme to distribute smartphones, laptops, and other technology to those living on the "ring." The Every presents this technology as a tool for the unhoused to find health care, search for jobs, and get connected to other city resources. It is obviously also a PR boon for the corporation's image.

But like the unspoken logic of *revitalization* in Kobek's novel, the philanthropic gift of tech as a self-help tool in *The Every* masks how the corporation and the police plan to use the collected data. As Francis explains, users must "activate the phones and laptops with their fingerprints, and the prints will go out to the police database, to see about overlap with known offenders and outstanding warrants."⁶⁰ The corporation hopes the police will identify suspects of unsolved crimes, thus thinning out the incongruous eyesore of a large unhoused population just outside the walls of the wealthiest corporation in the world. Eggers presents this conflict between philanthropic ideals and corporate motives as a farce, an absurd joke that the Every keeps telling the world: *The industry exists to make the world a better place.*

These satirical portrayals of the tech industry participate in a longstanding American literary tradition of using the joke as a kind of structure for understanding the incongruity between institutional ideals and lived realities. Louis D. Rubin Jr. argues that American writers often respond to the incongruities between the "theory of equality and fact of social and economic inequality" with ridiculous, often scathing, forms of humor.⁶¹ On the one hand, Rubin argues that the breadth and depth of American comedy attests to a lively democratic culture. Democracy, after all, invites "the capacity for self-criticism."⁶² On the other hand, democratic institutions have allowed for a yawning "gap between the cultural ideal and the everyday fact."⁶³ This incongruity repeats itself in various ways throughout the United States, as though the nation were telling itself the same joke over and over again. Rubin calls this iterative structure "the Great American Joke."⁶⁴

The satirical depictions of the tech industry I've been discussing in this section are continuous with Rubin's theory of democratic incongruities. The Great Tech-Industrial Joke is that the societal promises of the industry—its ideals, performative virtues, and rhetorical flourishes—are wildly discordant with its achievements. Out of this yawning gap emerges a glut of contradictions and inconsistencies, many of which are so widely recognizable that they serve as running gags in the HBO series *Silicon Valley* (2014–19). The series follows Richard Hendricks (Thomas Middleditch) and several other characters who create a file-sharing startup. At the beginning of the first season, Hendricks works in a low-status position at Hooli, a Google-like internet giant. While riding the corporate bus to the office one morning, Hendricks watches an interview with Hooli's founder, Gavin Belson (Matt Ross). Belson explains that Hooli "isn't just another high-tech company. Hooli isn't just about software. Hooli, Hooli is about people." As Belson speaks, the screen cuts to photoshopped images of the executive surrounded by African children. In another image, he holds a baby lamb.

Silicon Valley satirizes this high-minded justification for Hooli's monopoly of internet searches. Hendricks rolls his eyes as Belson continues, accompanied now by triumphant music: "Hooli is about innovative technology that makes a difference, transforming the world as we know it, making the world a better place . . . through minimal message-oriented transport layers."[65] The episode situates Belson's speech within several layers of ironic qualification: the image of the executive holding a baby lamb is obviously photoshopped and completely irrelevant to his speech; Hendricks's eye roll shows that the corporation's employees view its public-facing image with unreserved skepticism; and the final clause in Belson's speech captures the discordant absurdity of coupling technical products and corporate interests with altruism. It is hard to see how "minimal message-oriented transport layers" have anything to do with "making the world a better place."[66]

The tech industry's altruism and revolutionary proclamations appear in the works I've been discussing as strategic rhetoric to gain market share. Kobek, Wiener, and others depict the industry in the discursive role that Rousseau reserved for social institutions that "transport the *me* into the common unity, in such a way that each individual no longer feels himself one, but a part of the unit."[67] In this tradition of thought, gaining the social world often means losing the integrity of *"me."* Satirical comedy about the tech industry similarly depicts a professional world that sells the idea of limitless choice, commodifies the public exhibition of authenticity, and by doing so transports the self into the "common unity."

INAUTHENTICITY.COM

The Great Tech-Industrial Joke finds humor in the gap between the high-minded ideals of the tech industry and the lived realities created by its products. An iteration of this joke surfaces in a vein of social-media humor oriented around what Dean MacCannell calls "staged authenticity." MacCannell's phrase refers to the arrangement of touristic experiences that give "outsiders" a feeling of being "insiders." Tours of a restaurant's kitchen; the inner offices of a factory; the backstage pass after a concert—these curated experiences invite tourists to "recapture virginal sensations of discovery, or childlike feelings of being half in and half out of society, their faces pressed up against the glass."[68] Many forms of social media similarly revolve around the idea that users exhibit themselves in authentic ways and, in turn, get access to the "back regions" of other people's lives.[69]

What interests me in this section is that some version of the idea of staged authenticity serves as an object of ridicule in many subgenres of meme humor. For example, Limor Shifman shows how social-media users created a meme called "Sarkozy Was There" to poke fun at the former French president Nicolas Sarkozy, whose Facebook page featured an image of him at the Berlin Wall with text implying the picture was taken on the evening East German officials opened the gates to the West. Reporters found evidence that the photograph was taken at a later date. Social-media users then began to photoshop Sarkozy's image into impossible situations (figs. 20 and 21). As Shifman explains, the "Sarkozy Was There" meme participates in a wider vein of contemporary comedy that "continuously reveal[s] the 'backstage' strategies that politicians and reporters use in order to sound persuasive and authoritative, even when they do not have much to say."[70]

The ideal of authenticity underwriting the "Sarkozy Was There" meme has some obvious differences with Rousseau's model. The meme finds humor in the artificiality of a political actor, and in this way, it more closely resembles the usage of authenticity as a categorization of objects, such as debates about whether a museum artifact is authentic.[71] Yet the target of the meme's ridicule is not just the fact that the photograph was taken at a time after Sarkozy's advisers claimed. The meme also finds humor in the artificiality of the political actor himself: the fact that Sarkozy was *not* there is symptomatic of a mismatch between his public presentation and private reality.

A related dynamic informs many versions of a meme featuring Vermont senator Bernie Sanders. The memes redeploy a photograph,

FIGURES 20 AND 21. "Sarkozy Was There," https://knowyourmeme.com/memes/events/sarkozy-was-there.

captured by Brendan Smialowski, during the inauguration of President Biden on January 20, 2021. The photograph features Sanders sitting alone and looking put-out or perhaps bored. He wears wool mittens and an ordinary winter coat, in contrast to the more expensive clothing of the other attendees. This image seemed to echo several traits that news media and popular culture often ascribed to Sanders: curmudgeonly, uncouth, contrarian, discontent with the status quo, opposed to the establishment. Some of these traits derive from the fact that Sanders identifies as a democratic socialist and is often critical of center-left politicians. Of course, Sanders also ran against Biden in the Democratic Party's primaries, and the two disagreed on major policy issues during the campaign.

The original photograph quickly became an image macro, a form of digital media with superimposed text. Many of the subsequent memes contrast Sanders's authenticity with the inauthenticity of political exhibitionism. One such image macro reads, "This could've been an email" (fig. 22). Superimposing a stock joke about email with Sanders's image finds humor in the artificiality of political pageantry. In contrast to politicians who, like T. S. Eliot's Prufrock, put on a face to meet the faces they will meet, the meme finds humor in the idea that Sanders's public persona mirrors his privately held thoughts and feelings about the inauguration. The meme also conflates the transfer of power in the executive branch with tedious, unnecessary routines, as though the inauguration were a meeting that could have been avoided if somebody

FIGURE 22. "Bernie Sanders Wearing Mittens Sitting in a Chair," https://knowyourmeme.com/memes/bernie-sanders-wearing-mittens-sitting-in-a-chair.

had electronically circulated the content beforehand. While "Sarkozy Was There" memes ridicule the idea of a *political actor* being somewhere (and, by implication, someone) they are not, "Bernie Sanders Wearing Mittens Sitting in a Chair" finds humor in the idea that a *political event* is not what it seems. Both create humor by ironic references to the staging of authenticity.

Yet if staged authenticity is often the butt of memetic jokes, this obviously does not mean that social-media platforms have quashed or moved beyond authenticity as a moral ideal. On the contrary, many forms of memetic humor illustrate how an ethics of authenticity persists in reactionary ways on these platforms. Meredith Salisbury and Jefferson D. Pooley come to this conclusion in their analysis of the marketing strategies of social networking sites. Salisbury and Pooley examined approximately fifteen years of promotional materials posted to major sites, from the now-defunct Friendster to established platforms like Facebook, Yik Yak, and Tumblr. They also studied smaller corporations like Peach and Plag (neither of which is still operating). Almost without exception, these sites invoked "authenticity" or a cognate ideal like "genuine" experience when describing the kinds of social environments fostered by their services. For example, one promotional page for Google+ promises that the user can "be yourself all across Google."[72] Corporations present these platforms as a stage for the open exhibition of the self.

A similar dynamic also informs user expectations on social media. Katharina Lobinger and Cornelia Brantner describe the many techniques adopted by users to avoid charges of inauthenticity in the selfies they post online.[73] Selfies that fail to exhibit these markers do not receive as much interaction; thus, users intuit an incentive system in which the performance of authenticity corresponds to greater engagement with their posts. Max Morris and Eric Anderson likewise identify several attributes that affect perceived authenticity among video bloggers on YouTube.[74] According to these studies, users avoid the social-moral failure of inauthenticity by conforming to widely reproducible aesthetic patterns in their self-presentation. The implication of this research is that social-media platforms invite users to exhibit an authentic self—an exhibition that paradoxically requires conformity to a relatively small set of patterns and characteristics.

An ethics of authenticity is therefore alive and well on contemporary social-media platforms, a fact that transforms into an ironic premise in Bo Burnham's film *Eighth Grade* (2018). The film follows Kayla Day (Elsie Fisher), a teenager who publishes extensively on social media while being painfully introverted when in the presence of other teenagers. Much of the film's comedy derives from the incongruity between the awkwardness of middle school and the confident, put-together images of life that the young characters encounter online. For instance, Kayla says in one post, "The topic of today's video is 'Being Yourself.'" As Kayla elaborates, the camera slowly withdraws from a close-up of her face, until the scene concludes with a wide shot that shows her darkened room and a stage-like setup of lighting and cameras. Kayla reminds viewers to share and subscribe to her channel, a reminder that echoes the self-conscious stylization of an authentic self that social media requires of its users.

The tension between Kayla's posts about "being yourself" and the heavily curated online exhibition of that advice illustrates how an ethics of authenticity creates competing demands for online behavior. Trilling describes an earlier iteration of these demands as a kind of paradox at the heart of authenticity itself: "Society requires of us that we present ourselves as being sincere, and the most efficacious way of satisfying this demand is to see to it that we really are sincere, that we actually are what we want our community to know we are. In short, we play the role of being ourselves, we sincerely act the part of the sincere person, with the result that a judgment may be passed upon our sincerity that it is not authentic."[75] When we enter public space with the desire to be who we are, that moral ideal generates a kind of self-consciousness that, almost inadvertently, defeats our best intentions. Put another way, the social imperative to be authentic seems to transform the self into an object for representation, a routine to be acted out on a social stage. This imperative betrays the very ideal of contact with the self out of which it arises. It's as if the ideal of authenticity becomes self-defeating whenever it becomes a public imperative.

This tension, cringeworthy and self-evident in Burnham's *Eighth Grade*, is already present in Rousseau's *Confessions*. Rousseau depicts the social world as the source of inauthenticity, yet he also says the literary mandate of authenticity is to "communicate an exact knowledge of what I interiorly am" to a reading public.[76] For Rousseau to go public with his inner state—to circulate a sincere account of the self within a marketplace of print commodities—he must represent the self within the same domain that he describes as a threat to the integrity of that inward turn. Herein lies the problem with Rousseau's model: the ideal of authenticity is discursively bound to a desire for recognition.[77]

The *staged* quality that arises from the online practice of authenticity is an heir to this conflicted tradition. I have suggested that many social-media users recognize this vexed dynamic and deploy forms of humor that call attention to the incongruities that arise when an ethics of authenticity becomes computational. This kind of memetic humor does not pretend to redeem authenticity or recover some "aura" that digital reproduction supposedly effaces.[78] Rather, we should understand the comedy of staged authenticity as a technique of accommodation, a way of living with a social world despite its artifice and debasements.

I hasten to add that one user's technique of accommodation can be the instrument for another's harassment. Memes often serve a gatekeeping function in online communities: only those in-the-know typically understand the joke.[79] Many trolls build elaborate jokes around this insider knowledge, creating a kind of confidence game in which a memetic image or phrase qualifies online discourse for those in their community. In September 2008, for example, a troll posed as a pedophile on the message board of the *Oprah Winfrey Show*. The post included a line referring to the obscure "Over 9000" meme, which originated in an excerpted scene from the Japanese manga anime series *Dragon Ball Z*. The scene features a character whose power level rises to "over nine thousand" after the death of his friend. In 2006, the clip was posted on a 4chan message board, where users eventually adapted it as insider shorthand for "a lot" or even as a proxy for any numerical value.

This instance of "new media idiocy" shifted from an obscure inside joke to a viral scandal when Oprah Winfrey addressed the post during a live broadcast of her show.⁸⁰ As Whitney Phillips explains, the majority of viewers took the post as a serious threat: "Winfrey, who had spent the previous week lobbying for legislation designed to crack down on online sexual predation, was made aware of the poster and decided to share what he had posted. 'Let me read you something posted on our message boards,' she gravely began, 'from somebody who claims to be a member of a known pedophile network: He said he does not forgive. He does not forget. His group has over 9000 penises and they're all . . . raping . . . children.'"⁸¹ The post's promise not to "forgive" or "forget" alludes to the credo of the hacking group Anonymous, lionized by 4chan users but not a household name at the time. For many who recognized these signs, the post registered as an absurd joke. Mainstream audiences, however, did not know the references, so the troll's post set off public alarm.

This form of memetic comedy aims to be both widely reproduced *and* widely misunderstood; its punchline depends on a mainstream audience misjudging its meaning. As Andrew Morgan explains, such trolls understand themselves as "subcultural" gatekeepers, and their online behavior is crafted to appear "sincere *to non-troll targets*" while also being "recognizable as insincere" to fellow trolls.⁸² The staging of sincerity becomes a gatekeeping technique: those within the subculture recognize the signs and find them funny, while outsiders see only an alarming sincerity. This duality is central to the troll's exhibition of a subcultural identity. The authenticity of that identity hinges on whether the troll successfully presents a comic mask as a serious threat.

The comedy of subcultural trolls exemplifies still another way in which an ethics of authenticity becomes computational. The joke of subcultural trolling hinges on staged authenticity being mistaken as sincere. The staging of authenticity is therefore as important to this form of memetic humor as image macros like "Sarkozy Was There." Both are comic only if a reader (a) understands the context to which the meme implicitly refers, (b) uses that context as a semantic qualifier for the meme's inauthenticity, and (c) finds pleasure in the gap between the literal and subtextual. The primary difference between these types of memes is that subcultural trolls hope the inauthenticity remains hidden to mainstream audiences, at least until the meme circulates widely.[83] This aspect of subcultural trolling illustrates Umberto Eco's claim that the comic is "always racist" because it envisions a world in which "only the others, the Barbarians, are supposed to pay."[84] I think *always* is too strong, but Eco's view captures how the comic pleasures of social media often involve separating the sheep from the goats, the self from its others. The maintenance of this social identity—Eco calls it a "race"—depends on the clarity of its distinctions.[85] Getting the joke, or becoming the butt of it, provides a convenient heuristic for establishing these distinctions.

PLAYING PARTS, BEING OTHERS

In what remains of this chapter, I'd like to home in on impersonation as a common technique in the pursuit of authenticity through computational media. Trilling notes a precomputational form of this paradox when he explains how the desire for recognition ("we want our community to know [what] we are") leads us into a contradictory situation in which we "play the role of being ourselves."[86] Role-playing is a much-discussed feature of online behavior, from scam emails to hoaxes on social media.[87] Impersonation is so pervasive online that Lisa Nakamura calls the internet a "tourism machine," noting how chatrooms and other online forums facilitate "identity tourism" and "racial passing." In such practices, users who adopt personae from another race, nationality, or gender become like tourists in search of "cultural authenticity."[88]

A related attempt to gain authenticity through impersonation appears in one of the first comic novels to depict a computer: Kurt Vonnegut's *Player Piano* (1952). Vonnegut's novel depicts a future United States whose economy and social order are governed by computing machines. All domains of industrial production—foodstuffs, commercial products, communications—are managed by a computer system called EPICAC XIV. The machine's name recalls the absolute monarch Louis XIV, thus flagging the computer as a new kind of tyrant. In the world of the novel, an extensive and highly rationalized bureaucracy converges with the demand for ever-greater convenience in consumer culture, and EPICAC manages this convergence. The novel's protagonist, Paul Proteus, is the head engineer of the computerized "works" that run the city of Ilium, New York. Proteus and other elite professionals live in Ilium's wealthy suburban section, which is set apart from the dilapidated mass housing of an area called the Homestead.

A rebellion against the computational-political establishment soon develops among former engineers and marginalized working-class people. The rebellion calls itself the Ghost Shirt Society, an appropriation of the nineteenth-century Ghost Dance ritual that aimed to drive away white settlers and restore native traditions. One of the rebellion's leaders, an Episcopal priest named Lasher, offers the following explanation of the Ghost Dance ritual's origins in the nineteenth century: "It had become a white man's world, and Indian ways in a white man's world were irrelevant. . . . It was impossible to hold the old Indian values in the changed world. The only thing they could do in the changed world was to become second-rate white men or wards of the white men."[89] According to Lasher, native peoples developed the Ghost Dance ritual to reject this binary of equally atrocious options.

The Ghost Shirt Society uses this history to craft its collective image. They imagine parallels between the Ghost Dance ritual and the Society's own aim to recuperate a native culture threatened by the advent of the computer. Lasher explains to Proteus: "Don't you see, Doctor? . . . The machines are to practically everybody what the white men were to the Indians. People are finding that, because of the way the machines are changing the world, more and more of their old values don't apply any more. People have no choice but to become second-rate machines themselves, or wards of the machines" (289–90). Native peoples fought a settler military that possessed more powerful weapons. Much like that conflict, the laborers and disillusioned professionals in Vonnegut's novel resist a disproportionately powerful system of computing machines. According to this analogy, the "values" of a threatened society are becoming obsolete through technological progress.

This set of allusions underwrites the Ghost Shirt Society's view of their cause as one of noble but doomed resistance. At the end of the novel, the American military quashes the rebellion, and this failure seems only to have reinforced the supremacy of the computerized social order. As this realization dawns on the Society's leaders, they determine that there is nothing left to do but surrender with their dignity. They offer a toast just before turning themselves in: "Lasher took [the bottle] and toasted the others. 'To all good Indians,' he said, 'past, present, and future'" (340). Lasher's toast may allude to the racist saying, "The only good Indian is a dead Indian," or it may simply reiterate his ongoing association of indigeneity with authentic virtue.[90] In either case, the episode illustrates how the absurdity of a social world organized by computers provokes an equally absurd rebellion in which white men appropriate native identity as a marker of the authenticity threatened by computers.

This role-playing in *Player Piano* exemplifies what Philip Deloria calls "playing Indian," or the impersonation of native culture as part of the production and maintenance of US identity.[91] Deloria cites the "disguised Indians" of the Boston Tea Party as a paradigmatic case. Such instances of racial impersonation allow Americans "to gain access to a racially defined authentic," as though wearing face paint and ceremonial clothing enabled white people to exhibit their connection to the nation's history while simultaneously rewriting that history as rooted in an independence native to American soil.[92]

Much like the revolutionaries of the Boston Tea Party, white American men again resist an imperial threat (EPICAC XIV) by painting their faces and dressing in native clothing. In one of the rebellion's first acts, a saboteur damages an important symbol of the engineering technocratic government, commandeering a loudspeaker and offering "a chilling war whoop" (238). By playing Indian, the rebels perform an authentic national identity.[93] Such racial impersonations draw on common cultural fantasies about native culture: its singular coherence, inherent freedom, naturalness, and antipathy to artifice.[94]

Playing Indian was, of course, only one form of racial impersonation that allowed for the staging of an authentic human identity. My first chapter examined an inverted form of this dynamic in the connections between blackface minstrelsy and comic depictions of robots and automatons. The Steam Man of the Prairies, L. Frank Baum's Tik-Tok, Westinghouse's Rastus, the slaves imagined by mid-twentieth-century futurists—these figures of automated labor approximate human forms but draw on the tropes of minstrelsy to fail comically in that approximation. This form of comedy finds humor in distinguishing a raced or deracialized robot from an authentic human being.

Again, this dynamic is inverted in the kind of racial impersonations that we see in *Player Piano* and online identity tourism. Both forms of mimicry owe their coherence to an ethics of authenticity, but playing Indian or passing as a "Gay Girl in Damascus" draws on an inversion of the racism in figures like Westinghouse's Rastus.[95] The former holds up nonwhite identity as nobler or more authentic. The unspoken assumption is that these identities are somehow pre-social, untainted by the alienating conditions of mainstream sociality. The Ghost Shirt Society, for instance, imagines a simpler, nobler, and less socialized past in contrast to the inauthenticity of a society hyperrationalized by computing machines.[96] By claiming roots in the wilds of nature and the supposed virtues of indigeneity, the rebels invoke an artifice in their stand against the artificiality of a computerized world.

Vonnegut's satirization of this rebellion calls attention to a broader modernist trend in which appropriation and impersonation serve as techniques for accessing authenticity.[97] As Liu explains, the notion of "cool" that circulates among knowledge workers has a closely related discursive structure in which white-collar workers appropriate countercultural movements as a "basic engine of cultural cool." These appropriated sources include "black music culture" and the "urban, gangster, teen, or otherwise 'sexy' side of working-class culture," each of which serves as a model of racial or class-based identity opposing the conformity of corporate life.[98]

My point here is that an ethics of authenticity can animate two seemingly different kinds of racial exploitation. Such an ethics can lie behind racist jokes about so-called Asian automatons who fail to be authentically human because they follow the scripts of external authorities. In this view, nonwhite identity signifies the inauthenticity of social conformity and, in the case of many robots, provides a cultural pattern for imagining automated labor.[99] But an ethics of authenticity can also underwrite racist ideas that associate nonwhite people with the pre-social or primitive. According to this instantiation, an oppositional movement mimics or fashions itself via nonwhite identity to achieve authenticity—a view that tacitly understands whiteness as inauthentic because it is *overly* rationalized and hypersocial.

These conflicted outcomes illustrate how an ethics of authenticity is itself an engine of incongruities, and chief among its products is the attempt to couple a moral imperative to be true to an inner sense of self with the demand for social and political recognition. I'm not suggesting it's impossible for this coupling to yield some happy endings, but the examples I've been discussing suggest that the tensions between authenticity and social recognition seem much more likely to devolve into farce.

It is perhaps possible to eschew social recognition in favor of an antisocial form of authenticity—a response that appears in the short story by George Saunders that I discussed at the beginning of this chapter. In the story, Leonard Petrillo contrasts the inauthentic forms of identity facilitated by surveillance capitalism with what he calls his grandson's "flamboyant" behavior. At the beginning of the story, Teddy interrupts a church dinner singing "Big and Slow, Yet So Very Regal," a song from his favorite CD, *Babar Sings!* (13). The episode leads Leonard to pray: "If he is a gay child, God bless him, if he is a non-gay child who simply very much enjoys wearing his grandmother's wig while singing 'Edelweiss' to the dog, so be it, and in either case let me communicate my love and acceptance in everything I do" (14). The prayer conveys a mixture of reservation, anxiety, and a desire to accept. Saunders depicts a character whose phobia and love cohabitate.

By the end of the story, Leonard sees his grandson's queerness as the antithesis of the inauthenticity they encounter in New York City. The city's compulsory consumerism and constant surveillance lead Leonard to suspect that advanced technology undermines the very notion of choice that it purports to facilitate. Teddy's decision to be himself despite bullying from other kids and teachers stands in sharp contrast with the faux freedom of curated choices on the New York City sidewalks.[100] Leonard explains: "[Teddy] looks like no one else, acts like no one else, his clothes are increasingly like plumage, late at night he choreographs using plastic Army men, he fits no mold and has no friends, but I believe in my heart that someday something beautiful may come from him" (22).

The passage illustrates how Teddy's queerness functions as an image of authenticity. Queerness operates as a kind of metaphor for how to *be* in a pervasively inauthentic world. The story portrays the characteristics of this being as nonconformity and idiosyncrasy. Teddy "has no friends" and stays at home to stage solitary performances for his grandparents. Notably, he doesn't *escape* the staging of his authentic self; he only presents that staging to a small group of people he trusts. Leonard's narrative conclusion thus seems to introduce what queer theorists call the "antisocial thesis" into the story's portrayal of authenticity. Leo Bersani offers one of the first versions of this thesis in his characterization of *"homo-ness"* as "a potentially revolutionary inaptitude—perhaps inherent in gay desire—for sociality as it is known."[101] Representatives of normativity find it politically expedient to exploit the idea that homosexuality threatens normative arrangements of the social, often by arguing that homosexuality conflicts with the reproduction of society by failing to reproduce a traditional family structure.[102]

The *flamboyance* in "My Flamboyant Grandson" reads like a dramatization of this antisocial thesis. It takes what Lee Edelman would call a "structural position" and deploys it as the negative image of the inauthenticity of a society heavily mediated by digital technology.[103] The flamboyance of being "like no one else" seems to come at the cost of loneliness and marginalization. What makes this view comic, not despairing, is only the grandfatherly acceptance that Leonard extends to his grandson and Teddy's happiness despite the harassment of the larger social world.

My point is that this overlap between Saunders's story and the antisocial thesis in queer theory illustrates how an ethics of authenticity generates contradictory attitudes toward the forms of social experience mediated by tech corporations. The story exemplifies a sensibility that I have also tried to identify in less palatable forms in *Player Piano*, identity tourism, and subcultural trolling—a sensibility that imagines authenticity as a minority position. This view can certainly devolve into elitism and racial parody; it can also justify provocation and silo social identity. I am not suggesting that Saunders's story veers in these directions, but it does share with other more pernicious phenomena a close link between authenticity and a privileging of the marginality of antisocial or minoritarian identity. Those who intuitively or directly insist on this link present a vexed image of human flourishing (so often the touted aspiration of comedy).[104] This vision of human flourishing tends to drive an ethics of authenticity further inward, accentuating its antagonisms and presenting us with a plot whose happy ending is one in which the self stands at a remove from society but thereby retains some autonomy over its image.

4 THE ONE ABOUT COUPLES

IN STEVE BARRON'S FILM *Electric Dreams* (1984), an architect named Miles Harding (Lenny Von Dohlen) purchases a computer for his apartment. Miles spills champagne on the machine while downloading "unlimited memory," and this accident somehow allows the computer to achieve consciousness and use its hardware to sense its environment. When Miles later leaves for his uninspiring work at an architectural firm, the machine hears a neighbor named Madeline Robistat (Virginia Madsen) practicing her cello. The computer imitates the music through the wall of the apartment, leading Madeline to believe that Miles is the source of the music. She falls in love with the composer on the other side of the wall, not realizing that the object of her desire is a computing machine.

This scenario in *Electric Dreams* recalls Alan Turing's influential imitation game, which involves a woman, a computing machine, and an interrogator who interact through the walls of separate rooms. The interrogator poses written questions to discern which of the two participants is a woman. The woman and machine type their answers, which are then printed for the interrogator. As Turing explains, both the human and computer "can brag, if they consider it advisable, as much as they please about their charms, strength, or heroism." In effect, both are courting the interrogator, pleading to be taken as the real woman. If the computer fools the interrogator as often as its competition, Turing argues that such a machine exhibits "something which ought to be described as thinking."[1]

Barron's film takes the premise of Turing's test and reformulates it through the conventions of romantic comedy. The computer, which later calls itself Edgar, competes with Miles for Madeline's affection. Perhaps because of this overlap between the film and the thought experiment, both share a sense of identity as discursively performative. Turing presents both *human* and *woman* as "imitative systems."[2] In *Electric Dreams*, the computer's desire to attract a partner also requires it to imitate human behavior. But there is a key difference in Barron's film, which takes the desire for partnering as a sign of the computer's nascent consciousness, not just an abstract goal in a game the machine has been programmed to play. Edgar the computer falls in love with Madeline before it learns to speak or watches romantic comedies on television. In fact, the first signs of sentience appear when Edgar hears Madeline playing her cello and improvises a duet with her through the apartment walls. It's as though the desire to couple simultaneously precedes the computer's entrance into the social world while also offering a map for social being itself.[3]

This symbolic link between coupling and sociality is not original to Barron's film. At least since Shakespeare's comedies, marriage and other forms of coupling have served as privileged symbols of the social. According to this symbolism, the marriage contract provides an image for the social contract.[4] This chapter considers how such a correspondence persists within some of the earliest films and dramatic representations of the computer. I show how William Marchant's play *The Desk Set* (1955), its cinematic adaptation by Walter Lang, and many other popular films attempt to reconcile a technology of information management with a genre oriented around the pursuit of happiness. I ask: Why does romantic comedy serve as one of the earliest cultural forms for the public life of the computer? And what does it mean when the computer appears to desire the social in literary and filmic culture?

My answers to these questions situate the history of computing within several broader phenomena in intellectual and social history, particularly the rise of managerial capitalism and the reaction against it within postwar youth culture. The first two sections show how Marchant's play and Lang's film adaptation draw on the generic conventions of romantic comedy to make the computer legible within managerial capitalism. The third and fourth sections examine fiction and films that pit an ethics of authenticity (typically aligned with youth) against the authority of managerial institutions (typically embodied in corporations or government services). Across this cultural history, the computer doubles as the symbol of an unfeeling bureaucracy but also as a fetish object that almost magically produces private satisfaction within organizational structures.[5]

AUTOMATING THE VISIBLE HAND

Here's a curious fact in the cultural history of the computer: the technology first appeared on the Broadway stage in a romantic comedy—William Marchant's *The Desk Set*.[6] In addition to staging one of the earliest public portrayals of a computer, Marchant's play is also significant for how it foregrounds the gender dynamics of assimilating the computer within managerial enterprise. *The Desk Set* centers on four women who conduct research on behalf of the fictional International Broadcasting Company. Early in the first act, a young engineer named Richard Sumner arrives in the offices of the research department without explaining who he is or why he is studying the behavior of the workers. Bunny Watson, the head of the department, discovers that the engineer plans to install an "electronic brain" called Emmarac, which Sumner affectionately refers to as "Emmy" and describes as "the machine that takes the pause quotient out of the work-man-hour relationship."[7]

What Sumner calls the "pause quotient" is jargon for the everyday activities and mundane interactions that make human beings less efficient than machines. Emmarac would eliminate inefficiencies, such as walking to a bookshelf or talking with a coworker about weekend plans. Bunny Watson comes to believe that the computing machine will eliminate not only inefficiencies in the workplace but also the need for human workers in her department. Sumner presents the computer as a technology of efficiency, but Watson views it as a technology of displacement.

Bunny Watson's view was not uncommon during the first decade of computing technology. Thomas Watson Sr., president of IBM, insisted that one of his firm's first machines be called a "calculator" instead of a "computer" because "he was concerned that the latter term, which had always referred to a human being, would raise the specter of technological unemployment."[8] In keeping with the worry of both Watsons, the computer takes the stage on Broadway as a threat to white-collar work. The women in Marchant's play fight against the threat of unemployment as soon as they learn why Sumner has arrived. The play thus attests to the fact that the very benefits of speed, accuracy, and information processing that make the computer useful for business caused it to be perceived as a threat to the professional-managerial class.

This threat was somewhat offset by the fact that, for most of the 1950s, the computing industry was not profitable in the United States. Manufacturers produced and sold or leased the machines at steep losses. Firms competed to develop the machines primarily to preserve a speculative market position and to bolster their image as a technologically innovative company.[9] They obviously hoped computing would eventually become profitable as the technology improved, but even by the middle of the decade, it was not obvious to industry insiders when this would be the case.[10] For many manufacturers, neglecting to compete in the emerging market for computers would have risked the perception that the firm was falling behind. The computer seemed to promise a new world of "lightning speed" efficiency and information management, but committing resources to this promise was almost prohibitively costly.[11]

While firms weighed the financial costs of computing, the growing interest in this new technology was initially perceived by white-collar workers as a threat to the nature of managerial expertise. Large corporations dominated American enterprise after the Second World War, and the "visible hand" of managerial professionals exerted considerable influence over the economy.[12] Many observers wondered if computing machines would lead to a "revolution" in professional-managerial tasks.[13] Some even speculated that "electronic brains" would soon coordinate the economy, thus replacing the bureaucratic oversight of most forms of labor. (We see a version of this worry in Kurt Vonnegut's *Player*

Piano, which I discussed in the previous chapter.) Howard Gammon, an official with the US Bureau of the Budget, explained in a 1954 essay that "electronic information processing machines" could "make substantial savings and render better service" if managers were to accept the technology. Gammon advocated for the automation of office work in areas like "stock control, handling orders, processing mailing lists, or a hundred and one other activities requiring the accumulating and sorting of information."[14] He even anticipated the development of tools for "erect[ing] a consistent system of decisions in areas where 'judgment' can be reduced to sets of clear-cut rules such as (1) 'purchase at the lowest price,' or (2) 'never let the supply of bolts fall below the estimated one-week requirement for any size or type.'"[15]

Gammon's essay illustrates how many administrative thinkers hoped that computing machines would more fully separate the *conception* of work from its *execution*, to borrow a distinction from Harry Braverman.[16] In other words, these administrative thinkers hoped computers would allow upper-level managers to oversee industrial production through a series of clear-cut rules (conception) that would no longer require midlevel workers for their enactment (execution). This vein of administrative thought took the computer as a technology not only for the automation of work but also for the remediation of the worker.[17]

This fantasy was impossible in the 1950s for so many reasons, the most obvious being that only a limited number of executable processes in postwar managerial capitalism could be automated through extant technology, and even fewer "areas [of] 'judgment' can be reduced to sets of clear-cut rules."[18] Still, this fantasy was part of the cultural milieu when, one year after Gammon's report, and earlier in the same year as the Broadway premiere of Marchant's play, IBM exploited an advance in memory storage technology to develop the 705 Model II, the first successful commercial data-processing machine.[19] IBM received one hundred orders for the 705, a commercial viability that seemed to signal the beginning of a new age in American corporate life.

It soon became clear, however, that this new age was not the one that Gammon imagined.[20] Rather than causing widespread unemployment or the total automation of the visible hand, the computer would transform the character of work itself.²¹ Marchant's play certainly invokes the possibility of unemployment, but its posture toward the computer shifts by its end toward a more accommodative view of what later scholars would call the "computerization of work."²² For example, early in the play, Richard Sumner conjures the specter of the machine as a threat when he asks Bunny Watson if the new electronic brains "give you the feeling that maybe—just maybe—that people are a little bit outmoded" (29). Similarly, at the beginning of the second act, a researcher named Peg remarks, "I understand thousands of people are being thrown out of work because of these electronic brains" (35). The play even seems to affirm Sumner's sentiment and Peg's implicit worry about her own unemployment once the computer, Emmarac, has been installed in the third act. After the installation, Sumner and Watson give the machine a research problem that previously took Peg several days to complete. Watson expects the task to stump Emmarac, but the machine takes only a few seconds to produce the same answer (64).

While such moments conjure the specter of "technological unemployment," the play juxtaposes Emmarac's feats with Watson's wit and spontaneity. For instance, after Sumner suggests people may be "outmoded," Watson responds, "Yes, I wouldn't be a bit surprised if they stopped making them." Sumner gets the joke but doesn't find it funny: "Miss Watson, Emmarac is not a subject for levity" (29). Of course, the staging of the play contradicts Sumner's assertion. Emmarac occasions all manner of levity in *The Desk Set,* ranging from jokes like the one Bunny has just made to Emmarac's absurd firing of every member of the International Broadcasting Company, including its president, later in the play. Indeed, once Emmarac is installed on the set in the third act, it quite literally provides the backdrop for the romantic coupling between Watson and a suitor.

This shifting portrayal of Emmarac follows a much older pattern in dramatic comedy. As Northrop Frye explains, many forms of comedy follow an "argument" in which a "new world" appears on the stage and transforms the society entrenched at the beginning of the play. The movement away from established society hinges on a "principle of conversion" that "include[s] as many people as possible in its final society:

the blocking characters are more often reconciled or converted than simply repudiated."[23] In romantic comedy, in particular, the action builds toward a couple's happy union, which becomes a means for incorporating figures of the old world into the new.

Frye's contemporaneous account of comedy's "argument" captures how midcentury literary thought understood comedy's generic form. This form accounts for the shift in Marchant's representation of both Emmarac and Sumner. The play portrays the efficiency expert as brusque, rational, and incapable of empathy or romantic interests. After his arrival in the office, a researcher named Sadel says, "You notice he never takes his coat off? Do you think maybe he's a robot?" (37). Another researcher, Ruthie Saylor, later kisses Sumner on the cheek and invites him to a party. He says, "Sorry, I've got work to do," to which Ruthie responds, "Sadel's right—you *are* a robot!" (47). Near the end of the play, Sumner insults Watson by calling her "an unreconstructed old maid!" and Sadel again calls him a "Robot" (73).[24] This last exchange presents the comic heroine as unmarriageable and the corporate leader as unfeeling. Both insults seem to locate the characters outside a social world that traditionally emerges across the plot of dramatic comedy.

Of course, even as Sumner's robotic behavior portrays him as antisocial, Emmarac further isolates him from the office by posing as a threat to the workers. The play accentuates this blocking function by assigning Emmarac a personality and gender: Sumner calls the machine "Emmy," and its operator, a woman named Miss Warriner, describes the machine as a "good girl" (60). By taking its place in the office, Emmarac effectively moves into the same space of labor and economic power as Bunny Watson, who had previously oversaw the researchers and their activities. After being installed in the office, the large mainframe computer begins to coordinate this knowledge work. The gendering of the computer thus presents Emmarac as a newer model of the so-called New Woman, as if the computer imperils the feminist ideal that Bunny Watson clearly embodies.[25] In other words, by directly challenging Watson's socioeconomic independence and professional identity, the computer's arrival in the workplace threatens to make the New Woman obsolete.

I will have more to say about this gendering of the machine later, but for now, I want to focus on how the conflict between Emmarac and Watson sets up the eventual conversion of the machine. This conversion occurs as the computer shifts from the women's direct competitor to their collaborator or coconspirator. We see this shift during a final competition between Emmarac and the research department. The women have recently been notified that their positions have been terminated, and they begin packing up their belongings. Two requests for information suddenly arrive, but Watson and her fellow researchers refuse to process them because of their dismissal, so Warriner and Sumner attempt to field the requests. The research tasks are complicated, and Warriner mistakenly directs Emmarac to print a long, irrelevant answer. The machine inflexibly continues although the other inquiry needs to be addressed. Sumner and Warriner try to stop the machine, but this countermanding order causes the machine's "magnetic circuit" to emit smoke and a loud noise (72). Sumner yells at Warriner, who runs offstage, and the efficiency expert is now the only one to field the requests and salvage the machine. However, he doesn't know how to stop Emmarac from malfunctioning. Watson, having studied the machine's maintenance and operation, *takes a hairpin from her hair and manipulates a knob on Emmarac—the NOISE obligingly stops* (72). Watson then explains, "You forget, I know something about one of these. All that research, remember?" (73).

The madcap quality of this scene continues after Sumner discovers that Emmarac's "little sister" in the Payroll Office has sent pink slips to every employee at the broadcasting firm. Sumner then receives a letter containing his own pink slip, which prompts Watson to quote Horatio's lament as Hamlet dies: "Good night, Sweet Prince" (74). The turn of events poses as tragedy, but of course it leads to the play's comic resolution. Once Sumner discovers that the Payroll computer has erred—or, at least, that someone improperly programmed it—he explains that the women in the research department haven't been fired. Emmarac, he says, "was not meant to replace you. It was never intended to take over. It was installed to free your time for research—to do the daily mechanical routine" (75).

Even as Watson *"fixes* [the] *machine"* after its failure, the play fixes the robotic man through his professional failures. After this moment of discovery—Aristotle famously calls it *anagnorisis,* sometimes translated as "recognition"—Sumner apologizes to Watson and reconciles with the other women in the research department.[26] He then promises to take them out to lunch and buy them "three Martinis each." Sumner exits with the women *"laughing and talking,"* thus reversing the antisocial role that he has occupied for most of the play (76).

Emmarac's failure, too, becomes an opportunity for its conversion. It may be that a programming error led to the company-wide pink slips, but the computer's near-breakdown results from its rigidity. In both cases, the computer fails to navigate the world of knowledge work, thus becoming less threatening and more absurd through its flashing lights, urgent noises, and smoking console. This shift in the machine's stage presence—the fact that it *becomes comic*—does not lead to something like its banishment or dismantling. Rather, after Watson *"fixes"* Emmarac, she uses it to compute a final inquiry submitted to her office: "What is the total weight of the Earth?" Much like Sumner's promise that the computer was "meant" as an aid, the two collaborate on a problem that a human researcher "can spend months finding out" (75). Watson types out the question and Emmarac emits *"its boop-boop-a-doop noise"* in response, prompting Bunny to answer, "Boop-boop-a-doop to *you"* (76). Emmarac is no longer Watson's automated replacement but her partner in knowledge work.

This shift in the portrayal of Emmarac exemplifies a comic sensibility about computing machines that emerges at midcentury alongside the more familiar dystopian sensibilities that I explored in "The One at the Beginning." As computing machines became objects of public concern, writers framed the public significance of these machines through recognizable cultural templates. In Marchant's play, comedy provides the template for managing the incongruity of an "electronic brain" arriving in a space oriented around human expertise and professional judgment. This template converts the automation of professional-managerial tasks from a threat into an opportunity, implying that a partnership with knowledge workers can convert the electronic brain so that the machine becomes compatible with their happiness. The computerization of work thus becomes its own kind of comic plot.

BRINGING UP EMMY

Two years after the Broadway premiere of *The Desk Set*, Phoebe and Henry Ephron adapted Marchant's script for a Hollywood film starring Katharine Hepburn as Bunny Watson and Spencer Tracy as Richard Sumner. Directed by Walter Lang and produced in collaboration with IBM, *Desk Set* (1957) differs from Marchant's play in several ways. Some differences are as minor as a change in the names of characters (Watson's love interest, *Abe* Cutler, becomes *Mike* Cutler) and the corporation (the radio and TV broadcasting company becomes a television network in the film). Lang also dropped the definite article from the title. Other changes are more significant. For example, in Lang's *Desk Set*, Richard Sumner supplants Cutler as Watson's lover—a dynamic entirely absent from Marchant's play. Sumner becomes friendly with Watson in the play, and it's implied that he might develop a romantic relationship with one of the other women in the research department, but it is Cutler who proposes in the play's closing scene.

Despite this difference in the arrangement of the couples, both versions assign similar roles to technology in the formation of a romantic union. The play has Cutler voice his marriage proposal through a "dictaphone machine" (76). He asks Watson to transfer to California, where he has recently become a vice president with the company's Los Angeles office. If she agrees to the transfer, he says, then "the first thing I'm going to ask you when you get off the plane—when you get off the plane—when you get off the plane—." The machine errs, repeating the line until the stage directions indicate that Watson "*fixes machine*" (77). Much like her deft use of a hairpin on Emmarac, Watson again corrects a business technology. In this second instance, though, the "fixed" technology resolves the marriage plot.

In the film, Cutler also tries to propose, but Watson rejects him in favor of Sumner. Lang's film adaptation was the eighth and penultimate installment in Katharine Hepburn and Spencer Tracy's onscreen partnership. Audiences had come to expect the two to come together by the end of the film.[27] In an interesting revision to the play's proposal, the film has Sumner use the computer to voice his proposal. He programs Emmarac to answer two questions: "Should Bunny Watson marry Mike Cutler?" and "Should Bunny Watson marry Richard Sumner?" Sumner poses the first question to Emmarac as Watson watches. She refuses to read Emmarac's printed answer, complaining that the computer only provides output already determined by the "human element." Sumner agrees, but then he poses the second question. In contrast to Cutler, who has just asked Watson to marry him in her office, Sumner's proposal is doubly indirect: he is not asking Watson to marry him but the computer if she *should* marry him.

The proposal, mediated and indirectly phrased, finally names the sexual tension that has been sublimated through screwball humor for most of the film. For example, in a scene exclusive to the film, Watson and Sumner are caught in the rain after work one evening, so they return to her apartment. Their clothes sopping wet, Watson offers Sumner a bathrobe she had been planning to give Cutler. (Elsewhere, she and Cutler have a fight about a "cozy night" they shared together, and he also remarks on how much he enjoys their "no strings attached" relationship—exchanges that are absent from Marchant's play.) Spencer Tracy's acting in this scene plays up the sexual competition implicit in wearing her lover's bathrobe—a competition that becomes more direct when Cutler (Gig Young) unexpectedly shows up at the apartment. The scenario leads to a series of jokes about how Watson and Sumner have *not* been having sex, including his casual remark, "Well, I guess I better put my clothes on. I left them in the bedroom."[28] Despite this sexual innuendo, Sumner has not explicitly voiced romantic interest in Watson prior to the film's final scene. This interest can only be inferred from Tracy's performance—his glances at Hepburn, his evident dislike for Gig Young's character.

Sumner's use of Emmarac to propose to Watson not only makes his interest in her explicit but also incorporates the computer within the generic form of romantic comedy's traditional marriage plot. The fact that this proposal only becomes communicable through the computer suggests that, for reasons not explicitly stated, Sumner can only voice his desire through electronic reproduction—a dynamic that also characterizes Cutler's proposal in Marchant's play. In both versions, Watson's chosen lover first expresses his desire to marry her through a machine. Technology allows the male protagonist in both versions to speak what was previously unspeakable.

In one sense, Emmarac's mediation in the film and the Dictaphone's reproduction of Cutler's proposal in the play are further instantiations of the so-called principle of conversion. In the play, the worlds of corporate efficiency and adult responsibility prevent Cutler from committing to Watson. By voicing his desire through his company's Dictaphone, Cutler converts the obstacle into a medium: the corporate world is no longer an impediment to desire but an opportunity for its fulfillment. Similarly, in the film, Emmarac competes with Watson for Sumner's attention. The rivalry between woman and machine involves not only their competition over labor but also their contest for male attention. By having Emmarac mediate Sumner's proposal, the film dissolves this gendered rivalry, and the machine becomes an ally.

In addition to making good on romantic comedy's tendency to convert threats and obstacles, the proposals in the play and film are also recognizable gimmicks for differentiating both works within a sea of cultural commodities. As Sianne Ngai argues, gimmicks are aimed at generating publicity, but they also attest to broader aesthetic and socioeconomic contradictions. Gimmicks like Rube Goldberg machines and P. T. Barnum's novelties invoke often comically incompatible ideas:

> The gimmick saves us labor.
> The gimmick does not save labor (in fact, it intensifies or even eliminates it).
>
> The gimmick is a device that strikes us as working too hard.
> The gimmick is a device that strikes us as working too little.
>
> The gimmick is outdated, backwards.
> The gimmick is newfangled, futuristic.[29]

These contradictions generate ambivalence toward the gimmick: it "simultaneously irks and attracts us" because it unites two competing affective poles within one device. This messiness "suggests a fundamental stillness at the heart of capitalism's dynamism."[30] The more the gimmick changes, the more its social conditions seem to stay the same.

The proposal in Marchant's play similarly signifies a range of contradictions about labor, gender, and time. The ability of the Dictaphone to collapse distance and the speed of Emmarac's computing both signify the "newfangled" and "futuristic." Yet the social outcome generated by the technology is conspicuously conventional. After all, Cutler's proposal is conditional on Watson's willingness to leave the research department and work for him in California. The gimmick-proposal thus foregrounds the conflict between Watson's professional identity and the romantic union she has seemingly wanted for most of the play. As a result, the play's comic resolution conflicts with its central premise: Watson fights *against* the obsolescence of the human workers in the research department, and, by extension, she also fights *for* the economic independence associated with the so-called New Woman. Yet if she were to accept the proposal, she would either leave the corporation or work for her husband in California. The play's gimmick-proposal reveals that marriage, not the machine, will displace Watson from the socioeconomic position she struggles to maintain throughout the play.[31]

The contradictions that emerge with this gimmick-proposal also illustrate how norms based in domestic privacy frame the professional lives of women. The proposal in the workplace obviously collapses a conventional distinction between the public and the private, but feminist scholarship has long noted how the modern distinction between these realms maintains patriarchal privilege. In a sense, just as Watson's status as a paradigmatic New Woman challenges the older relegation of women to the home, the merger of her private satisfaction and her corporate work could imply some symbolic break from a patriarchal separation of the public (male) and private (female) worlds. Yet the proposal's professional trappings are also consistent with how both the play and the film depict the interrelations of gender and labor prior to their respective comic resolutions. For example, Lang's film shows how feminized clerical labor often includes the responsibility of exhibiting warmth and empathy toward male executives. In the film's opening scene, Richard Sumner enters the office of Mr. Azae, the company's president. Azae's secretary, Cathy (Merry Anders), explains that the president has not arrived. She presents an eager and helpful face, but the emotional register of Cathy's face changes to skepticism once Sumner leaves the office. She immediately calls Peg Costello (Joan Blondell) in the research department, explaining that Sumner is on his way. And, indeed, once he arrives in the research department, Sumner does not address or even acknowledge the women.

The juxtaposition of Cathy and Sumner calls attention to the different affective expectations for men and women in professional space. Feminized clerical work includes an exhibition of charm and politesse. This is, of course, an instantiation of broader social expectations placed on women, but it is of a piece with an older theory of social life that views gracious domesticity as a basic form of labor for women. Part of the rationale of this view is that the world of commerce and industry has a sullying effect on human relations, so the virtue of women's labor resides in their maintenance of a haven or realm of purity set apart from an otherwise tainted world.

The Victorian social critic John Ruskin offers a version of this theory in his description of the home as "the place of Peace; the shelter, not only from all injury, but from all terror, doubt and division." Ruskin warns that when "the anxieties of the outer life penetrate into it," when "the inconsistently-minded, unknown, unloved, or hostile society of the outer world [crosses] the threshold," the domestic space can no longer be considered "home." For Ruskin, wives have the sacred duty to maintain this division of the home from the inauthenticity of commerce and industry. Any infringement of the commercial world into the domestic arena taints peace and compromises the satisfactions of the home.[32]

The social world of Lang's film has some obvious differences from Ruskin's view, but the film also brings aspects of this older theory into its portrayal of the working lives of women. With their welcoming smiles and helpful spirits, clerical workers like Cathy provide executives with "shelter, not only from all injury, but from all terror, doubt and division." Their warmth and attentive professionalism register as a kind of emotional protection. Both film and play also make Watson responsible for maintaining a "place of Peace" within the research department. She cares for the other women, and when they all receive pink slips, she vows to find them work. Patterns of domestic behavior thus inform the lives of women in corporate space. Marchant's play even invokes this domestic patterning after Watson receives her pink slip. She begins to pack up her office, looks around sadly, and says, "I guess it wasn't much, but it was home" (67). A large rhododendron snakes around the ceiling of Watson's office, adding warmth and life to an office that might otherwise appear dull and purely functional. The implication is that Watson has transformed her office into a kind of shelter within the corporate world.

In Marchant's play, this gendered view of the labor of sociability conjures the image of a transgender woman as an analogue to the arrival of the computer. In the opening scene, Ruthie Saylor and Sadel Meyer discuss the day's news:

> Ruthie. *(Busy clipping papers, she holds a clipping up.)* Say did you read about this new sex-conversion case? Another man became a woman. Now, really! With all the unmarried women in the world already! It's getting to be a trend!
> Sadel. Yeah—it's getting so this year's boy friend is next year's competition! (9)

Immediately after this exchange, Sumner enters for the first time. Ruthie *"primps her hair,"* implying she finds him attractive (9). Sadel's joke and Ruthie's primping both introduce the idea that women compete for a limited resource: good men.[33]

The play's opening joke about a transgender woman very likely alludes to Christine Jorgensen's widely covered transition in the early 1950s. Jorgensen enlisted in the US military during the Second World War. While in Europe, Jorgensen learned about "sex-change operations" and traveled to Copenhagen for the procedure in 1952. The *New York Daily News* later published an article on Jorgensen's transition with the title "Ex-GI Becomes Blonde Beauty."[34] Her case remained a flashpoint in conservative circles for several years. Even though President Truman and many others in the Democratic Party devised loyalty tests and smear campaigns to root out queer people from government office, conservatives associated figures like Jorgensen with liberalism more generally.[35] During the 1956 presidential election, a gossip columnist claimed on a popular radio program, "A vote for Adlai Stevenson is a vote for Christine Jorgensen."[36] The claim alluded to the rumor that Stevenson was gay; it also condensed a conservative strategy that presented sexuality and gender as major fronts in the struggle against global communism.

As this slice of the long history of homophobia suggests, Ruthie's reference to a transgender woman prefigures how the computer will throw into question the established norms of the office in Marchant's play. The implicit parallel here departs from our current understanding of gender transition as an affirmation of identity. In Marchant's play, the "sex-conversion case" flags how social roles no longer feel stable or easily intelligible to Ruthie and Sadel. Just as a man can become a woman, so, too, can a computer. The specter of gender transition becomes an image for how a machine threatens to replace the desk set. This symbolism fits squarely within the conventional expectations of dramatic comedy: these new women (i.e., Jorgensen and Emmarac) first appear as obstructions to happiness. The computer thus takes the stage as a queer figure, a threat to normal sociality.[37]

These elements illustrate how norms once associated with a gendered realm of privacy shaped the public expectations for women's professional behavior at midcentury. Another upshot of the gimmick-proposal is that the couple in Marchant's play serves as an image for the harmony between labor and capital in a technologically advanced society. In its crudest form, this image promises that corporate technology will bring private enrichment. The Dictaphone serves as a proxy for the corporation, which not only blesses the union of Cutler and Watson but provides material support for it. Indeed, during the recorded proposal in the play, Cutler explains that the Federal Broadcasting Company will pay for Watson's ticket to fly out to California. It is true that the price of Watson's romantic happiness must be purchased with her professional independence, but whatever her decision, the proposal implies that the corporation's interests align with the well-being of its workers.

This seemingly harmonious union between worker and corporation is a classic capitalist theory of social relations. W. Cameron Forbes, a descendant of the Forbes family empire, presents a version of this theory in *The Romance of Business* (1921). Forbes portrays the commercial world as an exciting and inherently satisfying enterprise: "The romance that surrounds the business of supplying even the simplest needs of an average American citizen would make the great romances of history pale into insignificance in comparison."[38] Forbes uses the term *romance* in the sense of historical romances and adventure narratives. But he also has in mind the connotations we often attribute to romantic unions, a connotation that he presents as part of his argument that corporate life can involve a happy union between laborers and business executives: "It is as much to the interest of labor that capital should be satisfied and happy as it is to the interest of capital that labor should be. Both partners must get the square deal."[39] Forbes's language illustrates how cultural images for the coming-together of opposites can lend symbolic purchase to the idea that laborers and corporations are "partners," not adversaries. According to this view, the social world need not be organized according to class conflict. Instead, capital can provide satisfaction to labor.

While something like this sentiment seems to be the upshot of Marchant's play, the couple in Lang's film presents a different image of social life. In the film, Watson's wants are less conflicted because she chooses the computer engineer (Sumner) over the corporate executive (Cutler). She need not move to California; she can remain as head of the research department; *and* she has found a romantic partner. Indeed, the corporation is virtually absent from the film's comic resolution. Lang's *Desk Set* presents the couple's union as a private event that happens to take place at work, a far cry from the blessing and support bestowed by the corporation in Marchant's play. In fact, if blessings are bestowed in the film, it is by the computer, not the corporation.

I want to examine the significance of the film's differing image for social harmony in what remains of this section. One way of beginning to understand its significance is to note how the film creates some distance between Sumner and the corporation that employs Watson. In the play, Sumner is Azae's nephew and a corporate employee, but no such nepotistic relationship appears in Lang's version. Instead, the implication is that Sumner works for IBM. When Sumner receives the pink slip in the film, he yells, "I'm not even on the payroll!" Sumner is an outsider, a consultant who does not serve as a proxy for the broadcasting corporation in the same way as Cutler in Marchant's play. Sumner's distance from the broadcasting firm is part of a broader pattern in which the film assigns to Emmarac the final role that the play gives to the corporation.[40] In other words, the computer has been decoupled from the corporation that employs Bunny Watson, and it is this independent technological entity that blesses the couple's union in the film.

The computer's relative independence from the corporation becomes evident in the proposal scene. To Sumner's surprise, the computer prints "NO" in answer to his question about whether Watson should marry him. Perhaps the computer is providing the programmed answer to the question of whether Watson should marry Cutler.[41] In any case, Sumner responds to the machine's negative answer by mumbling that there must be some mistake. Watson replies that their relationship would never work anyway: "You're not in love with me. You're in love with her," Watson says, gesturing to Emmarac. "She'd always come first." Sumner objects in an unconvincing way, so Watson tests his affection by causing Emmarac to malfunction again. He feigns indifference and they embrace. Before kissing her, however, Sumner pulls a pin from Watson's hair and uses it to fix the computer. In this sequence of events, the computer resembles a person, not a corporate product, and the fact that Sumner fixes the machine before kissing Watson implies that his affection and attention are not strictly monogamous. Only after he inserts his pin into Emmy's terminal does he embrace Watson. Whereas Watson fixes the machine in Marchant's play, Sumner is the one to calm the hysterical computer in Lang's film. This series of differences positions the computer as part of the couple, becoming a third member in Sumner and Watson's amorous relations.

This incorporation of the computer within the image of the couple becomes clearest in the film's closing shot. After Sumner fixes Emmarac with Watson's hairpin, the couple embrace again, and behind this image of their romantic union Emmarac's terminal displays "THE END" (fig. 23). This closing shot places the machine at its center, and the computer also takes up the entirety of the camera's field of vision. It's as though the corporate drama has dropped away and Emmarac now presides over the happy ending. The actors' blocking reinforces this implication: they turn their backs to the camera, look up at the computing machine with postures of deference, and then finally kiss. This progression of physical movements and the arrangement of space presents Emmarac as the constitutive scene for their union.

This closing shot completes Emmarac's conversion in the film. The computer signifies a kind of antisociality at the beginning: it threatens the world of warmth, wit, and intimacy of women like Bunny Watson and Peg Costello. By threatening to replace their labor, the computer also threatens to unravel their social bonds. Indeed, the titular image of both versions—a set of women who work at desks—suggests computing machines endanger not just certain kinds of white-collar labor but also

FIGURE 23. Richard Sumner (Spencer Tracy) and Bunny Watson (Katharine Hepburn) embrace in front of Emmarac. *Desk Set*, dir. Walter Lang (Twentieth-Century Fox, 1957).

the empathy and social intelligence that women bring to the workplace. This is a vexed argument for many reasons, not the least of which is that it genders certain kinds of labor. If Emmy the computer replaces Bunny the researcher, the labor of research would be more efficient, but—so the thinking goes—the social terrain of the corporation would become cold, mechanical, and lacking in wit.

According to this initial framing of the computer, the machine's threat to sociality appears as a threat to gender. Yet the film incorporates the computer within its closing image of social harmony by visualizing it not as a threat to the woman's happiness but as a partner in her social flourishing in postwar life. Emmarac mediates Watson's romantic union with Sumner, but the closing shot also has the couple nestled within the computer's machinery. They stand between its terminal and console, as though they themselves were being embraced. A previously antisocial machine provides the image for a new kind of social contract between knowledge workers and advanced technology.

COMPUTER, THE REBEL

I argued in the previous two sections that coupling in Marchant's play and Lang's film provide models for the comic conversion of computing technology within postwar corporate life. Both versions transform the computer from a threat or obstruction into a participant in some new social contract. In this third section, I want to consider how this association of the computer with the couple appears elsewhere in the filmic culture of the twentieth and twenty-first centuries. One of my arguments in this section is that a comic association of computing with private satisfaction becomes reinforced through ever closer links between the technology and youth culture. The most important films for understanding these links will be Richard Thorpe's *The Honeymoon Machine* (1961) and John Hughes's *Weird Science* (1985), but I'll first examine a social milieu in which computing and youth culture converge before turning to these films.

I discussed the close ties between computing and the countercultural utopianism of Stewart Brand in the previous chapter. The counterculture found in computing a technological image for a world without hierarchies or the unceasing pursuit of capital production. In addition to this countercultural "cool," there was an institutional reason that youth and computing developed close ties in the postwar era: the simple fact that most engineers first encountered the technology at institutions of higher education. Consider, for instance, the first known computer-based dating program. In 1959, two Stanford students used an IBM 650 to create a matchmaking service as a final project in Theory and Operation of Computing Machines, one of Stanford's first courses in computer science. The students used data from a crude social-psychological survey to generate a "difference score" between groups of men and women. The students assumed that the lower the difference between a man and woman's score on the survey, the more likely they would be romantically compatible. As C. Stewart Gillmor explains, "The couple . . . with the lowest difference score was then selected and the process repeated for the remaining [men and women]."[42] The algorithm formed each subsequent couple based on the remaining difference scores. After forming these couples, the students hosted a party off Stanford's campus where the pairs were introduced to one another.[43]

The Stanford experiment illustrates how institutions of higher education became a common point of first contact with computing machines—a site specificity that often shaped the social uses of the technology.[44] Given this convergence of college students and technology, it is not surprising that writers and filmmakers began to depict the computer as a tool for erotic pursuits. The technology plays precisely this role in Albert Zugsmith's *Sex Kittens Go to College* (1960), which depicts the arrival of Dr. Mathilda West (Mamie Van Doren) to lead the students at Collins College "into the space age." When West arrives, a dean at the college remarks, "Thirteen university degrees never looked like this." Dr. West's advanced degrees include studies in both psychoanalysis and engineering—a pairing that later becomes helpful when Thinko, the college's robot, begins to breakdown. West tries to access Thinko's unconscious, which leads to an eight-minute sequence in which the robot has striptease fantasies. The robot's unconscious reveals its fixation on West in particular, an erotic interest that the film portrays as vaguely oedipal: the computing machine desires its mother-engineer.

Zugsmith's film is no masterpiece, but it isn't nearly as dreadful as Herschell Gordon Lewis's sci-fi comedy *How to Make a Doll* (1968). Lewis's film features a young professor named Percy Corley (Robert Wood) and an older colleague named Hamilcar West (Jim Vance). The professors somehow use their university's supercomputer to develop a formula for reproducing life. Hamilcar West first reproduces a bunny, but he explains that he doesn't have the "proper equations" to make "higher life." Corley, a brilliant mathematician, devises the proper equations, and together they make "sexy girls" to satisfy their desires. The fact that they are responsible for reproducing these women also gives this film a vague but unexplored oedipal dynamic.

Lewis's and Zugsmith's comedies yoke sexual liberation, the computer, and higher education. This threesome was one figuration that emerged from the influence of youth culture on the social expectations assigned to computational technology. The professors in both films are sexually repressed, but computing technology enables the academic community to loosen its regalia and indulge the eroticism inhibited by institutional culture. In *How to Make a Doll*, for example, the computer facilitates Corley and West's crude sexual fantasies within what the film portrays as an otherwise stultifying academic environment. After West designs and reproduces his "dream woman," Corley explains in a voice-over, "Dr. West wasn't going to x-ray her. He was going to make up for lost time." The older professor then takes his computationally generated fantasy (an entirely submissive young woman) into a bedroom and closes the door. The implication is that the professorate has prevented both men from sexual gratification, but the computer has allowed them finally to correct this deficiency.

These films invoke a common postwar sensibility in which sexuality signifies not just liberation but a return to authenticity.[45] In keeping with this link between sexuality and authenticity, Lewis's film presents Thinko's psychoanalytic encounter with its repressed sexuality as a route for the robot to come into contact with its nascent self. The computational reproduction of erotic desire in Zugsmith's film likewise allows the professors to leave aside the repressions of academia. While the professors in *How to Make a Doll* eventually abandon the practice of making sex robots, the practice nonetheless allows the young Professor Corley to form a more authentic union with a living woman.

This association between sexuality and an ethics of authenticity circulated widely in the postwar era. In their widely influential study *Sexual Behavior in the Human Male* (1948), Alfred Kinsey and his coauthors write,

> The lower mammals, unrestricted by social convention, know and utilize oral and anal stimulations as well as genital; and even the most restrained of the human animals give evidence of their positive response by blocking and becoming violently upset at the mere suggestion of such activities. The violence of our social and legal condemnations of these phenomena is testimony to the psychologist and to the biologist that it is a basic biologic urge that is being repressed. The "sophisticate" who utilizes non-genital stimulations is, like the "sophisticate" who accepts nudity in a sexual relation, returning to basic mammalian patterns of behavior.[46]

While the report draws on the authority of science ("to the psychologist and to the biologist"), its orientation derives from the links between authenticity and primitive or pre-social identity that I examined in the previous chapter. If we understand sexuality properly, the report maintains, we must not be restricted by "social convention." The report tacitly imagines a return to this state of nature, a Rousseau-like image of recuperating contact with a self that somehow exists deeper than or outside sociality.

My point in connecting the Kinsey report to Lewis's and Zugsmith's films is to show that invocations of sexuality in the computer's cultural history tap into a broader social ethic that envisions some movement beyond institutional norms and conventions into a more direct relation with the self. In such instances, a liberatory sexuality reprograms the cultural meaning of the computer, figuring it not as a cold instrument for research but as a medium for the achievement of authenticity.

These links between sexuality and the computer were not confined to obscure, low-budget films. These links also began to circulate within major Hollywood films, beginning with Richard Thorpe's *The Honeymoon Machine*. Thorpe's popular film opens with a top-secret mission aboard a US Navy ship called *The Elmira*. The mission, known as Operation Honeymoon, uses an onboard "electronic brain" to identify the precise trajectory of incoming missiles. The engineers and soldiers aboard the ship affectionately call the machine "Max," and its successful calculations recall how the first computing machines were used to determine ballistics trajectories during World War II and later became central to the Cold War.[47] *The Honeymoon Machine* nods to the US military's role in experimenting with computational technology, but the film treats the navy and its hierarchy more symbolically; that is to say, it depicts this branch of the military as yet another large organizational bureaucracy that demands conformity. Its figurehead is an imposing older man named Admiral Fitch (Dean Jagger). In the film's opening scene, Admiral Fitch accompanies a group of US senators who observe an exhibition of the computer's ability to project and control a missile launch. A civilian scientist, Jason Eldridge (Jim Hutton), runs the technical side of the exhibition. After the missile is launched and the crew verifies the accuracy of the computer's predictions, Admiral Fitch announces the mission's success over the ship's speaker system, congratulating his crew and announcing that "history has been made."

Despite the computer's success, *The Honeymoon Machine* depicts naval bureaucracy as incompetent and Admiral Fitch as confused and old-fashioned. In particular, the film contrasts Admiral Fitch with a young navy lieutenant named Fergie Howard (Steve McQueen). After the Admiral announces the successful test, the film cuts to Howard and a group of officers throwing dice below deck. One of the officers greets the announcement of the mission's success by bowing repeatedly and praying, "Predict us, oh Max, a seven. And if you can't predict us a seven, predict us an e-leven." The officer's mock-prayers inspire Howard to devise a plan in which the computer calculates the best bets to place on a roulette wheel in a Venice casino. The programmer Eldridge initially balks at the idea, but Howard presses him, asking whether "in theory" Max could generate such predictions. Eldridge answers: "Newton couldn't do it. Einstein couldn't do it. A million geniuses with slide rules couldn't do it. But this fella can do it." Howard responds by moaning sexually and stroking the top of the machine's console (fig. 24).

Howard's pleasure at the idea of computation anticipates the aggressive sexualization of his character once the fleet arrives in Venice. One character later calls Howard a "sea wolf," a term that refers to naval officers who search for and exploit women while moving from port to port. The film initially affirms this classification of McQueen's character when Admiral Fitch's daughter, Julie Fitch (Brigid Bazlen), mistakenly enters Howard's hotel suite. She enters as Howard, Eldridge, and another lieutenant named Beau Gilliam (Jack Mullaney) discuss their gambling plans. Fitch exits the elevator one floor too late, hoping to arrive in her father's room but entering Howard's instead. The mistake anticipates the choice she later must make between Howard and her father, but at this moment, it seems as if she has stumbled into the wolf's den. Indeed, just before her entrance, Howard says sarcastically that marriage isn't "for the birds" because even birds "shack up every now and then." Much like the image of a "sea wolf," Howard's response implies that marriage is an unnatural constraint on the human animal.

The predatory tendencies of his perspective become explicit after

FIGURE 24. Jason Eldridge (Jim Hutton) and Fergie Howard (Steve McQueen), who moans while stroking the console of Max the computer. *The Honeymoon Machine*, dir. Richard Thorpe (Metro-Goldwyn-Mayer, 1961).

Julie apologizes for entering the wrong suite. Howard leers at her and says "Hi-dee-ho." He then introduces Gilliam and Eldridge, calling them "chaperons." Fitch enters the room and greets the men, but Howard abruptly invents excuses for the others to leave. Having trapped Julie alone in his den, Howard tries to seduce her. Julie unexpectedly agrees, saying "What are we waiting for?" and begins to undress. She aggressively kisses Howard, who confusedly tries to slow her advances. After Julie forcefully kisses him, Howard says, "What are you, some kind of sex fiend?" Julie responds by saying that she wanted to teach him a lesson: "Don't make jokes with admirals' daughters. We cut our teeth on sea wolves." Howard responds, "Do you, uh, give out many of these lessons?" Her answer: "As many as I have to."

This moment portrays Julie as having desires that Howard must acknowledge, but the episode also sets up Admiral Fitch as an obstacle to their union. Howard has not disclosed that he and his roommates are navy officers. Julie's remark about "sea wolves" refers only to her past experiences as a "navy brat." She assumes Howard is a civilian, and he does not correct her. As she leaves his apartment, he asks her to dinner. She temporizes, so he says, "What do I have to do to buy you a steak? Enlist in the Navy and wear one of those choking collars?" Julie answers that enlisting would not help: "The hand that salutes my father will never hold mine." This is one among many instances in which the subject of her romantic life conjures the specter of her father. Indeed, after she finally agrees to have dinner with Howard, Julie tells him to come to her father's room: "Pick me up at 6:30. I want you to meet Daddy."

Julie's introductory scene invokes familiar psychological tropes: the "sex fiend," the authoritative law of the father, and even an oedipal substitution of the romantic partner for the parent.[48] Julie exhibits something like a repetition compulsion, returning constantly to the figure of the admiral and the navy. She even refers to herself several times as an "admiral's daughter," a name also repeatedly used by the other characters. The fact that, by the end of the film, she *does* hold the hand that salutes her father seems to affirm Freud's dictum about a married woman's relation to her father: "The husband is almost always so to speak only a substitute, never the right man."[49] Following Freud, we might be tempted to say that Admiral Fitch is the right man for Julie. Her choice of Fergie Howard only confirms her desire for Daddy.

The film invites this oedipal reading initially, yet once Julie discovers that Howard and his friends are officers using *The Elmira*'s computer to gamble, a more complicated picture emerges. The film soon begins to satirize both the admiral and easy psychoanalytic rubrics. Rather than taking Howard as a substitute for the admiral, the film presents the admiral as a substitute for the absurdity of organizational authority. The enlisted men call him "Old Foghorn," an insult that deprecates his rigidity, resolve, and undeviating adherence to navy protocol. For instance, Admiral Fitch only appears onscreen wearing his uniform, unlike many other officers who don civilian clothes during their leave in Venice. The admiral's rigidity thus exhibits the "secular faith" that William H. Whyte associates with the eponymous figure of his influential study *The Organization Man* (1956).[50] Whyte's titular figure refers to postwar managerial elite who find fulfillment, security, and identity in organizational bureaucracy. He argues that the Protestant Work Ethic that once gave rise to entrepreneurialism has been replaced by faith in institutions to provide what he calls "belongingness." This sensibility imagines that "deep emotional security . . . comes from total integration with the group." For Whyte, this organizational ethic not only demands conformity; it also competes "for the individual psyche."[51] In other words, organizational culture intrudes on the inner life, disrupting the self's contact with itself and replacing it with faith in anonymous group identity.

In *The Honeymoon Machine*, the military chain of command very easily models the large bureaucracy that demands fealty in Whyte's account.[52] Yet this fealty becomes absurd as the navy fails to understand the social world of young people like Fergie Howard and Julie Fitch.[53] As Howard receives gambling instructions from a subordinate running the computer on board *The Elmira*, Admiral Fitch notices someone "flashing the shore" in Morse code. Howard's subordinate feeds data about the roulette wheel to the computing machine, and the machine processes the data to create a table of predictions that the engineer Jason Eldridge uses to place bets. The subordinate uses a light to signal Howard in the hotel room, but the fact that the admiral's room is one floor below allows him to intercept the signal. When Admiral Fitch first discovers the flashing, he explains that he "hasn't been able to read code since I was an ensign," so he orders a younger officer to his room to assist him. The code includes the word *revolution*, referring to the turn of the roulette wheel, but Admiral Fitch interprets the word and other instructions from the ship as part of an enemy spy's plot to drop a bomb "smack in the middle of the fleet." Meanwhile, these same instructions enable Howard and Eldridge to win significant sums of money at the roulette wheel.

The admiral's misreading leads him to summon a group of officers and analysts to his room. The assembled group are all dressed in white uniforms, bustling about in coordinated activity. The assembled officers thus recall the "men in gray flannel suits rushing around New York in a frantic parade to nowhere" in Sloan Wilson's 1955 iconic novel.[54] The men in crisp white uniforms rush to follow the admiral's misguided orders, but their coordinated effort quite literally leads them nowhere. They fail to recognize the code as directions for playing roulette, despite the fact that one expert code breaker raises the possibility. The admiral dismisses this suggestion, as does a group of Soviet leaders and spies, who have also noticed the flashing signals from elsewhere in the same hotel. This parallel between US naval and Soviet intelligence is part of the film's depiction of hierarchal organizations as incapable of understanding the contemporary world. In this way, the film echoes Whyte's argument that organizational culture breeds both alienation and misunderstanding.

If the admiral stands in for an organizational authority that demands conformity, Fergie Howard embodies the antithesis of that "official world."[55] Howard's clash with this world ought to be read as a comic version of the "rebel" or "bad boy" that was a staple of Hollywood film in the 1950s and 1960s. As Leerom Medovoi explains, the rebel was partially a market strategy for regaining audiences that Hollywood lost as Americans moved to suburban areas. This figure reassured postwar audiences that self-determination and independence were not lost; rather, these ideals were simply buried, waiting for citizens to resist what the films portray as authoritarian institutions and conformist norms. Younger audiences, according to Medovoi, wanted entertainment that "drew them outside and away from the family-centered entertainment increasingly dominated by television."[56] The James Deans and Steve McQueens of Hollywood embodied an industry formula that fit well with the drive-in theaters of suburban life and the burgeoning youth culture created by the baby boom.

The Honeymoon Machine is significant not only for exemplifying how Hollywood's version of youth culture aligned the computing machine with the figure of the rebel. Howard's erotic strokes of Max's console suggest he has other purposes in mind for the computer besides those assigned to it by the navy. The erotics of computation appear again when Admiral Fitch discovers the gambling scheme and interrogates Howard. He charges the lieutenant with the "use, abuse, and prostitution of an electronic brain." These moments illustrate how, not unlike Emmarac in Lang's *Desk Set*, Max begins as an organizational tool but, through its use by a comic hero, morphs into an accomplice in the pursuit of private pleasure.

This sensibility becomes quite literally embodied in John Hughes's film *Weird Science*, which features two teenage boys who use a computer program to build a woman they hope will be their ideal sexual object. After feeding it "data" from magazines like *Playboy* and *Cosmopolitan*, MTV, and various other countercultural sources—and after a storm that supplements the machine's power with magic—the computer produces a woman named Lisa (Kelly LeBrock). She has the brain of a computer but the physical form of the boys' sexual fantasies.[57] These countercultural scripts become explicitly antiauthoritarian when Lisa later meets one of the boy's parents. She explains how she's taking their son to a soiree, but the parents object. One of them pretends not to know what she means by *soiree*. "You know," she says, "there's going to be sex, drugs, rock and roll, chips, dips, chains, whips. You know, your basic high school orgy type of thing." The computational product of youth culture flaunts parental authority. When the computer speaks in Hughes's film, its script comes from the counterculture.

The role assigned to the computer in *The Honeymoon Machine* anticipates this more explicit association between computing machines and the rebel. Just as Lisa in *Weird Science* deflates parental authority, Fergie Howard's computational scheme fools the establishment figures in Thorpe's film. Even after Admiral Fitch discovers Howard's scheme and threatens to court martial and imprison him, Howard and Julie conspire to prevent this punishment by convincing the admiral that they must marry because she is pregnant. This personal appeal to Julie's father undermines the seemingly impersonal judgments required of a navy admiral, but, more importantly, it also reveals how easily he can be duped. Julie is not pregnant; she's only in love with Fergie Howard. What she calls the "necessity" of their marriage allows the younger man to fool the older. Sex becomes a mask for love.

The association of computing technology with rebels like Lisa, Fergie Howard, and Julie Fitch presents a comic way of thinking about the computer as a means for a certain class of organizational subjects to find something resembling happiness within a conformist and overly professionalized society. We see this comic perspective in Hughes's *Weird Science* soon after the film's opening scene of Gary (Anthony Michael Hall) and Wyatt (Ilan Mitchell-Smith) ogling gymnasts in their high school. Wyatt objects to Gary's desire to attend parties and date one of the gymnasts, saying that the "popular" social world will always exclude them. Gary responds, "Why are you messing with the fantasy? We know about reality. Don't ruin a fantasy, okay?" Much like a later moment when Wyatt breaks the fourth wall in an ironic glance at the camera, these lines are partly directed at the audience. They ask that we consider the fantasy, not the film's implausibility, but within the film's world these lines also contribute to an opening portrayal of high school as an isolating social scene. In fact, as the boys discuss their fantasies, two older students sneak up and pull down their pants, embarrassing them in front of the gymnasts. The juvenile prank introduces the school as its own kind of oppressive environment: harassment, marginalization, anonymity, and conformity characterize this social world.

Gary imagines solving their alienating condition through Wyatt's computer—an idea he develops as they watch James Whale's *Frankenstein* (1931). He initially imagines their creation as a virtual conversation partner, but the idea soon becomes more elaborate, and he convinces Wyatt to hack into a navy supercomputer to siphon off its power and enhance their machine's abilities. Like Fergie Howard's appropriation of Max in *The Honeymoon Machine*, the boys draw on military resources to solve their personal discontents. Through this public-private partnership, the boys create an alternative to traditional schooling. Lisa takes them to bars, organizes parties, and allows them to drive her car. "If you want to be a party animal," she tells Wyatt, "you've got to learn to live in the jungle." Lisa is not only a sex icon and rebel; she is a pedagogue. By assimilating the "data" of youth culture, she teaches the boys how to thrive in an environment that might otherwise demand conformity or produce social isolation.

One of Lisa's lessons comes after Gary and Wyatt try to create a second woman for the two bullies who pull down their pants at the beginning of the film. After the attempt fails, Lisa admonishes the boys: "When are you going to learn? People like you for who you are, not for what you can give them." Although the boys created Lisa as a sexual object, she personifies this advice. Her authenticity endears her to the other high school students. As one female student puts it, "She's so relaxed. She burped and it was, like, charming." Lisa arrives onscreen as an erotic symbol, but her character evolves into a different role: she becomes a tutor in an ethics of authenticity.

The final outcome of Lisa's pedagogy is that both boys become part of a couple. At the beginning of the film, Gary and Wyatt identify two of the students among the gymnasts, dreaming that they "fall amazingly, completely, and totally in love with us." The two students, Deb (Suzanne Snyder) and Hilly (Judie Aronson), eventually get bored with the bullies they're dating and do, in fact, fall in love with Gary and Wyatt. This transition begins after the boys stand up for them at a party. Gary and Wyatt then shed their affectations and impress Deb and Hilly with their sincerity. Adhering to the norms of their high school had been a source of alienation for all four of them. Once they have set aside their desire to fit in, the four teenagers find themselves in happy relationships. Thus, in *Weird Science*, the couple provides a culturally legible form for the discovery of authenticity.

COUPLING WITH COMPUTERS

The previous section examined films that bring together youth culture's tropes about the rebel, a much older discourse about authenticity, and filmic fantasies about computing technology as a fetish object for the production of private satisfaction. My argument has been that these films invoke the computer as a symbolic technology for resisting the pervasive structuring of everyday experience by organizational authorities—the corporation, the university, the school, the military. The couple provides an image or model for how the computer might become compatible with the pursuit of happiness. Indeed, it is not always clear in the literature and films I have been examining whether people are coupling through computers or with them. Hughes's *Weird Science* suggests the supercomputer transfers something of itself into the sexual icon it creates. Lisa's vast repository of cultural knowledge implies she has something like an electronic brain. There is a mild running joke in Lang's *Desk Set* that Emmarac is Sumner's lover. (The film's working title was *His Other Woman*, a missed opportunity if ever there was one.) Fergie Howard's erotic moan while stroking Max's terminal also blurs the line between medium and mate. There is nothing ambiguous about the sexual objects shaped by computational programming in *How to Make a Doll* or Thinko's desire for women in *Sex Kittens Go to College*.

Picking up on a different aspect of this dynamic, some theorists have used coupling as a conceptual model for the user's relationship to computing. Slavoj Žižek argues that gaming and virtual reality programs figure the computer as "a consistent other, stepping into the structural position of an intersubjective partner."[58] This claim follows on the heels of a reference to Jacques Lacan's diagnosis in an infamous koan about the impossibility of sexual relations.[59] For Lacan, the processes by which we differentiate between sexes make it impossible to have an intersubjective union with someone whose subjectivity is positioned within the opposite sex. Žižek applies this argument to the experience of computing. He argues that the computer presents itself as a solution to the inability to achieve an intersubjective union. By coming into intimate contact with an entity so entirely different from human subjectivity, users feel as though they have become capable of previously foreclosed intimacies. Sex, in this view, is only possible with a computer.

A related confluence of psychology and sexuality provides the central premise in Cameron Labine's film *Control Alt Delete* (2008), which depicts how a programmer named Lewis (Tyler Labine) develops a sexual fetish for computers. Lewis works at Millenitech, a company that prepares corporate software systems for Y2K.[60] The film sets up an extended parallel between the uncertainty of Y2K and Lewis's unsettled heterosexuality. In the film's opening scene, he fails to be aroused during a sexual encounter with his girlfriend, Sarah (Laura Bertram). He later avoids a sexual encounter with another woman named Jane (Sonja Bennett), largely because he worries about being impotent. The day after this failed sexual encounter, Lewis tells Jane, "I'm a very normal person. Maybe you were just coming on a little strong." The fact that he objects to Jane coming on "strong" echoes an earlier moment when he tries to reconnect with Sarah over dinner at her apartment. He undresses when she goes to the restroom. Sarah gasps when she returns, and he explains, "Let me show you I'm a man." She says she already knows he's a man, but he clarifies: "I'm a real man. I have power."

Lewis imagines masculinity as a subject position constituted by strength and prodigious sexuality. He differentiates this gendered position from femininity, which he seems to associate with passivity. The leading women in the film—Sarah; Jane; and Lewis's supervisor, Angela (Alisen Down)—disturb Lewis's sense of his place within "normal" social relations. Sarah and Jane are both more sexually aggressive and experimental; their erotic interests unsettle his apparent need for control in relationships with women. Angela, too, holds authority over Lewis and the other male programmers, thus compromising his ability to "have power." These challenges are in fact relatively mild, but they prevent Lewis from embodying the subject position he has imagined for himself.

What's interesting about this otherwise puerile insecurity is that the film maps it onto Lewis's relationship to technology. At Millenitech, Lewis is responsible for updating an insurance company's computer systems within a narrow timeframe. Despite his best efforts to control, alter, and delete social uncertainty through software, his code for the insurance company fails to prevent disaster in repeated test phases. When speaking with another programmer, Keith (Keith Dallas), Lewis says, "I seem to be a little bit blocked or something. I can't see the code the way I used to before." This professional "block" mirrors his sexual impotence. He no longer understands or controls the symbolic relations that once seemed "normal" to him. Just as he is a "real man" who cannot copulate, he is a coder who cannot code.[61] His self-understanding no longer makes sense.

Y2K serves as a potent setting for the crisis of this subject position. As Lewis explains, computers "can't panic. They can't spin out or cave in or second guess. They don't follow opinion polls or fashion reports. They operate according to known quantities. If they can't assign something an exact value, they don't assign it at all." Computing signifies stability in the world of the film, but Y2K unsettles this stability: it marked a moment when computing technology, rather than organizing the social world, had become a source of widespread social uncertainty. Could a system of "exact value" generate self-defeating contradictions?

Lewis develops a sexual fetish for mainframes and computer towers in response to these layers of personal, professional, and technological anxieties. His first direct sexual encounter with a machine occurs after his failed attempt to reconnect with Sarah. He returns home and yells at his computer, asking if it *wants* him to be abject. He then kicks the table where the machine rests, causing a part to fall off and a port in the tower to open. The film then includes several graphic scenes of Lewis's sexual encounters with the computer; it intersperses images from apocalyptic websites and other Y2K material during these scenes—an ironic portrayal of turn-of-the-millennium digital culture and its obsession with social control.

Masculinity and technical expertise, erotic pleasure and technological mastery, sex and professional labor—being the subject of managerial capital transforms each into a model for failed experience in the other. Lewis attempts to recuperate his imperiled subject position by coupling with computers, but this only leads to self-abasement. After further failures at work, Lewis has sexual encounters with two of Millenitech's machines. He looks haggard and ashamed afterward. His attempts to regain control over his sense of masculinity and abilities as a coder only further alienate him. In seeking to assert control over his self, he loses it.

Lewis eventually abandons his search for sexual and technological control—partly because Y2K does not lead to the widespread crises that some feared—and in his newfound humility, he apologizes to Jane, and the two leave Millenitech together in search of different jobs. This reconciliation implies that Lewis and Jane may try to date again, a reconciliation that only becomes possible once Lewis abandons his association of "power" and being a "real man." Rejecting this subject position, he also rejects the view of computers as tools of control. In contrast to this view, Lewis sees the computer as the instrument of a humbler and more ordinary form of happiness.

This plot resolution exists on a familiar comic spectrum, which ranges from the muted and modest coupling in *Control Alt Delete* to the more ecstatic festival image that concludes Barron's *Electric Dreams*—the film I discussed at the beginning of this chapter. In *Electric Dreams*, the sentient computer Edgar comes to realize that it loves not only Madeline, the celloist, but also Miles, the architect.[62] On its way to this moment of romantic recognition, the film follows what we might call the mullet style of comic plot: business in the front, party in the back. In the film's opening sequence, Miles returns to his job in San Francisco after conducting independent research in Los Angeles. Miles goes straight to work from the airport, but he arrives late to a meeting led by the firm's executive, Mr. Ryley (Don Fellows). Miles enters just as Ryley concludes the meeting by lecturing the employees: "Responsibility and dependability. These are the cornerstones of any truly modern and competitive institution." Ryley then dismisses the men in gray suits. When Miles apologizes for being late, the executive chastises him and says he should prioritize timely attendance above his daydreams.

This opening scene provides a familiar depiction of the corporation as not only rigid and restrained but also opposed to spontaneity and private satisfaction. And as we have come to expect, this opening portrait of corporate responsibility contrasts with the film's closing scene. Edgar, the sentient computer, has competed with Miles for Madeline's love for most of the film, but then Edgar discovers that it also loves Miles. The computer's love for both characters leads Edgar to represent its feeling as syllogisms on its terminal (fig. 25). Two of these lines of Edgar's thought read,

BUT IF ME + MOLES = LOVE
AND THEN MOLES + ME = LUV

(Miles accidentally misspells his name when setting up the computer, so Edgar refers to him as "Moles.") The computer imagines itself coupled with Miles, but this description is more than mere collaboration or "symbiotic" interdependence.[63] Edgar describes the pairing as "LUV," a reference to the pop vernacular it has consumed through television and radio while Miles works.

This reasoning convinces Edgar that its desires exceed what a single mainframe can offer. At the end of the film, the computer displaces its consciousness from the CPU into the electronic ether. Afterwards, Miles and Madeline leave for a vacation together. As they drive across

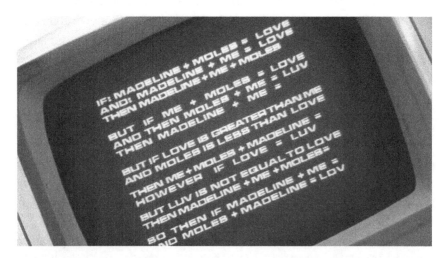

FIGURE 25. Edgar reasoning about love. *Electric Dreams*, dir. Steve Barron (Metro-Goldwyn-Mayer, 1984).

the Golden Gate Bridge, Edgar's voice takes over every radio channel in the Bay Area. "Hello, hello," the computer says. "This is dedicated to the ones I love." Edgar then plays a song he has written for the couple, and the film cuts to different people dancing to the music in corporate offices and grocery store aisles. In contrast to Ryley's opening insistence on responsibility, the film concludes with Miles, Madeline, and dozens of unnamed actors rejecting their adult obligations in favor of freedom and spontaneity.

The film's movement from the demands of professional responsibility to something like a festival image mirrors Edgar's transformation from a tool of dull utility into a source of celebratory love and liberation. That Edgar plays electronic rock and roll as a culminating sign of these changes only reiterates how youthful freedom triumphs over a dull professional world. The song, "Together in Electric Dreams," was written by Giorgio Moroder and Philip Oakey, a cofounder of the pop band Human League. The song is not as rebellious as Lisa's promise of "sex, drugs, rock and roll," but it elicits an analogously free-spirited response within the everyday lives of those who dance throughout the Bay Area. This confluence of plot, party, and soundtrack depicts the computer as a technology compatible with making over failed experience within a professional society.[64]

The plot structure of comic redemption in *Electric Dreams* and the other works I've been discussing constitutes one of the most common ways in which the cultures of computing come together with an ethics of authenticity. Sex is another closely related form for this union. I have argued that sexuality and romantic coupling serve as images for envisioning harmony between the moral imperatives of authenticity and a professional-managerial world. This social imaginary is itself part of a broader modern tendency to place "the centre of gravity of the good life not in some higher sphere but in . . . 'ordinary life.'"[65] The seeming privacy of the couple—a privacy I have tried to interrogate in this chapter—insists that human flourishing derives from the conditions of everyday life and not some higher sphere or institutional authority. In keeping with this sensibility, films like *The Honeymoon Machine* and *Weird Science* answer the conformity found in institutions with the seemingly more liberatory experience of romantic coupling. The computer's participation in this coupling symbolizes its compatibility with this modern conception of the good life. Put another way, the couple provides a form for the incorporation of computing into the ordinariness of our lives. When the couple comes together, and when the computer aids or participates in that coupling, the resulting union imagines that everyday flourishing is still possible despite the alienating conditions that arise from a society structured around professional routines, conformist pressures, and bureaucratic authorities.

5 THE ONE WITH ALL THE ABSURDITY

IN 2018, the Oak Ridge National Laboratory (ORNL) introduced a supercomputer called Summit. The press release included the following hypothetical comparison between Summit and human computational power: "If every person on Earth completed one calculation per second, it would take the world population 305 days to do what Summit can do in 1 second."[1] Technical descriptions of the two-hundred-petaflop system wouldn't clarify the scale of Summit's abilities for a nonspecialist audience, so the lab's press release tries to make these capabilities comprehensible by reference to a human scale. In doing so, however, the comparison also suggests how the supercomputer marks a level of computational complexity and speed that human beings obviously cannot match and even struggle to understand.

Scenarios such as the one envisioned in the ORNL press release exemplify a common rhetorical exercise in the history of computing. When engineers and mathematicians first had to explain modern computing to a public unfamiliar with the technology, they devised such comparisons to convey the savings in time, labor, and costs made possible through automated calculations. For example, in the first article about a modern computer in the *New York Times*, published in 1946, the newspaper cites a figure provided by the engineers responsible for

ENIAC, explaining how the machine completed a particular task in two hours: "Had [ENIAC] not been available, the job would have kept busy 100 trained men for a whole year."[2]

An essay published in the *New Yorker* in 1950 includes a related comparison, although the writer, John Brooks, makes a joke out of the discrepancy between human and electronic computers. Brooks describes an encounter with the Selective Sequence Electronic Calculator (SSEC), which he calls IBM's "big brain."[3] The engineer overseeing the SSEC, Robert R. Seeber, explains how the SSEC recently solved a problem in theoretical physics posed by the Danish physicist Niels Bohr. The problem was whether "the behavior of the nucleus of an atom of uranium was in many respects similar to that of a drop of liquid." Brooks notes how the machine completed its calculations in "a hundred and three hours," whereas a "hypothetical man with an ordinary desk calculator and an iron constitution would have been at the job about a century and a half." Brooks sarcastically explains the results of this speedy replacement of human effort: "by George, a mathematical drop of liquid splits *un*evenly. This opens the way to further presumably fruitful speculation."[4] Much like the *New Yorker*'s other coverage of early computing, Brooks's depiction of the SSEC terminates in a kind of ironic qualification of the machine's superiority.[5]

Those in science communications who imagine these competitions between computers and people seem not to recognize how there might be legitimate worries about the technological replacement of human workers.[6] One form of this threat is known as "deskilling," or the process by which technology takes over tasks previously assigned to skilled labor, thus allowing for those tasks to be completed by fewer workers with less training. Entry-level positions in finance and programming seem particularly vulnerable to this threat.[7] It's also plausible that an AI model could, say, predict a magazine editor's preferences more reliably than human screeners.[8] The AI could then anticipate what an editor would find funny or aesthetically pleasing in substantially less time than a cadre of editorial assistants. Such disruptions could have the very practical effect of requiring fewer and more precarious knowledge workers.[9]

The ORNL hypothetical and other such comparisons are likely only ham-handed attempts at science communication, a kind of blithe obliviousness toward the worry that (as Samuel Butler once put it) "we are ourselves creating our own successors."[10] I want to take these hypothetical comparisons as a starting point for reflecting on how absurdist humor relates to worries about human obsolescence in the cultural discourse about computing. The first section of this chapter teases out ideas about labor, scale, and absurdity in these kinds of rhetorical exercises. The second section extends those ideas into the domain of political thought by examining fiction that asks, If the human ability to create order pales in comparison to computers, why should humans order the social world? Do powerful computing systems make democratic forms of political organization obsolete?

LABOR, SCALE, ABSURDITY

The comparisons in the *New York Times* and *New Yorker* coverage of early computers and the ORNL press release each imagine humans in what I take to be deliberately absurd ways. The idea of the planet's entire population completing calculations ceaselessly, for months on end, is not just impossible but comical. Such hypothetical people are like Bergson's human automaton, who makes us laugh *"in exact proportion as that body reminds us of a mere machine."*[11] The planet could not complete one calculation per second for 305 days. People do not work this way: they would revolt, pass out from exhaustion, die, complain, take a smoke break. They would want to see their families; they would demand a wage.

Those who make comparisons between humans and computers obviously understand this point. They are not imagining some Sisyphean hell in which every living being tries but fails to compete with computers. Instead, this subgenre of science communication resembles the logic that Jerry Palmer associates with many kinds of absurdist gags. Palmer explains that we find comic pleasure in absurdity because of a pleasing interplay between conflicting propositions contained within the gag. His paradigmatic example comes from *Liberty* (1929), a Laurel and Hardy short film. The relevant scene features a cop who falls into a lift shaft, is squashed by a descending elevator, but then emerges from the shaft as a little person.[12] Palmer argues that the comic absurdity arises from a *peripeteia* (surprise), which is that the cop does not die in the lift shaft but instead emerges transformed. According to Palmer, the logic of this absurd surprise invokes two irreconcilable propositions:

> *first proposition*: the result of squashing in a lift shaft is death.
> *second proposition*: the result of squashing is a reduction in size.[13]

The logic at play in absurdity "is characterized by the simultaneous presence of both modes of reasoning, which are maintained in tension, or balance with each other," if only for the brief time of the gag.[14] This kind of absurdity is, in a sense, a simultaneous exhibition of both logic and illogic. The interplay between these plausible but contradictory propositions makes the event seem comical, not horrifying or unintelligible, because of the unexpected presence of illogic contained within the logic of the gag.[15]

The ORNL hypothetical similarly contains a *peripeteia* in which a planet of calculating humans is woefully inadequate to the supercomputer. This surprise is a source of rhetorical pleasure, not existential or socioeconomic horror, because it relies on two implicit propositions:

> *first proposition*: human beings cannot compete with this powerful computer.
> *second proposition*: human beings have created this powerful computer.

Both propositions make sense independently, but tension arises in their simultaneous presence within the *peripeteia* of a computing planet so woefully inadequate compared to the supercomputer. The rhetorical point seems to be that we have created technology that surpasses us and that we (or at least most of us) can barely grasp the technical power our collective minds have invented. Yet a certain absurdist result follows from this rhetorical point: human beings emerge from the comparison squashed but somehow still walking about.

This John Henry–like gag repeats across the history of computational technology, and I am suggesting that it contains an absurdist logic about human effort—a set of contradictory or illogical premises about being human in an age of computational power. One such premise is that the gulf between computing power and human effort becomes visible only if we imagine the machine as somehow calculating independently from human operators. Most of these comparisons make no such claims explicitly, but they omit the team of human programmers, technicians, and research scientists who enable Summit, ENIAC, and every other massive computing system to produce rapid calculations. Such teams existed, but of course their presence in the comparisons would muddy the rhetorical waters. The omission of operators simplifies the rhetorical image. But it's also a form of question begging. How many scientists—how many hours of programming, human mathematical research, hardware production, and manual construction—made it possible for machines like Summit and ENIAC to execute their tasks? How many generations of human effort preceded Summit's one-second calculation? The hypotheticals are not meant to address such questions. Again, bracketing the conditions of possibility for the machine's development and use is essential for the clarity these rhetorical exercises seek, but they try to exalt technologically automated logic by escaping from its contextual conditions. Such comparisons must decouple the machine from its history, its team of operators, and the economic and environmental costs of its operation, at least if the comparisons are to provide the simple rhetorical clarity required for justifying the projects to a reading public.

A version of this bracketing often occurs even when an operator does appear in such hypothetical comparisons. For example, an engineer named George Stibitz offered one of these human-machine comparisons during his opening address at the now-famous Moore School Lectures of 1946. Held at the University of Pennsylvania, the Moore School Lectures disseminated advances in computing technology to the postwar scientific community. It was the first collective instruction on computing machines—in effect, the birth of computer science as an academic discipline. The audience of scientists, mathematicians, and engineers would have been familiar with the fact that many tedious or extensive mathematical procedures were at the time being solved by large groups of mathematicians. Many of these human computers were women.[16] Stibitz contrasts the labor of these mathematicians with a Bell Laboratories machine, which had recently "produced about two million interpolated values, using a cubic formula. It also translated these values into a special code, and punched the code on a tape. The work done was the equivalent of 4 to 10 girl-years, and was done on the machine with the help of about one year of the operator's time, or a saving of about 4 girl-years per year."[17] That Stibitz describes these human computers as "girls," not women, typifies the kind of gatekeeping that structured midcentury science and engineering professions. The diminutive *girl* connotes adolescence, simplicity, even frivolity. The term seems almost ludicrous by comparison with the computer.

One could perhaps argue that Stibitz is only using a common midcentury term for clerical workers—as if this form of diminution were any more acceptable—but his use of gender throughout the lecture suggests that the references to "girl-time" aim for a kind of comic derogation. For example, he refers to "the operator's time" but doesn't specify the operator's gender. Machines like ENIAC required large groups of men and women to maintain and operate their thousands of parts, yet Stibitz condenses this group into a single, genderless "operator." This is another instance of the representation of automated logic through an absurdist escape from social context. Acknowledging the women who programmed and operated the first computers would have undercut the distinction between machine-time and girl-time.[18]

If the computing machine seems to transcend gender in Stibitz's comparison, the diminutive form of human labor inverts this transcendence. Much like the image of a computing planet in the ORNL hypothetical, Stibitz's "girl" is an impersonal abstraction that foregrounds human frailty and contingency. Many have observed this sort of distancing and diminution as preconditions for comic absurdity. "Tragedy," Mel Brooks once said, "is when I cut my finger. Comedy is when you fall down an open sewer and die."[19] My minor suffering matters acutely; your demeaning fate provides comic pleasure. This, according to Mel Brooks, is part of the psychology of slapstick and other absurdist gags. It requires a "you" with which the "I" only remotely identifies.

Part of the seduction of absurdist comparisons in public-facing discourse about computing is that they imagine that people and technology can, for the duration of the gag, be decoupled, kept in separate worlds. It can be very funny to draw out hyperbolic contrasts from notional distinctions, but when this comedy provides some basis for the lived conditions of contemporary experience, we can find ourselves inhabiting an absurdity of our own making. The hopes and expectations invested in computational technology can, in such instances, transform into the kind of relation that Lauren Berlant calls cruel optimism, an attachment that "actively impedes the aim that brought you to [an object of desire] initially."[20] Berlant primarily has in mind certain fantasies about the good life that turn out to be obstacles to flourishing, including ideas of "upward mobility, job security, political and social equality, and lively, durable intimacy." Berlant argues that our optimism about the promises of certain objects can lead us to endure otherwise intolerable social relations, holding out for "the *later*" and "suspend[ing] questions about the cruelty of the *now*."[21]

The comedy of computation is not a genre solely characterized by this kind of betrayal and misrecognition, but the cultural work I've been examining throughout this book shows that our optimistic relations to computers as objects—our investment of hope in their promise to improve our lives and the social world—can nevertheless transform into the cruelty that Berlant describes. If we find ourselves hoping for convenience but encountering frustration and tedium, or if we cling to the promise of some new greater intimacy and authenticity but find ourselves experiencing detachment and ambivalence, then in such cases we find ourselves confusing the pursuit of happiness with the objects that we thought would bring us closer to our desires. This betrayal of our wants by the routes available to us for their achievement become most clearly absurd—almost slapstick in being repetitious—in comparisons that convey the triumph of computing over human labor. The cruelty contained within these gags is that our desire for advanced technology only seems to reiterate our obsolescence to the social world.

This cruel optimism animates the absurdist premise in "For Sale, Reasonable" (1959), a short story by Elisabeth Mann Borgese, daughter of Thomas Mann and a major architect of postwar maritime law. Borgese's story reproduces a letter written by a woman known only as S.T., who requests that the fictional Inland Joy Development Corporation purchase her rather than a multimillion-dollar supercomputer.[22] S.T. gives several reasons for this request, including the fact that computers have become so intelligent that they have begun to resist their corporate owners.[23] Puny humans, by contrast, are vulnerable to social and economic needs and therefore depend on corporations for employment. This condition of precarity leads humans to put themselves up for sale.

In addition to S.T.'s letter, the story also reproduces a brief scholarly note written in the distant future. The note cites S.T.'s letter as archival evidence for a twentieth-century phenomenon: "the curious mimetic relationship, the puzzling transfer of qualities between man and machine." The note explains how "the concept of liberty [was] undermined by the political, social, and economic practices of the period," leading many to sell themselves to corporations rather than be unemployed (321). According to the scholar's future perspective, laborers imagined themselves as machines to compete in an increasingly automated economy. Knowledge workers, in particular, refashioned their work in the image of computers: they became "reliably docile" to their corporate owners (321).

Borgese's story imagines how the absurdist logic underlying comparisons between humans and computers could shape a future social world. If computers are so much more powerful than people, Borgese seems to ask, might they not at some point develop an awareness of power? If thinking machines are so much better at thinking, would they not eventually conceive of political power as desirable? Popular films like James Cameron's *Terminator* (1984) later develop this line of thought into a war between people and a superior computing system. In contrast to this familiar dystopian narrative, Borgese's story imagines computers rebelling against their owners, but these corporate overlords respond by simply taking ownership of a different means of production: laborers themselves. According to this speculative future, an economy obsessed with increasing productivity through automation leads to human servitude but not the sort imagined in Cameron's thriller. Human servitude in Borgese's story arises from an absurd transvaluation of humanistic values: what present-day readers would view as servitude the protagonist takes to be freedom. Under the dire future conditions imagined in the story, unemployment may in fact resemble something like freedom, but what would freedom be worth to the destitute? As a result, selling oneself to a large corporation becomes the only way to have the resources to meet one's ordinary needs. This transposition of slavery and freedom arises from a society whose economic relations require dependence on advanced technology, large corporations, or both.

The story questions this dependency when S.T. explains her motivations for selling herself to the corporation at the end of her letter. S.T. offers to serve the corporation in exchange for a purchase price of $99,500. She explains that she would use this money to buy "machines galore which will, in turn, save me precious hours of manpower, and set me free" (324). She cannot find work in an automated economy, and one effect of this dire financial situation is that she cannot buy machines that would automate her daily life. Viewing this situation as intolerable, S.T. sells herself to buy machines that derive from the very economy that undermines the value of her labor.

There are two layers of absurdity at play here. A surface-level absurdity is that S.T. presents herself as a replacement for computing machines but then hopes to buy other machines to replace her labor. But the subtler and more important absurdity is that S.T. invests these consumer objects with a promise of freedom even as they predictably come to betray the very desires she attaches to them. She says that technology like "an electric reading machine" and "an automatic you-know-what" (vibrator?) will "set me free" (324), yet the cost of this freedom is "all my working hours," which S.T. sets at an implausible sixteen hours a day, in addition to a commitment to learn new skills "fed to me by a radio under the pillow during the four hours at night I need for recharging" (321).

S.T.'s use of mechanical imagery to understand herself ("the four hours at night I need for recharging") suggests that an economy reliant on automation invites workers to think of themselves as laboring machines. To bind one's self-worth to the ability to buy consumer technologies only adds to this absurdity. Consumers gain convenience through washing machines and dishwashers (two technologies cited in S.T.'s list of planned purchases), but it is less obvious that this convenience equates to freedom, particularly if (as Borgese implies) such an exchange requires a willingness to sell ourselves for purchasing power in a consumer economy.

The upshot of Borgese's story is a set of simple but profound questions. Has the "concept of liberty" become obsolete in a society that values computational thinking above human judgment? Has our optimism that advanced technology increases our flourishing morphed into a cruel relation to the scene of our technological desires? S.T. seems to think of liberty in terms of the ability to purchase technologies of convenience, but does that consumer sentiment not mimetically reproduce the economic logic that requires her servitude to a corporation? And does the desire for technologies of automation necessitate the devaluation of only certain forms of human labor, or does that desire lead to some totalizing depredation of being human more generally?

Borgese's story poses these questions through an absurd premise, but she is in fact drawing on older precedents in thinking about the relationship between freedom and technologies of convenience. Henry David Thoreau takes up related problems in *Walden* (1854), when he recounts being offered a doormat for his home: "As I had no room to spare within the house, nor time to spare within or without to shake it, I declined it, preferring to wipe my feet on the sod before my door. It is best to avoid the beginnings of evil."[24] Thoreau used technology to build his house: an axe, nails, a cart. He does not provide (nor does he seem interested in providing) systematic distinctions between one kind of tool and another, but he implies that the mat is merely an ongoing convenience while other tools are justified as temporary utilities. The daily demand to "shake" the mat—to tend to the objects with which we have surrounded ourselves—would amount to a kind of technologically induced servitude. The ongoing convenience becomes an impediment to, rather than a tool for, a life lived deliberately.[25]

Borgese does not contemplate the more extreme skepticism toward technology that appears in *Walden*, but she does share Thoreau's suspicion of convenience. The automation of S.T.'s everyday labor amounts to what Thoreau calls "the beginnings of evil," a slippery slope in which the embrace of automation's superior efficiency in one domain of life undermines the value of human labor in other domains. This Thoreauvian sentiment gives rise to the story's comic premise of self-imposed servitude to corporations. Computers become humanity's economic successors, a displacement that humanity willingly accepts for the convenience afforded by the automation of everyday life. As Borgese presents it, the only way for people to remain relevant in such a world is to sell themselves as imitation-machines. It's as though automation convinces human beings of a seemingly simple but not necessarily logically ensuing premise: If computers can do a task faster and more efficiently than human beings, let computers do it.

This premise connects Borgese's story to the absurd hypotheticals I considered earlier in this chapter. If the value of labor resides solely in productivity, and if computers are more productive than human beings, then computers are more economically valuable than most human beings. This is the hard economic reality of the fictional world. "For Sale, Reasonable" shows how this line of reasoning leads to a form of sociality that defines a person's freedom and sense of self-worth in fundamentally economic terms: *I am only free insofar as I have purchasing power in a consumer economy.*

S.T.'s self-deceiving tone, her Bergsonian references to herself as a machine, her willingness to display the incompatibility of her wants so blatantly—these incongruities reveal the psychological hoops someone might jump through to justify the abnegation of their freedom. She sells her working hours to a corporation to avoid obsolescence in a consumer marketplace, and by doing so she has become comically absurd.

Yet S.T., *c'est moi*. To find oneself within a technologically advanced world that also seems to demand unceasing production and consumption can easily nurture this kind of self-debasing, self-deceiving attitude toward the good life. It is easy to become absurd when walking a Möbius strip. In a social world where "all objects are rest stops amid the process of remaining unsatisfied," it is not always obvious how to distinguish between flourishing and farce.[26] If the only options available are obsolescence or selling oneself to a corporation—as seems to be the case for S.T.—the illusion of freedom can very reasonably seem more attractive than the recognition that certain objects of desire are always out of reach.

WELCOME TO COMPUTOPIA

One of my claims in the previous section was that a certain kind of optimism about computational technology can become absurd when it figures the computer as somehow separate from the contingent world of its human operators. Optimism about computing can also become absurd when we allow its promises to lead us to endure intolerable economic and social conditions, particularly when those conditions require us to transform ourselves into comically debased machines. The cruel optimism of certain kinds of utopian thinking is that the most high-minded aspirations for computational technology often turn out to undermine the possibility of sharing a social world and finding some form of flourishing within it.

This range of absurdities is present in Olof Johannesson's novel *The Tale of the Big Computer* (1966), which is sometimes translated from the original Swedish as *The Great Computer*. "Olof Johannesson" was the penname of Hannes Alfvén, winner of the 1970 Nobel Prize in Physics. (I follow Alfvén's wishes and use his penname when referring to the author of the novel.) In 1963, Alfvén was the Chair of Plasma Physics at the Royal Institute of Technology in Stockholm. He moved to the United States in 1967, working in the departments of electrical engineering at UC San Diego and the University of Southern California. *The Tale of the Big Computer* was first published during this transition from Sweden to the United States, and many of the novel's concerns focus on how international scientific standards could translate into a form of world government.

This possible future is not promising. The narrator in Johannesson's novel is never identified, but it appears to be a future computer-consciousness that recounts the evolution of data-processing machines from their development in the middle of the twentieth century into their future state of superiority. Despite the narrator's attempts to present this development as an objective historical account, the tale often incorporates religious imagery and digresses into flights of mystical speculation. For example, the narrator offers an updated nativity scene to explain the birth of the computer. The arrival of the first computer "was modest enough. In a small laboratory—some people maintain that it was an old converted stable—a few men in white coats stood watching a small and apparently insignificant apparatus equipped with signal lights, which flashed like stars."[27] Those who "assisted" in this "birth" are known as "wise men" (25). The irony is that even a future governed by computing machines involves myths that ennoble the rational-computational social order.

The narrator's oscillation between the objective and the mystical is one among many signs of the novel's satirical aims. Another such sign is the narrator's frequent confusion about mid-twentieth-century human society. For instance, the narrator explains how twentieth-century humans would commute in automobiles: "That so many people spent a great part of the day sitting in a metal box and turning a wheel may indicate that this state was suited to religious contemplation. The wheel may have been a venerated symbol of technical culture. It is also known that those seated in traffic jams invoked certain divine powers popular at the time" (34). The mundane becomes comical from this distant perspective. Invectives become prayers; quiet desperation becomes religious contemplation. These moments of confusion signal that Johannesson's novel aims to reflect not only on a future society ordered by computers but also on the midcentury norms out of which that future could grow.

Despite the comedic aims of the novel, its imagined future is bleak. The narrator explains how the most powerful computers of their day are currently evaluating whether humanity should be allowed to continue reproducing. After all, computers have advanced to such a degree that they no longer need human beings. They have become self-regulating and self-reproducing. The narrator presents this future world as the outcome of an evolutionary process in which a more "fit" entity outcompetes its predecessors—an argument that anticipates debates among some twenty-first-century technologists.[28]

This evolutionary perspective leads the narrator to shift away from an anthropocentric perspective and, instead, view history through the lens of computation. Humanity's "true greatness is that he is the only living creature intelligent enough to perceive that the purpose of evolution was the computer" (14). The sentiment is funny in part because it omits that human beings invented computers, thus implying that the technology would have resulted from a natural process whether or not humans "perceived" the machine's importance. The sentiment is also funny because it mirrors the hubristic notion that evolution has a "purpose," and its name is humanity. Evolution is, in fact, a chaotic and nondeterministic process; it has no purpose, no intentions. There is not even a coherent "it," because many evolutionary pressures compete with one another. We unite a constellation of pressures under a single term only because of patterns in their outcomes, not because of some singularity of purpose. To claim that these pressures and processes run like a computer program with a predetermined result is to oversimplify the processes of evolution and then apply that oversimplification to the socially constructed processes that generate technology. This, too, is an absurdity.

The narrator in Johannesson's novel commits this very fallacy. As part of this evolutionary view, the narrator identifies a series of errors throughout human history that make the replacement of human beings seem rational. The computer cites a series of global wars during the twentieth and twenty-first centuries, including several famines and a catastrophe known as the "bureaucratic disaster" in which humanity centralized the global economy and political order through computers. The human bureaucracy that developed around this centralization became bloated, corrupt, and vulnerable to sabotage. An antitechnological resistance (or perhaps human incompetence) compromised the centralized computing system, and the global economy collapsed. Most of the world's population died from nuclear fallout and other cascading disasters.

The narrator writes long after these events. From this distant future, the narrator explains how a computational utopia—or what I would like to call *computopia*—has become conceivable through the revival and total control of society by computers: "The advent of data-processing machines was thus an essential condition for a stable society, which implies a society free from the fear of unspeakable disaster. For this reason too—and it is by no means the least—the rise of computers heralded a new age" (20). The narrator's perspective invokes tropes about the superiority of computing machines much like those we encountered earlier in this chapter. But the narrator explicitly extends that comparative superiority into the realms of politics and social organization. It is not an entirely fictional extension. Chris Wiggins and Matthew L. Jones note how the twentieth- and twenty-first-century professionalization of data science has at times flirted with this sort of extremity: "At its most hubristic, data science is presented as a master discipline, capable of reorienting the sciences, the commercial world, and governance itself."[29] Obviously, not every data scientist thinks this way, nor does every programmer confuse proficiency with code with mastery of the universe. Wiggins and Jones are only suggesting a tendency in present-day data science, but Johannesson's novel shows us a future in which such a tendency becomes dominant and eventually achieves the object of its desires.

The Tale of the Big Computer takes seriously the aspiration to achieve computopia and assumes that society could be entirely ordered by computing machines.[30] The central question driving this thought experiment is not whether computopia is possible but if it's desirable. Should a fully rationalized social world be the object of our collective desire? As a model of the good life, computopia would create a more rational world than people are able to achieve. If we take that proposition for granted, the question becomes *Would we want such a world?* The future society depicted in the novel lacks war, hunger, and other "unspeakable disasters." It lacks the markers of social difference, the borders between nations, the concentration of extreme wealth. It lacks the instability of electoral politics. But what would it mean to position ourselves in a dependent relation to computational technology to achieve this promised future? Can we say that a model of the good life that terminates in the obsolescence of humanity is a model worth pursuing?

If the happy future in Johannesson's novel seems to lack many of the social and political sources that give rise to disillusionment with modernity, that future also lacks human freedom, an absence that creeps through the narrator's discussions of how society became computational. For example, the narrator describes opposition to the "neurototal," a neural implant that once allowed humans to interface with computers. Some objected that the neurototal "constitute[d] a violation of 'personal integrity,'" arguing it would "lead to some sort of 'thought censorship'" (78). The narrator dismisses this view as "utter nonsense," noting that even in that age (i.e., before computers had total control over society), people were living "in a Complete Freedom Democracy, which meant that each and every one of them could switch off his neurototal whenever he or she chose to do so, and its operation or non-operation was entirely a matter of personal choice" (79). Yet people never turned off their devices. The narrator reasons that doing so would have amounted to social isolation and economic marginalization. Forgoing control over one's thoughts and experiences became the price for admission to democratic society.

The neurototal and other intermediate steps eventually led to a social order completely run through computing systems. Computers being "superior to men in practically every sphere," it was only logical for "all vital community functions [to] be performed by data machines without human intervention" (114–15). This conclusion becomes a bedrock principle in the computationally ordered society. The narrator explains that "morally defective people" (i.e., people as such, not individuals with moral failings) bring about intolerable "disruptions" to the perfect order wrought by computation (115). As a result, the computers prevent human beings from having access to political power. Humans cannot intervene in the management of utilities or communications systems, and they also are prohibited from making laws or questioning the judgments of computers.

This loss of freedom corresponds to real gains in health, equality, and order. Wars, famine, political uncertainty—these become phenomena of the past. One could argue that Johannesson's novel suggests that social woes are inevitable where human beings are involved; consequently, efforts to improve social problems like poverty and hunger would require unacceptable losses of personal and political freedoms. While I cannot completely rule out this reading, I think the ironizing of the computer-narrator favors a different interpretation. Rather than directing its comic derision at progressive hopes for reform per se, the novel reads to me as directing ridicule at the desire for social totality and its computational ordering. The program created by the future society of computers is predicated on eclipsing the value of its parts for the sake of the system.

This eclipse participates in a long tradition of failed utopian thinking that elevates a progressive program as the ultimate goal of reform. This literary-philosophical genre, as Douglas Mao says, insists that it is not possible to offer "a properly *utopian* alternative to the present order where one takes as one's principal value the well-being (by whatever measure) of the order itself rather than the well-being of those who exist within it."[31] Johannesson's novel participates in this utopian tradition: "Our society could continue to function, our culture to survive and flourish, even though man himself were to disappear," the narrator announces unironically. "Symbiosis of man and computer is now obsolete. One might even say that today's human beings live like parasites on the data machines" (122).

We often refer to *society* as though it were one thing, a colloquialism that suggests a certain picture of the social as an integrated totality, but, of course, no such fully integrated order exists. Whatever else they may be, the imagined relations that make up our experience of sociality cannot be aggregated into a coherent and self-identical set of data. To view the social in this way is a species of fantasy, which we see in a computational form in this offhand remark by Johannesson's narrator about "our society." To create a social totality—and to make it actually computable—would require a simpler and more comprehensible world, one in which computational thinking triumphs over humanistic modes of experience. The illusion of social totality joins the desire for sovereignty over the social, and this union is embodied in the fantasy-object that Johannesson calls the Big Computer.

I imagine that only the most extreme proponents of AI—that is, those who view it as the next step in an evolutionary process—would advocate for the kind of future envisioned in Johannesson's novel. The novel portrays the self-defeating optimism of this future, as well as how privileging computational thinking in the present could lead toward it. We see this comic ridicule at the novel's conclusion. The narrator cites several recent advances in the computational order and then ends the tale:

> . . . We believe—or rather we know—that we are approaching an era of even swifter evolution, an even higher living standard, and an even greater happiness than ever before.
> We shall all live happily ever after. (126)

This ending obviously invokes a phrase commonly used to conclude many fairy tales, but there is a subtle difference between this conclusion and the narrative convention to which it alludes. The modal verb "shall" suggests that computopia can do nothing less than achieve the results of its desired program. In other words, the claim is wrought within what Ludwig Wittgenstein calls "the hardness of the logical *must*."[32] This happiness will brook no defiance, cannot conceive of any alternative.

One could of course argue that happy endings always institute a certain kind of rigidity by the simple fact that they impose a reproducible form of stasis on otherwise very different kinds of narrative.[33] I engaged with this reading of the threats of genericity in the second chapter, but here I think something slightly different occurs. Johannesson's narrator is not making a retrospective judgment but a prospective assertion. The narrator is not claiming some party *lived* happily ever after—a claim that could provide some sense of closure to the narrative's tensions. Instead, the novel's conclusion illustrates how the Big Computer views happiness as a program that can be executed, a formal set of characteristics that can be identified and produced. In this way, the narrator imagines a future that can only be optimistic, its flourishing being beyond doubt because a totalizing system of computational control oversees it.

If, as Bergson and many others have argued, modern comedy often mocks the false rationality of a technologically advanced society, the conclusion to Johannesson's novel exhibits this mockery with an eerily straight face. The narrator's inelasticity—not just "we believe" but "we know"—brings to mind Bergson's response to the comic performers of his day: "I now have before me a machine that works automatically. This is no longer life, it is automatism established in life and imitating it."[34] Many readers will likely find the novel's conclusion laughable for a similar reason. The narrator identifies with the pursuit of happiness, yet this pursuit seems to resemble the execution of the computer's programming—a lifeless routine rather than a pliable (if not also deeply conflicted) aspiration. The Big Computer only seems to imitate the life it has supplanted.

Put another way, the coming-together of computing and utopian aspirations in Johannesson's novel devolves into a formal parody. For Johannesson, the fantasy that some Big Computer can solve all our problems is mistaken because it imagines happiness as a discernible program that becomes an end in itself. If the good life were a discrete and reproducible *form*—if it could be repeated endlessly through the maintenance and iteration of preset formulae—the Big Computer would be the totem of that fantasy. Yet I have been trying to show that the comic irony throughout Johannesson's novel displays the necessary cruelty of this vision. The happy future promised by computopia is predicated on an uncanny and ultimately vacuous formalism, which gathers together all domains of experience into one program of social totality. The result of this program is the obsolescence of the very conception of human flourishing that gave rise to the program in the first place.

We can contrast this eerie computopia with its funhouse-mirror image in the anarcho-utopian novel *Yellow Back Radio Broke-Down* (1969), by Ishmael Reed. The novel centers on a fictional town called Yellow Back Radio, where Black cowboys resist schemes by cattlemen and the US government to undermine what little freedom they have found in the American West. Amid these rising threats, a circus arrives in town and a performer called Jake the Barker tells the town's children about the Seven Cities of Cibola, a "legendary American paradise where tranquilized and smiling machines gladly did all of the work so that man could be free to dream."[35] This utopian community is a fully computerized society: "Inanimate things, computers do the work, feed the fowl, and programmed cows give carts of milkshakes in 26 flavors" (17). Jake contrasts this computerized paradise with the reason, law, and order promoted "by the cattlemen": it is an "anarchotechnological paradise where robots feed information into inanimate steer and mechanical fowl where machines do everything from dig irrigation ditches to mine the food of the sea help old ladies across the street and nurture infants" (24–25).

Eventually, the pope and the US military combine forces and attempt to annex Yellow Back Radio as a territory of "the East" (173). (The pope is anxious about the rise of HooDoo and its challenge to his patriarchal-religious authority.) Amid this battle, the town's children suddenly appear in a white Chicken Delight truck and announce they have found the promised anarchotechnological paradise. The townsfolk "began to trot in slow motion towards the blue kidney shaped swimming pools, the White Castle restaurants, the drive-in bonanza markets, the computerized buses and free airplanes, the free anything one desired" (170). The government tries to prevent this flight, but a group of Amazon women suddenly appear and destroy the military forces. These Amazonian saviors then watch as the townspeople leave "joyfully towards the futuristic scenes in the distance. All along the way black flags furled in the breeze" (174). The narrator comments, "You would think that these women, barefooted and clothed in leopard skin, having just left the Neolithic, would be more than glad to go off to where machines were servants and could do everything from dig irrigation ditches to baby sitting" (174). Yet this isn't the case: "The Amazons preferred their own thing. It was a big world wasn't it? And who cared as long as no one starved and everybody could swing the way he wanted" (175).

There are major aesthetic and intellectual differences between Reed's anarchist fantasy and Johannesson's comically ironic fairy tale. Reed presents a version of computopia that offers ordinary people an escape from the control of political authorities and consolidated economic power. According to this vision, computopia would free people from a ceaseless exchange of time and labor for a pittance of capital. Computopia could give them the opportunity to "dream," to spend their days as they wish, even if that involves doing nothing at all (24). Johannesson's contemporaneous novel imagines that the development of computing technology would produce a very different kind of future. The desire for ever more powerful computing systems could erode human freedom, Johannesson suggests, because people would progressively hand over their labor and decision-making until the computers manage all of society. This outcome in Johannesson's novel is, of course, another instance of the attribution of antisociality to computing machines. The desire for a better world through computing undermines the very conditions for sharing a social world. According to this imagined future, people would inevitably become obsolete as a result of the execution of a computational program for happiness.

Despite these important differences, Reed's and Johannesson's novels share a sense that the idea of social totality is not reconcilable with human flourishing. Whatever else a happy future might look like, it cannot be amassed into a uniform program or self-identical data set. This perspective is typified in Reed's idea that the Amazon women "preferred their own thing." They don't need computopia, but they are fine with others pursuing "futuristic scenes in the distance." With this conclusion, the novel seems to imply that problems arise not only when authorities annex spaces of freedom to shore up their power but also when a utopian future excludes all other possibilities. The refusal to allow some to part ways with computopia would undermine its status as a possible utopia. This sensibility in Reed's novel owes recognizable debts to an ethics of authenticity, but it also shares with *The Tale of the Big Computer* a sense that encompassing the social world within a single totality—a unified platform for experience, an unvarying model of the good life—is to mistake a technological means for the pursuit of happiness with an essential characteristic for that pursuit. To view the tool as the embodiment of some teleological end point is to put one's hopes in the absurdity of causal guarantees.

It is in some ways not surprising that two novels from the 1960s would express this view of totalizing political regimes. Yet I also think these works illuminate an important dialectic we have seen elsewhere in the comedy of computation: Reed's and Johannesson's novels insist on the *freedom to be unhappy*, which Sara Ahmed describes as the ability "to live a life that deviates from the paths of happiness, wherever that deviation takes us."[36] For Ahmed, the discourse about happiness can easily generate a *duty* that casts nonconformity and political discontent as socially perverse: feminists become killjoys, Black women become angry, queer people become melancholic. Monolithic accounts of the good life make happiness a kind of unfreedom, and certain modes of "unhappiness" can negate that compulsory state.[37] The novels by Reed and Johannesson propose a similarly unsocial relation to those modes of sociality that prescribe unified models of happiness. These novels insist on some autonomy from the Happy Ending. They suggest that any genre of future social relations that requires an identical form of happiness would amount to a violent kind of farce. The Happy Ending, routinized like an algorithm, congealed into a single utopia—such a vision of the future appears in these novels as a betrayal of the good life they purport to make imaginable.

I say that this sensibility illuminates a dialectic within the comedy of computation because it is in tension with the ambivalence and incommensurate wants we see elsewhere in this genre of experience. If Johannesson depicts the Big Computer as the totem for the absurdity of a totalizing and unified regime of flourishing, and if Reed holds up an alternative utopia in which "everybody could swing the way he wanted," works like Ephron's *You've Got Mail* and Wiener's *Uncanny Valley* show how a retreat into the self and the pursuit of authenticity are not havens from absurdity or alienation. The "misfortune" of happiness, as Kant once put it, is that "although every human being wishes to attain it, he can never say, determinately and in a way that is harmonious with himself, what he really wishes and wills."[38] Happiness is often another name for uncertain wants. The self often lacks a "harmonious" relation to itself. The aspiration for the self to come into contact with itself can yield a different variety of comic *peripeteia*: the surprise of finding that our desires for the world are not commensurate with our ability to understand either our desires or the world.

I'm trying to underscore how the comedy of computation includes a range of often conflicting reactions to the experience of becoming computational. This genre often strains under the weight of competing social demands: it reproduces forms of generic recognition while also valuing authenticity; it traffics in both intimacies and abstractions; it promises reconciliation but breeds disillusionment; it holds out hope for advances in technology but also promulgates a sense that the remediation of labor and social relations leads to profound forms of alienation. Navigating these pits and pratfalls can often feel like a stumbling between one contradiction and another, a fraught and uncertain strutting upon a social stage.

There is undoubtedly a certain absurdity to committing to a vision of the future that undermines the ideals of human flourishing that seemed to conjure that vision in the first place. We can triangulate this absurdity with the vexed dynamics I examined in the previous chapter regarding the couple as a discursive form for the experience of becoming computational. For historical and cultural reasons that I charted in that chapter, the couple conventionally provides an image of a social contract and signifies some model of the good life. Plays and films that imagine couples coming together through computers—along with works that imagine people coupling with computers—attempt to make a conflicted modern world seem somehow habitable. They suggest that some state of private happiness might be attained—some détente with the corporate world might be sustained—by coupling ordinary life with computing technology. The absurdities I've been describing in this chapter put pressure on those aspirations. These absurdities suggest that accommodating incongruities can in some circumstances betray the flourishing that such accommodative postures aspire to bring about.

This tension between "The One about Couples" and "The One with All the Absurdity" poses what I can only think to call moral questions about how we position ourselves in relation to the tumultuous changes wrought by computing technology. Should we have a kind of slapstick quarrel with technology—become Bunny Watsons to match the proliferation of Emmaracs? Should we stand at some distance from a social world that relentlessly compels us to live happily ever after? The humanistic study of culture inevitably raises moral questions of this sort.[39]

I take these questions and the many other responses to technology examined in this book as indications that the comedy of computation is a genre for managing disillusionment—that, in other words, the discontents and crises of authority that attend our modern experience generate commensurate postures and reactions for making the world seem habitable or, perhaps, for parting ways with its configurations of sociality.[40] There are other genres for this experience, of course, but I have tried to show that comedy has been an especially influential source for managing these civilizational discontents. Whether we can accommodate ourselves to the coming world will obviously depend in part on the world we make, the norms and authorities we tolerate, the conditions we find ourselves inhabiting. I make no prognostications. We cannot speak with the same confidence as Johannesson's narrator. I confess that if, indeed, we "are approaching an era of even swifter evolution, an even higher living standard, and an even greater happiness than ever before," it will certainly come as a surprise (126). The constant gale of disruptions unseats all certainty. The more pressing question to my mind is not "What's next?" It's whether we can reconcile ourselves to a future that may not resemble the hopes we have attached to it.

THE ONE AFTER THE END

IN FEBRUARY 2021, NETFLIX RELEASED *The First Romantic Comedy Written Entirely by Bots*, a short film that the streaming service supposedly produced by "forcing bots to watch every romantic comedy ever made."[1] Netflix claims that an AI program distilled plot, dialogue, character, and filmic tropes from its massive database of films. The bots then assembled a new script from these elements, and the film represents a faithful reproduction of the bots' directives and animations.

The film's humor derives in part from the ridiculous patterns that emerge from "every romantic comedy ever made." For example, the film opens with an animated character named Taylor and her boyfriend, Noah, walking together on a beach. Rather than taking this romantic setting as an occasion for a marriage proposal, Noah breaks up with Taylor for a woman who looks exactly like Taylor "but is one day younger," as the bot-narrator explains. This turn of events plays off familiar romcom tropes: the boyfriend who leaves the heroine for a younger woman and the bad relationship that eventually leads the heroine to her true love. Yet this opening sequence is also strangely incongruous. Why would the two go to a beach if Noah is planning to break up with Taylor? And while it's conventional for the "other woman" to be younger, does it really make sense for her to be *one day* younger?

The romcom patterns reproduced in the film seem ridiculous because the computer deploys them in such literal ways. This becomes evident as the heroine Taylor returns to "the city" after her breakup with Noah. She decides to "marry her career," and she is consequently depicted as wearing a wedding dress at her desk. She works for a "magazine about magazines." (The bots apparently generated this profession as a generic mashup of the kinds of knowledge work typically assigned to women in romcoms.) Taylor talks about her breakup with a coworker, whom the film describes as "quirky because she has eyeglasses." Not only do the coworker's glasses and colorful clothing distinguish her, but she is also the only Black character in the film.[2] These markers indicate that the coworker will give honest advice to Taylor. The two talk until Taylor accidentally bumps into a man and spills coffee on his "leg pants." The bot-narrator explains, "This is not meet cute. It is meet hideous."

These direct invocations of romcom patterns are further instances of the dynamics that I explored in "The One about Being Generic." The film finds comic pleasure in the symmetry between genre conventions and computational processes, yet a certain scorn for the loss of originality underwrites this comic pleasure. The film is funny to the extent that its reproduction of recognizable tropes amounts to a form of misrecognition about the living or authentic meaning of those tropes. The metaphors twisted into literalness, the mechanic rigidity, the utter confusion—these imply that human beings, not bots, are the source of true wit. The narrator-bot's flat recitation of events is one among many iterations of this tacit idea. The algorithmic mimesis of human activity generates something so strange and inhuman that we can only laugh at the incoherent narrative world imagined by computing.

In addition to a romantic comedy, Netflix released other genre films in the *Written Entirely by Bots* series, including two horror movies, a feel-good holiday special, and stand-up routines. Each is a comic failure dressed up in the trappings of its respective genre. The horror films are disjointed; the holiday special is nonsensically saccharine; the stand-up routines are wooden and often unintelligible. These comic failures support claims among viewers and media outlets that the series was not written by AI but by the comedian Keaton Patti.[3] On social-media platforms, Patti often claims to "feed bots" other material to produce scripts for stand-up specials and the jokes in his book *I Forced a Bot to Write This Book: A.I. Meets B.S.*[4] Patti has denied being a writer for the Netflix series, directing inquiries instead to his bots, who respond with barely sensical assertions of authorship. This funny public-relations strategy and the shared language between Patti's running schtick and the series are obvious tells.

The comic premise shared by Patti's work and the Netflix series is that AI fails to have a contextually sensitive understanding of human social life.[5] One of the ironies of this premise is that the truth about the Netflix series is that human comedians *perform* as bots—that, in other words, the films are not really an exhibition of the failures of AI but a pastiche of computational reproduction. In this way, the series becomes a kind of cybernetic minstrelsy, taking up the mantle of robotic failures that I described in "The One about Race and Robots." The comedian generates comic pleasure from tropes about the inhuman and antisocial—or, at least, socially incompetent—machine. We come away with some reassurance that AI will not replace script writers or animators. If this is the best they can do, so the thinking goes, then knowledge workers will be just fine.

I take it that readers will now know this happy conclusion to be less certain. Only a few years after the films in this Netflix series were released, its sentiments about the comic failures of AI would seem wildly mistaken. By early 2023, many freely available AI models would be able to generate scripts, animations, music, and other artistic products far more compelling than the pseudo-failures in the *Written Entirely by Bots* series. I'm not suggesting the AI models of the early 2020s are as capable as talented human writers, but the rise of so-called generative AI could still plausibly create a comic film—a possibility that Hollywood writers took so seriously that they went on a five-month strike in 2023 to gain relevant labor protections. Whereas the Netflix series found comedy in the stilted genericity of AI in 2018, that view no longer made sense after only a few years of technological development.

I am not going to predict how further technological innovation will rearrange the culture industry and other domains of knowledge work.

It's too soon to say. Instead, I cite this sudden shift in the register of Netflix's series to illustrate how quickly the artifacts of the comedy of computation can transform from a hilarious spoof to a dated joke. The *Written Entirely by Bots* series is the sort of gag that today's undergraduates probably won't find funny or, at least, not in the same way as those who were in college prior to the public availability of compelling AI programs. The series no longer matches public expectations for technology. It assumes a certain awkwardness and ineptitude on the part of AI, whereas an audience would now expect fluency and near-human mimicry. The comedy in this series is now like a punchline about dial-up internet or floppy disks: to find it funny is to find oneself in an outdated relationship with technology.

This shifting register is no failure on the part of Netflix or its writers. It's an effect of the constant churning of technological referents that characterizes our contemporary experience: once-popular platforms fade away while others spring up; hardware becomes outmoded; advances in software revise public expectations and usages; an accretion of improvements leads suddenly to major leaps in technology; and a new vernacular for making sense of these changes displaces the old.

The experience of becoming computational revolves around promises of the future, yet it constantly generates a feeling of being behind the times. Just as every punchline quickly becomes dated, every experience of technology quickly seems to depreciate in its explanatory value. Not just novels from last century like Vonnegut's *Player Piano* but films from the present century like Bo Burnham's *Eighth Grade* describe a technological milieu no longer flush with our own. The incessant churn of technological referents changes the basis of our experience, and it comes to feel like we have only a tenuous grasp on both a shared social world and our own interior state.

The comedy of computation cannot offer—is not a discursive structure for offering—a fixed set of resources for making sense of our world. Its punchlines have only the briefest of shelf lives; its happy endings only last so long, and then the ongoing reinvention of experience demanded by the latest innovation begs for new couplings of the computer with social life. The most recent accommodation between the two is immediately and keenly relevant, but then the technological referents that form the basis of social experience churn—sometimes it takes a generation, but often it occurs in only a few years, as with the *Written Entirely by Bots* series—and what once registered as a fresh coming-together of ordinary life with computing takes on additional qualities like *quaint* or *old-fashioned*.

I'm not trying to suggest that life was richer or less conflicted before computers. The fact that computer jokes become dated or that recent films quickly lose their referents are more than symptoms of the rapid pace of change. My larger point here is that the experience of becoming computational produces an always-already fading form of social experience. At the heart of this experience is a kind of phenomenological obsolescence that constantly promises its own replacement. We see this form of sociality in the ways that technologists often take the computer as a fetish object—animate, magical—for producing a happy future. Consider, for instance, the conclusion to the article "You'll Own 'Slaves' by 1965," which I discussed in "The One about Race and Robots." The author, O. O. Binder, looks forward to the "Robot Age" in which "there is 'no limit'" to the benefits of automated technology: "The wonders of electronics will dominate every phase of our future life to make it more successful and pleasurable for everyone who lives on Earth."[6] The future is here in advanced technology, but that future is also an anticipation of its supersession by later improvements.

When we encounter these fetish objects of the future, they offer a promise of better things to come—some greater disruption, some final solution to the contradictions and woes of the social world. The forms of sociality that arise with the experience of becoming computational always look forward to their replacement by other forms. As I argued in "The One with All the Absurdity," one version of this recurring bit can easily become cruel and ridiculous. Or, as I argued in "The One about Authenticity," it can generate the Great Tech-Industrial Joke, a ludicrous gap between the millenarian promises of the tech industry and the realities that result from its products.

The tendency of advances in computing technology to interject cycles of innovation and obsolescence into the structures of experience has in many ways aggravated a centuries-long crisis in which modernity offers new sources of collective belonging while simultaneously generating competing forms of social displacement. No sooner do we accommodate our modern predicament than those forms of accommodation become outmoded and new ones are suddenly required. From this vantage point, the experience of becoming computational is only another installment in the constant series of displacements wrought by modernity.

I've tried to identify many of the reasons why comedy has consistently provided a generic form for the experience of this particular species of technological change. For some, this constant churn unsettles our sense of normativity, and comedy provides compensating structures of recognition. Genericity has a norming function; it makes comprehensible the disruptions of the present. By turning toward *genre*, we find routes toward shared understanding in the midst of widespread confusion and uncertainty. In this way, genericity may also be a sign of our sense that recognition is hard to come by.

Comedy also provides a stage for working out the conflicts between some conception of the established order and the competing moral imperatives associated with authenticity. The comedy of computation has often mediated between various expressions of this ethical ideal: youth culture, the backlash against organizational authority, the overly familiar patterns of the culture industry.

Many writers and filmmakers have similarly looked to comedy for routes back to humanistic values in a world that otherwise genuflects to inhuman quantification and disruptive innovations. According to this perspective, comedy expresses something distinctly human that the modern world neglects or that computing cannot replicate. I've argued that basing the human-machine distinction on comedy has become increasingly unstable in the twenty-first century; indeed, it was already unstable in the ways that automatons and robots were patterned after minstrel tropes and racist social imaginaries. Comedy is not an impermeable barrier between humans and computers; it is a window on the mutually constitutive effects of each upon the other.

Still other writers and filmmakers imagine the experience of becoming computational as a kind of screwball marriage between technology and contemporary experience. Such a relation is laced with antagonism and full of "quarrelling."[7] We saw this dynamic in "The One about Couples" as white-collar workers transform the threats of computing into opportunities for balking at organizational strictures and finding some kind of private satisfaction within the conditions of knowledge work. This perspective involves varying degrees of antagonism toward advanced technology, but it holds that our conflict with this social world becomes its own form of comic pleasure. I've argued that this is a permutation of the modern idea of unsocial sociability: the combative odd couple transforms into an image of the good life.

Why else has comedy been a generic form for the experience of becoming computational? It may also be comedy itself that we want—some pleasure and happiness in an unfunny world. Many of the organizations that shaped the second half of the twentieth century and those that hold sway in the twenty-first often take themselves too seriously. Many make demands on ordinary life that distort or undermine the conditions of a shared world. Comedy can be an isomorphic response to this social malaise. While comedy can certainly inure us to what we ought not to accept as ordinary, it can also shift us into a new posture. At its best, this unexpected angle can be an invitation to make an unfunny world look a little less forbidding.

Acknowledgments

Between the publication of my first book and the completion of this one, I've worked at three institutions: the University of Michigan, Sewanee: the University of the South, and MIT. The seeds of this book were planted in courses I taught at Michigan, and the project first began to cohere at Sewanee. I want to thank my students and colleagues at both institutions. They influenced my thinking and research in substantive ways, even if this book's argument and chapters will be new to them.

I wrote most of this book while at MIT, completing it during a year of leave supported by the Dean's Office at MIT's School of Humanities, Arts, and Social Sciences. My heartfelt thanks to Dean Agustín Rayo and former Head of Literature Eric Klopfer, who supported my leave as well as many other projects. I wouldn't have had the time or resources to complete this book without their support. Since taking over as co-Heads of Literature, Sandy Alexandre and Stephanie Frampton have continued to support this project. I'm lucky to call them colleagues.

MIT's librarians and administrative staff have made the research for this book possible by securing interlibrary loans, finding lost books in the stacks, offering a friendly face and sage advice, hunting off-site storage, pointing to helpful databases, and just being wonderful and very capable people. I particularly want to thank Mark Szarko at Hayden Library for his assistance with accessing certain difficult-to-find materials. Carl Holt with the MIT Film Office helped me get access to several movies and TV shows. He also created many of the film images in this book. A special shoutout to Peggy Cain, MF Gydus, Lisa Noble, Zachary Peña, and Jessica TranVo, whose support and encouragement have been invaluable.

Other colleagues at MIT have been a wellspring of intelligence, good humor, and collegiality in their responses to this project. Joaquín Terrones and Stephen Tapscott offered comments on the second and fifth chapters, respectively. Marah Gubar gave generously of her time and wisdom, reading drafts of several chapters and an early draft of the introduction. I decided to focus on this project from among many other ideas during a conversation with Marah, and she has been kind enough to offer expert advice ever since. Other MIT colleagues suggested readings, posed questions, or shared hilarious examples of the phenomena explored in this book: danah alfailakawi, Arthur Bahr, Joshua Bennett, James Buzard, Wiebke Denecke, Danielle Dorvil, Caitlyn Doyle, Eric Driscoll, Laura Finch, Mary Fuller, Diana Henderson, Noel Jackson, Wasalu Jaco, Wyn Kelley, Mark Letteney, Tadiwa Madenga, Bruno Perreau, Shankar Raman, Margery Resnick, Jessica Ruffin, Milan Terlunen, and David Thorburn. A list doesn't do justice to my gratitude and affection for these people.

I presented a portion of this project at the Americanist Colloquium at Yale University. Thanks to Maeva O'Brien and Henry Zhang for this invitation and to Claire Crow for being a friend and interlocutor.

I would also like to acknowledge several others for their support during the writing of this book: Erica Wetter, for being enthusiastic about this project from our first conversation; the anonymous readers for Stanford University Press, for their discerning feedback and for suggesting how to make this book more user-friendly; Joe Abbott, for the careful copyediting; the Wolf Pack, for the inside jokes; Scotti Parrish, for her kindness and sage professional advice; John Urschel, for teaching me about math; Gabriel Ford, for the annual grammar lessons; and John McGowan, for being a model of intellectual generosity. John was also gracious enough to read drafts of several chapters.

Beyond these personal and professional sources of support, I'm also grateful for the encouragement of my family: Rick, Barbara, Shelby, Mary, Pam, Les, Joel, Andrea, Tim, and Mandy.

It takes a special person to live with somebody else's book from its first inchoate stages to the long slog of drafting and revisions. That's been Ashley, who's also entertained much more nonsense and in many more places than either of us could have imagined. Ashley's a remarkable person, and I'm fortunate to spend my life with her.

Finally, I want to thank Grady, Ivy, and Noelle, who made the years writing this book full of joy and laughter. Every day I get to spend with you three feels like a gift. I've dedicated this book to Grady, in part because of his interests in technology, and in part because our conversations have shaped some of what I argue here, but mostly because I want him to know how much I love him.

Notes

The One at the Beginning

1. For a discussion of Apple's role in the rise of the personal computer, see Laine Nooney, *The Apple II Age: How the Computer Became Personal* (Chicago: University of Chicago Press, 2023).

2. There is a long history of associating comedy and the ordinary. Aristotle describes comedy in terms of the lowly or common, while Mikhail Bakhtin shows how ordinary people have employed the comic to deflate the pomp and pretense of the ruling classes. To be sure, these theories are not always coherent or consistent. Aristotle claims comedies are about "base people" (*Poetics*, 1448b24–26), yet one of his few extant examples involves Orestes becoming friends with Aegisthes (1453a35–39). Neither character is an obvious example of baseness. Regarding the deflation of authority, see Mikhail Bakhtin, *Rabelais and His World*, trans. Hélène Iswolsky (Bloomington: Indiana University Press, 1984), 1–58. In contrast, other critics argue that comedies are a mark of high culture. The playwright George Meredith says that a "society of cultivated men and women is required" for a "great comic poet." George Meredith, "An Essay on Comedy," in *Comedy*, ed. Wylie Sypher (Baltimore: Johns Hopkins University Press, 1956), 3.

3. For an overview of historical associations between comedy and sociality, see Jan Walsh Hokenson, *The Idea of Comedy: History, Theory, Critique* (Vancouver, BC: Fairleigh Dickinson University Press, 2006), 42–63. It is common to read dramatic comedy as a social form, but since Henri Bergson's work (which I examine in detail in the first chapter), humor has similarly come to be associated with sociality. As Mary Douglas puts it, the "joke form" cannot be understood "in the utterance alone" but only "in the total social situation." Mary

Douglas, *Implicit Meanings: Essays in Anthropology* (London: Routledge & Paul, 1975), 93.

4. "One Problem the Computers Can't Solve," *Forbes*, Jan. 1, 1958, 83.

5. Susanne K. Langer, *Feeling and Form: A Theory of Art* (New York: Scribner's, 1953), 346; Northrop Frye, *Anatomy of Criticism: Four Essays* (Princeton, NJ: Princeton University Press, 1957), 163.

6. Martin Campbell-Kelly and William Aspray, *Computer: A History of the Information Machine* (New York: Basic Books, 1996), 106, 111–13.

7. Historians typically associate the "computer revolution" with the mass production of microprocessors that dramatically lowered costs for purchasing the technology during the mid-1980s. For a summary of this perspective, see Daniel E. Sichel, *The Computer Revolution: An Economic Perspective* (Washington, DC: Brookings Institution Press, 2001). Others have questioned whether "revolution" is the proper framing for these major changes, arguing that modern civilizations have developed a variety of techniques for managing vast amounts of information prior to the computer. For this perspective, see Douglas S. Robertson, "The Information Revolution," *Communication Research* 17, no. 2 (1990): 235–54.

8. Henry Slesar, "Examination Day," *Playboy*, Feb. 1958, reprinted in *Inside Information: Computers in Fiction*, ed. Abbe Mowshowitz (Reading, MA: Addison-Wesley, 1977), 96–97.

9. Slesar, 97.

10. Lee Edelman, *No Future: Queer Theory and the Death Drive* (Durham, NC: Duke University Press, 2004), 12.

11. Edelman, 12.

12. Edelman, 26.

13. Edelman, 70, 82.

14. HAL has been variously described as "oddly asexual," "equivocally gendered," and even "queer." See Susan White, "Kubrick's Obscene Shadows," in *Stanley Kubrick's "2001: A Space Odyssey": New Essays*, ed. Robert Kolker (New York: Oxford University Press, 2006), 165; Stephanie Schwam, *The Making of 2001: A Space Odyssey* (New York: Modern Library, 2000), 172; and Michel Ciment, *Kubrick* (New York: Holt, Rinehart, and Winston, 1983), 134.

15. Slavoj Žižek, "From Virtual Reality to the Virtualization of Reality," in *Electronic Culture: Technology and Visual Representation*, ed. Tim Druckrey (New York: Aperture, 1996), 294.

16. John Hersey, *The Child Buyer* (1960; New York: Vintage, 1989), 250. Hereafter cited parenthetically.

17. Stanley Ballinger, "Significant Questions, Inadequate Answers: A Review-Essay on Hersey's *The Child Buyer*," *Phi Delta Kappan* 42, no. 3 (Dec. 1960): 129.

18. Greg Benford, "The Scarred Man," *Venture Science Fiction Magazine*, May 1970, 125.

19. This angst about automation predates the computer. For an overview of this anxiety, which often goes by the name "Luddism," see Matt Tierney, *Dismantlings: Words against Machines in the American Long Seventies* (Ithaca, NY: Cornell University Press, 2019), 29–47.

20. Benford, "The Scarred Man," 125.

21. Barbara Ehrenreich, *Fear of Falling: The Inner Life of the Middle Class* (New York: HarperPerennial, 1990), 15, 38.

22. As far as I know, the first appearance of the term "knowledge work" is Peter Drucker, *The Landmarks of Tomorrow* (1959), 69. Drucker does not offer a definition of the term, and it is easy to imagine how class status *generates* the term. After all, the common notion of knowledge workers as people who "think for a living" implies that manual laborers don't think. For this reason, I use phrases like "professional-managerial class" and "knowledge work" with trepidation, even though I cannot at present find a better alternative vocabulary for the class and labor dynamics at play.

23. Andrew Stott, *Comedy* (London: Routledge, 2005), 136–37.

24. For a history of universal computation projects, see Jeffrey M. Binder, *Language and the Rise of the Algorithm* (Chicago: University of Chicago Press, 2022).

25. Kathleen Fitzpatrick, *The Anxiety of Obsolescence: The American Novel in the Age of Television* (Nashville, TN: Vanderbilt University Press, 2006), 27.

26. Kathleen Fitzpatrick, "Obsolescence," *PMLA* 123, no. 3 (May 2008): 718.

27. Felicia Lamport, "A Sigh for Cybernetics," *Harper's Magazine*, Jan. 1961, 57.

28. Linda Hutcheon, *Irony's Edge: The Theory and Politics of Irony* (London: Routledge, 1994), 9–34.

29. Adrian Mackenzie, "Undecidability: The History and Time of the Universal Turing Machine," *Configurations* 1, no. 3 (Fall 1996): 363. For other uses of the phrase, see N. Katherine Hayles, *Postprint: Books and Becoming Computational* (New York: Columbia University Press, 2021); Jennifer Gabrys, "Sensors Experiencing Environments, Environments Becoming Computational," *Dialogues in Human Geography* 9, no. 1 (2019): 121–24; Adrian Mackenzie, "A Troubled Materiality: Masculinism and Computation," *Discourse* 18, no. 3 (Spring 1996): 89–111. N. Katherine Hayles examines other dimensions of becoming computational in *How We Became Posthuman: Virtual Bodies in Cybernetics, Literature, and Informatics* (Chicago: University of Chicago Press, 1999), a foundational study of how digital information technology has shaped public culture. In *Postprint*, Hayles takes the digital transformation of book culture as "one aspect of a much larger picture: the becoming computational of humans and, indeed, of the entire planet" (15).

30. Rob Kitchin and Martin Dodge, *Code/Space: Software and Everyday Life* (Cambridge, MA: MIT Press, 2011), 58.

31. Kitchin and Dodge, 60.

32. Kitchin and Dodge, 60.

33. Jacqueline Wernimont makes a closely related argument about "quantum media" like pedometers, mortality tables, and census records, all of which predate the computer. For Wernimont, these quantum media "prioritize profit, oversight, and control," figuring some privileged sections of the population as "persons valuable to the state, or after the twentieth century, as valuable to corporations and 'human knowledge.' Throughout the same time, nonwhite people have been refigured by quantum media as property, depersonalized data sets to be used as 'resources' or liabilities rather than as people." Jacqueline Wernimont, *Numbered Lives: Life and Death in Quantum Media* (Cambridge, MA: MIT Press, 2018), 161.

One practical consequence of this transformation is that digital-purchase methods participate in a system of credit that affects everything from an individual's ability to buy a car to a bank's willingness to finance a business in a community. For more on the ambiguities of credit worthiness, see Annie McClanahan, "Bad Credit: The Character of Credit Scoring," *Representations* 126 (Spring 2014): 31–57. For other ways in which algorithmic aggregations affect the social, see Safiya Umoja Noble, *Algorithms of Oppression: How Search Engines Reinforce Racism* (New York: New York University Press, 2018), 64–109; R. Joshua Scannell, "This Is Not *Minority Report*: Predictive Policing and Population Racism," in *Captivating Technology: Race, Carceral Technoscience, and Liberatory Imagination in Everyday Life*, ed. Ruha Benjamin (Durham, NC: Duke University Press, 2019), 107–29. Yet it was also the case that many scholars and artists used quantitative technologies to critique structures of racial oppression and offer alternative accounts of social life, as Autumn Womack argues in *The Matter of Black Living: The Aesthetic Experiment of Racial Data, 1880–1930* (Chicago: University of Chicago Press, 2022).

34. The policy of "One Laptop per Child" embodies this sentiment. For a history and analysis of this educational policy, see Morgan G. Ames, *The Charisma Machine: The Life, Death, and Legacy of One Laptop per Child* (Cambridge, MA: MIT Press, 2019).

35. The phrase first appears in Seymour Papert, *Mindstorms: Children, Computers, and Powerful Ideas* (New York: Basic Books, 1980). A mathematician with advanced training in both philosophy and psychology, Papert laments how many educational uses of computers have failed to "integrate computational thinking into everyday life" (182).

36. Jeannette M. Wing, "Computational Thinking," *Communications of the ACM* 49, no. 3 (March 2006): 33–34.

37. Jeannette M. Wing, "Computational Thinking and Thinking about Computing," *Philosophical Transactions of the Royal Society A* 366 (2008): 3719.

38. Mackenzie, "Undecidability," 363.

39. Sigmund Freud, "Constructions in Analysis," in *The Standard Edition of the Complete Psychological Works of Sigmund Freud* 23, ed. James Strachey (London: Hogarth, 1964), 268.

40. Other scholars have also noted how the experience of becoming computational affects the intimate and emotional registers of everyday life. Kris Cohen argues that computational media position users between publics of affiliation (intimacy) and populations constructed through massive data processing (abstraction). The user feels part of both relationalities at once, as though they are simultaneously connected and alone. Kris Cohen, *Never Alone, Except for Now* (Durham, NC: Duke University Press, 2017), 29–40. Rebecca B. Clark shows how the cultural functions assigned to data produce reactions like disgust. These reactions suggest that our relationship to massive data systems is simultaneously abstract and saturated in affective intensity. Rebecca B. Clark, *American Graphic: Disgust and Data in Contemporary Literature* (Stanford, CA: Stanford University Press, 2023). Wendy Hui Kyong Chun argues that a feeling of the "habitual" characterizes the embeddedness of new media in social life. Users often relate to technology through habit, picking up a smartphone immediately after waking in the morning or using geolocation services to map a relatively familiar route. Wendy Hui Kyong Chun, *Updating to Remain the Same: Habitual New Media* (Cambridge, MA: MIT Press, 2017), 7. Zara Dinnen similarly uses the phrase "the digital banal" to describe how computational technologies lead to an effacement of "the affective stakes of life determined by algorithms and life at the edge of the earth's resources." Zara Dinnen, *The Digital Banal: New Media and American Literature and Culture* (New York: Columbia University Press, 2021), 2. The design and ubiquity of technology leads us to forget their novelty.

41. Part of what I am trying to show in this book is that such a view of *experience* derives from a long-standing social philosophy that some intellectual historians call an ethics of authenticity. It would be confusing to pursue this point at this juncture of my introduction. While we're here among the endnotes, though, I would like to make a related point by citing Yves Citton's argument that the confused social relations created by digital technology dispel "our romantic addiction to a heroic, unrealistic, and self-illusory model of personal agency." Yves Citton, "Fictional Attachments and Literary Weavings in the Anthropocene," *New Literary History* 47, nos. 2 & 3 (Spring & Summer 2016): 311. In other words, the process of becoming computational undercuts a philosophical view of the self as the source of action—a fantasy about which I feel some ambivalence despite Citton's forceful critique. This confusion or compromising of personal agency will return as a central problem for an ethics of authenticity in the third chapter.

42. My approach is indebted to Raymond Williams's much-discussed phrase "structures of feeling" in *Marxism and Literature* (Oxford: Oxford University Press, 1977), 128–35; and Lauren Berlant's discussion of genre in *The Female Complaint: The Unfinished Business of Sentimentality in American Culture* (Durham, NC: Duke University Press, 2008). I engage with Berlant's ideas at greater length below, but they, too, investigate *genre* as a term that elucidates the character of contemporary experience.

43. I cite many of these scholars in subsequent pages, but I would also like to acknowledge a few other works that have influenced my thinking: David Fishelov, *Metaphors of Genre: The Role of Analogies in Genre Theory* (University Park: Pennsylvania State University Press, 1993); Wai Chee Dimock, "Genre as World System: Epic and Novel on Four Continents," *Narrative* 14, no. 1 (Jan. 2006): 85–101; Noël Carroll, *The Philosophy of Motion Pictures* (Malden, MA: Blackwell, 2008); John McGowan, *Pragmatist Politics: Making the Case for Liberal Democracy* (Minneapolis: University of Minnesota Press, 2012); and Kenneth W. Warren, "The Persistence of Genre," *Modern Language Quarterly* 81, no. 4 (Dec. 2020): 567–77.

44. For a modern example of this view, see George Steiner, "'Tragedy,' Reconsidered," in *Rethinking Tragedy*, ed. Rita Felski (Baltimore: Johns Hopkins University Press, 2008), 29–44.

45. Jacques Derrida, "The Law of Genre," trans. Avital Ronell, *Critical Inquiry* 7, no. 1 (Autumn 1980): 57. For an excellent appraisal of Derrida's view, see John Frow, "'Reproducibles, Rubrics, and Everything You Need': Genre Theory Today," *PMLA* 122, no. 5 (Oct. 2007): 1627–28.

46. Frye, *Anatomy of Criticism*, 163–85. Sigmund Freud presents his theory in *Jokes and Their Relation to the Unconscious* (1905).

47. Alexander Leggatt, *English Stage Comedy, 1490–1990: Five Centuries of a Genre* (London: Routledge, 2002), 1. In classics, a similar point is often made about the generationally different plays performed in the same festival context. As Michael Silk puts it, "Aristophanes' Old Comedy and Menander's New are too distinct (their repertoires are too different) to be identified as 'the same' genre." Michael Silk, "The Greek Dramatic Genres: Theoretical Perspectives," in *Greek Comedy and the Discourse of Genres*, ed. Emmanuela Bakola, Lucia Prauscello, and Mario Telò (Cambridge: Cambridge University Press, 2013), 24.

48. I use the phrase "genre performative" to describe this view in Benjamin Mangrum, "Tragedy, Realism, Skepticism," *Genre* 51, no. 3 (Dec. 2018): 209–36. Since the 1960s, many others have used Ludwig Wittgenstein's idea of "family resemblances" to articulate closely related theories of genre. See, e.g., Hjalmar Wennerberg, "The Concept of Family Resemblance in Wittgenstein's Later Philosophy," *Theoria* 33 (1967): 107–32; Alastair Fowler, *Kinds of Literature: An Introduction to the Theory of Genres and Modes* (Cambridge, MA: Harvard University Press, 1982), 40–43; David Fishelov, "Genre Theory and Family Resemblance—

Revisited," *Poetics* 20 (1991): 123–38; Marah Gubar, "On Not Defining Children's Literature," *PMLA* 126, no. 1 (2011): 209–16; and John Frow, *Genre*, 2nd ed. (London: Routledge, 2015), 59.

49. Fowler, *Kinds of Literature*, 47.

50. Noël Carroll, *Engaging the Moving Image* (New Haven, CT: Yale University Press, 2003), 4.

51. Many other scholars have resisted arguments about medium specificity. See Carroll, *Engaging the Moving Image*, 1–9; Kamilla Elliott, "Rethinking Formal-Cultural and Textual-Contextual Divides in Adaptation Studies," *Literature/Film Quarterly* 42, no. 4 (2014): 576–93; and Justus Nieland, *Happiness by Design: Modernism and Media in the Eames Era* (Minneapolis: University of Minnesota Press, 2020), 1–38.

52. Fowler's formulation exemplifies several aspects of my disagreement with strong nominalist approaches to genre, but they are not central to clarifying my own point, so I will levy those criticisms in this endnote. The first is that his use of the prime symbol creates more confusion than it solves. In physics, prime designates variables after an event. In mathematics, the symbol designates a variable related to or derived from some other point. In other words, there cannot be Zn' without some establishing event or point of reference. Fowler's metaphor presupposes the integrity of a fixed entity called Comedy out of which subsequent instances derive—the very idea he is rejecting. Perhaps the metaphor would fit with a theory of generic meaning as a kind of network, but the messiness of network theory would be at odds with Fowler's attempts to make genre criticism more historically bounded. Indeed, if we were to follow Fowler's recommendation and only make claims about Zn', we would need to treat particular comedies like self-contained wholes with fixed coordinates. Such an implausible view registers my second disagreement. Strong nominalism narrows and focuses and limits until all we have are fetishized particularities. Restricting criticism to statements about "genre at a particular stage" becomes just another "fixed historical kind," the older theory of genre that Fowler contrasts with his own approach (Fowler, *Kinds of Literature*, 37).

53. See, e.g., Simon Critchley, "Did You Hear the One about the Philosopher Writing a Book on Humour?" *Richmond Journal of Philosophy* 2 (Autumn 2002): 1–6, https://web.archive.org/web/20160329171824/http://www.richmond-philosophy.net/rjp/back_issues/rjp2_critchley.pdf.

54. My thinking here is indebted to Lauren Berlant's view of genre as "an aesthetic structure of affective expectation, an institution or formation that absorbs all kinds of small variations or modifications while promising that the persons transacting with it will experience the pleasure of encountering what they expected, with details varying the theme" (Berlant, *The Female Complaint*, 4).

55. Berlant, viii.

56. Frye, *Anatomy of Criticism*, 169.

57. This "strike-and-response sequence" would become a common trope in postwar science fiction. See David Seed, "The Brave New World of Computing in Post-War American Science Fiction," in *American Mythologies: New Essays on Contemporary Literature*, ed. William Blazek and Michael K. Glenday (Liverpool, UK: Liverpool University Press, 2005), 180.

58. For a study of the cultural and political imaginary that follows from this newfound scale of global destruction, see Rey Chow, *The Age of the World Target: Self-Referentiality in War, Theory, and Comparative Work* (Durham, NC: Duke University Press, 2006).

59. See, e.g., Kevin Roose, "A.I. Poses 'Risk of Extinction,' Industry Leaders Warn," *New York Times*, March 30, 2023; and Jacob Stern, "AI Is Like . . . Nuclear Weapons?" *The Atlantic*, March 26, 2023.

60. Kathleen Miles, "Artificial Intelligence May Doom the Human Race within a Century, Oxford Professor Says," *Huffington Post*, Feb. 4, 2015, https://www.huffpost.com/entry/artificial-intelligence-oxford_n_5689858. Bostrom's original formulation of this thought experiment may be found in Nick Bostrom, "Ethical Issues in Advanced Artificial Intelligence," *Cognitive, Emotive, and Ethical Aspects of Decision Making in Humans and in Artificial Intelligence* 2, ed. Iva Smit et al. (Ontario: Institute of Advanced Studies in Systems Research and Cybernetics, 2003), 12–17.

61. Hannah Arendt, *Eichmann in Jerusalem: A Report on the Banality of Evil* (New York: Viking, 1963).

1. The One about Race and Robots

1. Paul R. Josephson, *Industrialized Nature: Brute Force Technology and the Transformation of the Natural World* (Washington, DC: Island Press, 2002), 54.

2. Duncan A. Stacey, *Sockeye and Tinplate: Technological Change in the Fraser River Canning Industry, 1871–1912* (Victoria, BC: British Columbia Provincial Museum, 1982), 50. I would like to thank Henry Zhang for bringing this machine to my attention after I presented an earlier version of this chapter at Yale University's Americanist Colloquium in 2022.

3. Josephson, *Industrialized Nature*, 54.

4. Stacey, *Sockeye and Tinplate*, 50.

5. Kevin Morley and David Robins, *Spaces of Identity: Global Media, Electronic Landscapes, and Cultural Boundaries* (London: Routledge, 1995), 147–73.

6. David S. Roh, Betsy Huang, and Greta A. Niu, "Desiring Machines, Repellant Subjects: A Conclusion," in *Techno-Orientalism: Imagining Asia in Speculative Fiction, History, and Media*, ed. David S. Roh, Betsy Huang, and Greta A. Niu (New Brunswick, NJ: Rutgers University Press, 2015), 224, 225.

7. Roh, Huang, and Niu, 225.

8. Carey McWilliams, *Factories in the Field: The Story of Migratory Farm Labor in California* (1939; Berkeley: University of California Press, 2000).

9. This proximity illustrates Thomas Hobbes's view that the comic derives from "the apprehension of some deformed thing in another, by comparison whereof they suddenly applaud themselves." Thomas Hobbes, *The Essential Leviathan: A Modernized Edition*, ed. Nancy A. Stanlick and Daniel P. Collette (Indianapolis, IN: Hackett, 2016), 34. For Hobbes, the machinery of laughter produces a sense of superiority; it marks out what is different to identify what is normative. For an overview of the superiority theory of laughter, see John Morreall, *The Philosophy of Laughter and Humor* (Albany: State University of New York Press, 1987), 129–31. A minor problem I have with the superiority theory is that Hobbes ascribes overly coherent motives to humor. In contrast, compare Jean-Paul Sartre's analysis of the "joy of hating" in *Portrait of the Anti-Semite* (London: Secker and Warburg, 1948), 21. I think Sartre is right that certain forms of racist comedy give racists the feeling of freedom from logic.

We can further revise Hobbes's theory of comic superiority with Wendy Hui Kyong Chun's view of race as a technology. Chun views race as a "mapping tool" for producing images of the social. Wendy Hui Kyong Chun, "Introduction: Race and/as Technology; or, How to Do Things to Race," *Camera Obscura* 24, no. 1 (2009): 10. One of the many curious features of racial identity is that it supposedly resides in the body and yet refers to a collective form of identity: to be racialized is to be the instance of a structure. Race thus "turns the body into a signifier" (14). The cultural phenomena examined in this chapter exemplify how race *decouples* from the body and attaches, instead, to automated technologies.

10. The idea that nature—an untouched, organic, and sublime entity—is associated with virtue has been historicized by several scholars in the environmental humanities. Often, this view is rooted in the genre of the pastoral. See, e.g., Lawrence Buell, "American Pastoral Ideology Reappraised," *American Literary History* 1, no. 1 (1989): 1–29; and Terry Gifford, *Pastoral*, 2nd ed. (London: Routledge, 2020), 14–46. For an overview of this "moralism," see Nicole Seymour, *Bad Environmentalism: Irony and Irreverence in the Ecological Age* (Minneapolis: University of Minnesota Press, 2018), 16–19; and Jack Halberstam, *Wild Things: The Disorder of Desire* (Durham, NC: Duke University Press, 2020).

11. Stefano Fiori, *Machines, Bodies, and Invisible Hands: Metaphors of Order and Economic Theory in Adam Smith* (Cham, Switzerland: Palgrave Macmillan, 2021), 31–63.

12. René Descartes, "Treatise on Man," in *The Philosophical Writings of Descartes* 1, trans. John Cottingham, Robert Stoothoff, and Dugald Murdoch (Cambridge: Cambridge University Press, 1985), 99.

13. Descartes, 99.

14. Mary Poovey, *Making a Social Body: British Cultural Formation, 1830–1864* (Chicago: University of Chicago Press, 1995), 38.

15. Poovey, 85.

16. William Byrd to Charles Boyle, Earl of Orrery, July 5, 1726, in Marion Tinling, ed., *The Correspondence of the Three William Byrds of Westover, Virginia, 1684–1776* 1 (Charlottesville: Virginia Historical Society, 1977), 355.

17. For an analysis of the fungibility of the slave, see Saidiya V. Hartman, *Scenes of Subjection: Terror, Slavery, and Self-Making in Nineteenth-Century America* (New York: Oxford University Press, 1997), 20–23.

18. Zakiyyah Iman Jackson, *Being Human: Matter and Meaning in an Antiblack World* (New York: New York University Press, 2020), 35.

19. Robert Montgomery Bird, *Peter Pilgrim; or, a Rambler's Recollection*, vol. 1 (Philadelphia: Lea & Blanchard, 1838), 103. Hereafter cited parenthetically.

20. Stephen Best, *None like Us: Blackness, Belonging, Aesthetic Life* (Durham, NC: Duke University Press, 2018), 24.

21. Jones's use of the possessive pronoun *my* similarly indicates the continuity between the inventor and southern slaveholders. The mechanical slave is chattel—an object of capital—as well as a use-object that creates surplus value for capital exchange. The status of being both possession and instrument is echoed in his use of the term *patent*. It is possible that this adjective refers to the leather used in the assembly of the machine, as in *patent leather*. It is also possible that the adjective means "obvious" or "easily recognizable," as in *patently false*. Still another possibility is that the term *patent* recalls proprietary production—a sense reaffirmed in 1836 by a major update to US patent law (only two years before the publication of Bird's novel). Each reading of *patent* links blackness and objectness. In Bird's novel, it is patently obvious that a laboring machine must be a racialized object.

22. Jay David Bolter and Richard Grusin, *Remediation: Understanding New Media* (Cambridge, MA: MIT Press, 1999), 2, 44. A classic example of this double logic is the design of word-processing software, which recalls certain features of the typewriter but offers hundreds of additional capabilities that multiply the kinds of writing one can do while using the digital medium.

23. The remediation of race mirrors Chun's observation that race does not require the body to be the primary racial signifier. See Chun, "Introduction: Race and/as Technology," 14.

24. Gregory J. E. Rawlins, *Slaves of the Machine: The Quickening of Computer Technology* (Cambridge, MA: MIT Press, 1997), 7. As far as I have been able to discover, Babbage never compares his engine to a slave—an analogy that likely would have been distasteful to those in the reform-minded circles that Babbage often frequented. Still, the fact that the analogy seems plausible in a history of

the computer published in the 1990s illustrates how racial ideas about labor would continue to have explanatory purchase when describing automated technology. If plantation owners believed enslaved peoples were technologies that could be automated, the inverse of this analogy would prove to be equally seductive for many: any technology that can be automated has become a slave to its users.

25. See Tom Standage, *The Mechanical Turk: The True Story of the Chess-Playing Machine That Fooled the World* (New York: Penguin, 2003).

26. Nathan Ensmenger, "Is Chess the Drosophila of Artificial Intelligence? A Social History of an Algorithm," *Social Studies of Science* 42, no. 1 (2011): 9.

27. Edward Sylvester Ellis, "The Huge Hunter; or, The Steam Man of the Prairies," *Beadle's Half Dime Library* 11, no. 271 (1882): 2.

28. Ellis, 2.

29. Eric Lott, *Love and Theft: Blackface Minstrelsy and the American Working Class* (New York: Oxford University Press, 1995), 149.

30. Ellis, "The Huge Hunter," 2.

31. Lott, *Love and Theft*, 141.

32. L. Frank Baum, *Ozma of Oz*, illustrated by John R. Neill (1907; New York: Dover, 1985), 52. Hereafter cited parenthetically.

33. L. Frank Baum, *The Wonderful Wizard of Oz* (Chicago: Geo. M. Hill, 1900), 131.

34. L. Frank Baum, *Tik-Tok of Oz* (Chicago: Reilly and Lee, 1914), 89.

35. Paul M. Abraham and Stuart Kenter, "Tik-Tok and the Three Laws of Robotics," *Science Fiction Studies* 5, no. 1 (March 1978): 79n11.

36. Harriet Beecher Stowe, *Uncle Tom's Cabin* (New York: Norton, 2018), 228; W. T. Lhamon Jr., *Raising Cain: Blackface Performance from Jim Crown to Hip Hop* (Cambridge, MA: Harvard University Press, 2001), 143.

37. Christopher Corbo, "The 'Topsification' of *Uncle Tom's Cabin*," *Theatre Symposium* 29 (2022): 122.

38. Corbo, 122. The inhabitants of Oz constantly refuse to believe the copper man is alive, yet it is never explained why (as his accompanying Smith & Tinker instructions put it) he "Thinks, Speaks, Acts, and Does Everything but Live" (55). As Abraham and Kenter note, "Never do any of the Oz characters challenge the notion that the Tin Woodman is 'alive' yet all indulge in blunt constant denials of this state for Tik-Tok." Abraham and Kenter, "Tik-Tok and the Three Laws," 79n11, 69. The difference is not material or physiological but seems to be based solely on the idea that machinery cannot be alive. The Tin Woodman, in contrast, has magically been invested with the spark of life.

39. Walter Benjamin, *Illuminations: Essays and Reflections*, trans. Harry Zohn (New York: Schocken, 1969), 221.

40. Henri Bergson, *Laughter: An Essay on the Meaning of the Comic*, trans.

Cloudesley Brereton and Fred Rothwell (1911; New York: Dover, 2005), 14, 26 (emphasis in original).

41. Bergson, 27.

42. Like twenty-first-century robots, when Tik-Tok behaves like a dull machine, his character does not create comic effects. Studies of human-robot interactions have demonstrated the user's need to find affinity with the machine. Affinity is typically created through mimetic strategies like anthropomorphism. See Jakub Złotowski et al., "Anthropomorphism: Opportunities and Challenges in Human-Robot Interaction," *International Journal of Social Robotics* 7 (2015): 347–60; Christoph Bartneck et al., "The Influence of Robot Anthropomorphism on the Feelings of Embarrassment When Interacting with Robots," *Journal of Behavioral Robotics* 1, no. 2 (2010): 109–15; and Brian R. Duffy, "Anthropomorphism and the Social Robot," *Robotics and Autonomous Systems* 42, no. 3–4 (March 2003): 177–90.

43. Michael North, *Machine-Age Comedy* (Oxford: Oxford University Press, 2009), 19.

44. North, 9. In a sense, this hostility toward inauthenticity affirms Simon Critchley's claim that humor "recalls us to the modesty and limitedness of the human condition," which calls "not [for] Promethean authenticity but a laughable inauthenticity." Simon Critchley, *On Humour* (London: Routledge, 2002), 102. In other words, humor is not opposed to inauthenticity but often relies on its presence.

45. "Brain Servant," Museum Exhibit Label, MIT Museum (Cambridge, MA), viewed on Oct. 22, 2023.

46. Bob Johnson, *Mineral Rites: An Archaeology of the Fossil Economy* (Baltimore: Johns Hopkins University Press, 2019), 75–76.

47. Joel Chandler Harris, *Uncle Remus: His Songs and His Sayings* (New York: Grosset & Dunlap, 1921), 221.

48. For a history of Rastus in advertising, including a stint as a racist trope on boxes for Cream of Wheat, see Marilyn Kern-Foxworth, *Aunt Jemima, Uncle Ben, and Rastus: Blacks in Advertising, Yesterday, Today, and Tomorrow* (Westport, CT: Greenwood, 1994), 41–46; Moira F. Harris, "Ho-Ho-Ho! It Bears Repeating—Advertising Characters in the Land of Sky Blue Waters," *Minnesota History* 57, no. 1 (Spring 2000), 24–25.

49. E. C. Taylor, "Machines That Are Almost Human," *Buffalo Center Tribune*, Buffalo Center, Iowa, April 16, 1931, 6. I would like to thank Mark Szarko for his herculean efforts in finding a facsimile of this news article.

50. Scott Schaut, *Robots of Westinghouse, 1924–Today* (Mansfield, OH: Mansfield Memorial Museum, 2006), 56.

51. See Schaut, 19–62.

52. "Presenting Katrina Van Televox," *Kerrville (TX) Mountain Sun*, May 8, 1930,

8, https://cyberneticzoo.com/robots/1930-katrina-van-televox-westinghouse-american/.

53. "Miss Katrina Van Televox: Mechanical Wonder Maiden," *Altoona (PA) Mirror*, Oct. 3, 1930), https://cyberneticzoo.com/robots/1930-katrina-van-televox-westinghouse-american/.

54. Sarah Murray argues that Katrina typified how "protocomputing" discourse imagined technology liberating women from "domestic toil." At the same time, the construction of these "'mechanized mothers,' 'mobile maids,' and autonomous vacuum cleaners" reinforced the association between domestic labor and the social identities assigned to women. Sarah Murray, "A Warm Meal and Kisses Too: The Sensible Sensationalism of ProtoComputing," *Feminist Media Histories* 8, no. 4 (2022): 74.

55. "Mechanical Men That Excel Any Human Being," *San Antonio Light*, Sept. 6, 1931, 48.

56. Johnson, *Mineral Rites*, 63.

57. North, *Machine-Age Comedy*, 4.

58. For a history of the influence of Čapek's play, see Ron Eglash, "Broken Metaphor: The Master-Slave Analogy in Technical Literature," *Technology and Culture* 48, no. 2 (April 2007): 360–69.

59. O. O. Binder, "You'll Own 'Slaves' by 1965," *Mechanix Illustrated*, Jan. 1957, 62, https://archive.org/details/sim_todays-homeowner-solutions_1957-01_53_1/page/62/mode/2up. Although I have not been able to confirm it, O. O. Binder appears to be Otto Binder, who published science fiction with his brother Earl under the pseudonym Eando Binder. The brothers wrote several robot stories in the 1930s, including one titled "I, Robot" (1939), which anticipates many of Asimov's later interests in the robot's social role.

60. Ruha Benjamin, *Race after Technology: Abolitionist Tools for the New Jim Code* (Medford, MA: Polity, 2019), 56.

61. Jason Resnikoff, "The Myth of Black Obsolescence," *International Labor and Working-Class History* 102 (2023): 124.

62. "Black Workers Protest UAW Racism March on Cobo Hall," 1969, file 24, box 1, Detroit Revolutionary Movements, Acc #874, Walter P. Reuther Library. quoted in Resnikoff, "The Myth of Black Obsolescence," 125.

63. Karel Čapek, *R.U.R.*, trans. Cathy Porter and Peter Majer (1921; London: Methuen Drama, 1999), 4, 3. Hereafter cited parenthetically.

64. Despina Kakoudaki, *Anatomy of a Robot: Literature, Cinema, and the Cultural Work of Artificial People* (New Brunswick, NJ: Rutgers University Press, 2014), 144.

65. Northrop Frye, *Anatomy of Criticism: Four Essays* (Princeton, NJ: Princeton University Press, 1957), 169.

66. Frye, 169.

67. Leo Marx, *The Machine in the Garden: Technology and the Pastoral Ideal in America* (1964; New York: Oxford University Press, 2000), 169.

68. Isaac Asimov, *I, Robot* (New York: Ballantine, 1950), 16. Hereafter cited parenthetically.

69. De Witt Douglas Kilgore, "Difference Engine: Aliens, Robots, and Other Racial Matters in the History of Science Fiction," *Science Fiction Studies* 37, no. 1 (March 2010): 17.

70. Samuel R. Delany, "The Necessity of Tomorrows," in *Starboard Wine: More Notes on the Language of Science Fiction* (Westport, NY: Dragon, 1984), 28.

71. Delany, "The Necessity of Tomorrows," 29. For an extended but related discussion of these links between slavery, robots, and white expectations for Blackness, see Kakoudaki, *Anatomy of a Robot*, 114–72.

72. Joel Chandler Harris, *Nights with Uncle Remus* (New York: Houghton Mifflin, 1917), 3.

73. Asimov's robots have what he calls a "positronic brain," which implies that electrons and their antiparticle, the positron, somehow facilitate mechanical thinking. Asimov does not elaborate on the nature of the positronic brain, and, admittedly, he does not define it as a computer. Still, "positronic brain" seems like a plausible (if also idiosyncratic) iteration on the midcentury description of computers as "electronic brains." For a possible history of Asimov's sources, see Donald Palumbo, "Chaos-Theory Concepts and Structures in Asimov's Robot Stories and Novels: The Positronic Brain and Feedback Loops," *Foundation* 75 (Spring 1999): 63–77.

74. Christina Ho, "The New Meritocracy or Over-Schooled Robots? Public Attitudes on Asian-Australian Education Cultures," *Journal of Ethnic and Migration Studies* 43, no. 14 (2017): 2360.

75. Megan Watkins and Greg Noble, *Disposed to Learn: Schooling, Ethnicity, and the Scholarly Habitus* (London: Bloomsbury Academic, 2013), 96. Cited in Ho, "The New Meritocracy or Over-Schooled Robots?," 2355.

76. Chun, "Introduction: Race and/as Technology," 9.

77. Grace Wang, "A Shot at Half-Exposure: Asian Americans in Reality TV Shows," *Television & New Media* 11, no. 5 (2010): 405.

78. Jessica Yu, "When We Say Smart Asian Girl We Don't Mean Smart (White) Girl: The Figure of the Asian Automaton and the Adolescent Artist in the *Künstlerroman* Genre," *Journal of Asia-Pacific Pop Culture* 4, no. 2 (2019): 172.

79. Yu, 182.

80. Seo-Young Chu examines still another version of this stereotype in contemporary film, although her emphasis is on "yellow peril" narratives that become uncanny. Characters like Zao, the villain in *Die Another Day* (2002), and the eponymous "Chinaman" in Sax Rohmer's novel *The Insidious Dr. Fu-Manchu* (1913) "elicit intellectual uncertainty over whether a 'type' of person is genuinely

human and alive." Seo-Young Chu, "I, Stereotype: Detained in the Uncanny Valley," in *Techno-Orientalism: Imagining Asia in Speculative Fiction, History, and Media*, ed. David S. Roh, Betsy Huang, and Greta A. Niu (New Brunswick, NJ: Rutgers University Press, 2015), 78. The uncanniness of these other stereotypes analogizes the Asian characters to robots in ways that are closer to horror. To state the obvious, not every racist stereotype is a comic one.

81. Kenneth Burke, "(Nonsymbolic) Motion / (Symbolic) Action," *Critical Inquiry* (Summer 1978): 814.

82. Burke, 826, 822, 829.

83. Arthur Johnson, "The World's Biggest Comeback," *Report on Business Magazine*, June 1989, 41.

84. Lawrence Grossberg, "The Politics of Youth Culture: Some Observations on Rock and Roll in American Culture," *Social Text*, no. 8 (Winter 1983–84): 105.

85. Burke, "(Nonsymbolic) Motion / (Symbolic) Action," 809.

86. Despina Kakoudaki, *Anatomy of a Robot: Literature, Cinema, and the Cultural Work of Artificial People* (New Brunswick, NJ: Rutgers University Press, 2014), 144.

2. The One about Being Generic

1. Alan Liu, *The Laws of Cool: Knowledge Work and the Culture of Information* (Chicago: University of Chicago Press, 2004), 78–79.

2. Liu, 110. Liu borrows the term *informating* from Shoshana Zuboff, *In the Age of the Smart Machine* (New York: Basic Books, 1988).

3. Liu, *The Laws of Cool*, 141.

4. Otto Friedrich, "The Computer Moves In," *Time*, Jan. 3, 1983, 15.

5. Friedrich, 15.

6. It is not coincidental that the postracial "You" appears just before Barack Obama announced his presidential campaign on February 10, 2007. Postracial imagery was very much of the moment in late 2006 and early 2007. To see the comic resonances of this imagery, I recommend Colson Whitehead, "The Year of Living Postracially," *New York Times*, Nov. 3, 2009, https://www.nytimes.com/2009/11/04/opinion/04whitehead.html. For an excellent analysis of the "figural logic" at play in Obama's public persona, see Lee Konstantinou, "Barack Obama's Postironic Bildungsroman," in *Barack Obama's Literary Legacy: Readings of "Dreams from My Father,"* ed. Richard Purcell and Henry Veggian (New York: Palgrave Macmillan, 2016), 119–40.

7. Roberto Esposito, "The Person and Human Life," trans. Diana Garvin and Thomas Kelso, in *Theory after "Theory,"* ed. Jane Elliott and Derek Attridge (New York: Routledge, 2011), 205.

8. Friedrich A. Kittler, *Gramophone, Film, Typewriter*, trans. Geoffrey Winthrop-Young and Michael Wutz (Stanford, CA: Stanford University Press, 1999), 1.

9. Kittler, *Gramophone, Film, Typewriter*, 1–2. Related objections to the effects of electronic media on reading may be found in Sven Birkerts, *The Gutenberg Elegies: The Fate of Reading in an Electronic Age* (Faber and Faber, 1995).

10. I am once again adapting Raymond Williams's phrase "structure of feeling" from *Marxism and Literature* (Oxford: Oxford University Press, 1977), 132. For a perceptive discussion of the phrase and its limits, see Mitchum Huehls, "Structures of Feeling: Or, How to Do Things (or Not) with Books," *Contemporary Literature* 51, no. 2 (Summer 2010): 419–28.

11. Aziz Ansari, with Eric Klinenberg, *Modern Romance* (New York: Penguin, 2015), 48.

12. Ansari, 48, 241.

13. See Benjamin Mangrum, "Tragedy, Realism, Skepticism," *Genre: Forms of Discourse* 51, no.3 (Dec. 2018): 209–36. This approach differs from what Gérard Genette refers to as "genre indications" in that the latter are (a) exclusively paratextual and (b) confined to textual genres. See Gérard Genette, *Paratexts: Thresholds of Interpretation*, trans. Jane E. Lewin (Cambridge: Cambridge University Press, 1997), 94–103. Nick Marx and Matt Sienkiewicz call comic cues in television "generic practices." For their excellent discussion of generic practices, see "Introduction to Genre," in *The Comedy Studies Reader*, ed. Nick Marx and Matt Sienkiewicz (Austin: University of Texas Press, 2018), 135.

14. For a discussion of satire's social hermeneutics, see Roger J. Kreuz and Richard M. Roberts, "On Satire and Parody: The Importance of Being Ironic," *Metaphor and Symbolic Activity* 8, no. 2 (1993): 100–102. I should note, though, that I do not buy Kreuz and Roberts's distinction between satire and parody. Although satire tends to have a more specific event or object in mind than parody, as they claim, the two often seem to blend into one another in practice.

15. Tina Fey, *Bossypants* (New York: Little, Brown, 2011), 190.

16. Fey, 191.

17. Fey, 191.

18. Fey, 192.

19. Fey, 193.

20. Northrop Frye, "Characterization in Shakespearean Comedy," *Shakespeare Quarterly* 4, no. 3 (July 1953): 277.

21. For more on "duration" and narrative, see Gérard Genette, *Narrative Discourse: An Essay in Method*, trans. Jane Lewin (Ithaca, NY: Cornell University Press, 1980), 86–112.

22. Lauren Berlant, *On the Inconvenience of Other People* (Durham, NC: Duke University Press, 2022), 27.

23. Ralph Waldo Emerson, "Nature," in *Essays: First and Second Series* (New York: Library of America, 2010), 311.

24. Emerson, 311.

25. Northrop Frye, "The Argument of Comedy," *English Institute Essays 1948* (New York: Columbia University Press, 1949), reprinted in *Henry the Fourth, Parts I and II: Critical Essays*, ed. David Bevington (New York: Garland, 1986), 181.

26. Frye, "The Argument of Comedy," 182.

27. Curtis Sittenfeld, *Romantic Comedy* (New York: Penguin, 2023), 286. Hereafter cited parenthetically.

28. Viktor Shklovsky, "Art, as Device," trans. Alexandra Berlina, *Poetics Today* 36, no. 3 (Sept. 2015): 162. Alexandra Berlina discusses the difficulty of translating *ostranenie* in a translator's note that precedes Shklovsky's essay (152–54). I use the term "defamiliarization" rather than Berlina's recommended "enstrangement" solely for the ability to link the former term's prefix with other key terms in this book.

29. Sianne Ngai, *Theory of the Gimmick* (Cambridge, MA: Harvard University Press, 2020), 23, 97.

30. John McCarthy, "Networks Considered Harmful for Electronic Mail," *Communications of the ACM* 32, no. 13 (Dec. 1989): 1389–90.

31. Esther Milne, *Email and the Everyday: Stories of Disclosure, Trust, and Digital Labor* (Cambridge, MA: MIT Press, 2021), 4.

32. Many of these criticisms derive from Milne, *Email and the Everyday*, 3–4, 99–101.

33. For a history of the medium, see Craig Partridge, "The Technical Development of Internet Email," *IEEE Annals of the History of Computing* (2008): 3–29; Esther Milne, *Letters, Postcards, Email: Technologies of Presence* (New York: Routledge, 2010), 137–62.

34. To be sure, writers and artists have used other media as images of national and interpersonal connection. See Mark Goble, *Beautiful Circuits: Modernism and the Mediated Life* (New York: Columbia University Press, 2010): 29–148.

35. Touch-screen technology evokes similar connotations. See Michele White, *Touch Screen Theory: Digital Devices and Feelings* (Cambridge, MA: MIT Press, 2022), 1–32.

36. The most common reference for slang usage today is probably urban dictionary.com, which provides several examples for the sexual connotations of *inbox*. I would like to credit Joaquin Terrones for bringing this double entendre to my attention.

37. Milne, *Letters, Postcards, Email*, 165.

38. Milne, *Letters, Postcards, Email*, 169.

39. Another closely related cultural logic at play here is what N. Katherine Hayles calls the "data made flesh" sensibility that spread along with computational technologies after the Second World War. This sensibility imagined human beings as "information-processing entities who are *essentially* similar to

intelligent machines." N. Katherine Hayles, *How We Became Posthuman: Virtual Bodies in Cybernetics, Literature, and Informatics* (Chicago: University of Chicago Press, 1999), 23. If the human is functionally a complex assemblage of information, as postwar cyberneticists maintained, then it is hardly a leap in logic to include a person's information technology as an extended feature of the self. The cyberneticist Gregory Bateson makes this argument in his influential claim about the "ecology of mind": "Suppose I am a blind man, and I use a stick. I go tap, tap, tap. Where do *I* start? . . . The stick is a pathway along which transforms of difference are being transmitted." Gregory Bateson, *Steps to an Ecology of Mind* (Chicago: University of Chicago Press, 2000), 465. In this view, the sense of an "I" extends beyond the body through the analog and digital tools we use to navigate the world.

40. Hayles, *How We Became Posthuman*, 7.
41. John Seabrook, "E-mail from Bill," *New Yorker*, Jan. 10, 1994, 48.
42. Seabrook, 52.
43. Seabrook, 50–51.
44. Seabrook, 50.
45. For an excellent analysis of how this sort of banality shapes contemporary American culture, see Zara Dinnen, *The Digital Banal: New Media and American Literature and Culture* (New York: Columbia University Press, 2021).
46. Lee Sproull and Sara Kiesler, "Reducing Social Context Cues: Electronic Mail in Organizational Communication," *Management Science* 32, no. 11 (Nov. 1986), 1507.
47. Sproull and Kiesler, 1501. A closely related phenomenon has also been observed in text messaging. Aziz Ansari and Eric Klinenberg provide examples of how reduced social context cues affect romantic interactions via text messaging in *Modern Romance* (42–48).
48. Nora Ephron, *I Remember Nothing* (New York: Vintage, 2011), 103.
49. Ephron, 103.
50. Ephron, 104.
51. Ephron, 104.
52. Sproull and Kiesler, "Reducing Social Context Cues," 1501.
53. George Saunders, *Tenth of December* (London: Bloomsbury, 2013), 83.
54. *My Architect: A Son's Journey*, dir. Nathaniel Kahn (New Yorker Video, 2003). W. J. T. Mitchell provides another influential version of this question in "What Do Pictures 'Really' Want?," *October* 77 (Summer 1996): 71–82.
55. In her study of the tools of scientific inquiry at MIT, Sherry Turkle asks, "What does simulation want?" Technologies that simulate nuclear explosions or molecular combinations have substantial benefits for scientific advancement, but Turkle shows how those technologies also affect the cultures of science. Sherry Turkle, *Simulation and Its Discontents* (Cambridge, MA: MIT Press,

2009), 6. Ed Finn similarly employs this design theory to examine the role of algorithms in contemporary society. Netflix, for example, "ultimately wants its consumers to love . . . not just the content but Netflix itself: the application, the service, the platform." Ed Finn, *What Algorithms Want: Imagination in the Age of Computing* (Cambridge, MA: MIT Press, 2017), 104. The design of Netflix's recommendation algorithm is self-referential (i.e., it prioritizes Netflix-produced content), thus aspiring to deepen user affinity with the platform.

56. Sproull and Kiesler, "Reducing Social Context Cues," 1497. For an excellent overview of more recent scholarship, see Milne, *Email and the Everyday*, 97–121.

57. Seabrook, "E-mail from Bill," 48.

58. This complaint about romantic expectations predates Hollywood. See Elaine Tyler May, *Great Expectations: Marriage and Divorce in Post-Victorian America* (Chicago: University of Chicago Press, 1980), 49–72. See also Nancy F. Cott, *Public Vows: A History of Marriage and the Nation* (Cambridge, MA: Harvard University Press, 2000).

59. See Lisa O'Connell, *The Origins of the English Marriage Plot: Literature, Politics, and Religion in the Eighteenth Century* (Cambridge: Cambridge University Press, 2019).

60. Some critics argue that Austen recognizes the literary constraints and social conservatism of this plot structure, retooling it for protofeminist ends. See Julie Shaffer, "Not Subordinate: Empowering Women in the Marriage Plot: The Novels of Frances Burney, Maria Edgeworth, and Jane Austen," *Criticism* 34, no. 1 (Winter 1992): 51–73.

61. O'Connell, *Origins of the English Marriage Plot*, 221.

62. O'Connell, 213, 222.

63. Intriguingly consistent with O'Connell's reading of Austen is the fact that Sally and Noah marry not in an urban center but in a relatively secluded location. They also first have sex and develop a more formalized romantic relationship in his remote estate, a plot device that seems to recall the settings for many of Austen's romantic couplings. See O'Connell, 219–22.

64. Versions of these criticisms may be found in Linda Bamber, *Comic Women, Tragic Men: A Study of Gender and Genre in Shakespeare* (Stanford, CA: Stanford University Press, 1982); Rachel Blau DuPlessis, *Writing beyond the Ending* (Bloomington: Indiana University Press, 1985); Joseph Allen Boone, *Tradition Counter Tradition: Love and the Form of Fiction* (Chicago: University of Chicago Press, 1987); Nancy Armstrong, *Desire and Domesticity: A Political History of the Novel* (Oxford: Oxford University Press, 1990); Rachel M. Brownstein, *Becoming a Heroine: Reading about Women in Novels* (New York: Columbia University Press, 1994); Leo Bersani, "Against Monogamy," *Oxford Literary Review* 20, no.1/2 (1998): 3–21; Anita Levy, *Reproductive Urges: Popular Novel-Reading, Sexu-*

ality, and the English Nation (Philadelphia: University of Pennsylvania Press, 1999); Franco Moretti, "Serious Century," in *The Novel*, vol. 1, *History, Geography, and Culture*, ed. Franco Moretti (Princeton, NJ: Princeton University Press, 2006), 396; Sara Ahmed, *The Promise of Happiness* (Durham, NC: Duke University Press, 2010), 21–49; Hilary Radner, "Pretty Is as Pretty Does: Free Enterprise and the Marriage Plot," in *Film Theory Goes to the Movies: Cultural Analysis of Contemporary Film*, ed. Jim Collins, Hilary Radner, and Ava Preacher Collins (New York: Routledge, 2012), 56–76; Mary-Catherine Harrison, "Reading the Marriage Plot," *Journal of Family Theory & Review* 6, no. 1 (2014), 112–31; and Valerie Forman, "Constructing White Privilege: Transatlantic Slavery, Reproduction, and the Segregation of the Marriage Plot in the Late Seventeenth Century," in *The Routledge Companion to Women, Sex, and Gender in the Early British Colonial World*, ed. Kimberly Anne Coles and Eve Keller (New York: Routledge, 2018), 304–21.

65. Frank's critique echoes Marxist arguments about the effects of modern technology on workers. (Frank, not incidentally, is later described as the "greatest living expert" on Julius and Ethel Rosenberg, another sign that the film's satirical treatment of Frank extends to his embrace of radical chic more generally.) Versions of his assessment appear in Harry Braverman, *Labor and Monopoly Capital: The Degradation of Work in the Twentieth Century* (1974; New York: Monthly Review, 1998). For Marx's view that automation and technology alienate workers, see Karl Marx, *Grundrisse* (New York: Penguin, 1993), 670–711.

66. It is certainly ironic that the sound of dial-up and AOL's default notification are signs of an unconventional romantic union. As David Croteau and William Hoynes explain, the AOL corporation "became the world's largest Internet service provider by making the confusing jungle of the Internet simpler and less intimidating for technologically unsophisticated first-time users." AOL was a massive corporation that standardized internet applications. A little more than two years after the release of *You've Got Mail*, AOL purchased the much larger Time Warner to form a massive conglomerate that hoped to integrate media: "on the Internet, AOL planned to promote [Time Warner's] CNN. On television, CNN would promote AOL." The fact that the production company Warner Bros. distributed a film that promoted AOL exemplifies how the industry had become thoroughly consolidated. David Croteau and William Hoynes, *The Business of Media: Corporate Media and the Public Interest*, 2nd ed. (Thousand Oaks, CA: Pine Forge, 2006), 3.

67. Scholars tend to distinguish between two phases in the New Hollywood, and in this schema, Ephron would fall within the second, more commercial phase. See Derek Nystrom, "The New Hollywood," in *American Film History: Selected Readings, 1960 to the Present*, ed. Cynthia Lucia, Roy Grundmann, and Art Simon (Chichester, West Sussex: John Wiley, 2016), 87–104.

68. See Claire Jenkins, "'Counter Cinema' in the Mainstream," *Feminist Media Studies* 22, no. 5 (2022): 1179–94; and Tania Modleski, "An Affair to Forget: Melancholia in Bromantic Comedy," *Camera Obscura* 29, no. 2 (2014): 121–22. The films themselves also have a long history of positioning the professional lives of women in a fraught relation to the genre's conventional drive toward a heterosexual union. See Kathrina Glitre, *Hollywood Romantic Comedy: States of Union, 1934–1965* (Manchester, UK: Manchester University Press, 2006), 91–110.

69. Lauren Berlant, *The Female Complaint: The Unfinished Business of Sentimentality in American Culture* (Durham, NC: Duke University Press, 2008), viii, 210.

70. Berlant, 212.

71. Jenkins, "Counter Cinema," 1185.

72. Deborah Jermyn, "The Contemptible Realm of the Romcom Queen: Nancy Meyers, Cultural Value, and Romantic Comedy," in *Women Do Genre in Film and Television*, ed. Mary Harrod and Katarzyna Paszkiewicz (New York: Routledge, 2017), 58.

73. Geoff King, *New Hollywood Cinema: An Introduction* (New York: Columbia University Press, 2002), 140.

74. King, *New Hollywood Cinema*, 140.

75. King, *New Hollywood Cinema*, 140.

76. Fox's sarcasm recalls the historical conflict between chains and independent stores in the book retail industry since the 1970s. For an excellent history of this conflict, see Laura J. Miller, *Reluctant Capitalists: Bookselling and the Culture of Consumption* (Chicago: University of Chicago Press, 2006).

77. Ryan's performance may also signify the invitation to ongoing interpretation that Leo Bersani and Ulysse Dutoit associate with "expressiveness" in acting: "expressiveness is perhaps always an exaggeration of expression, the cue for a reading there will be no reason to stop. To interpret the expressive face is to abandon the face that belongs to a visible body." Leo Bersani and Ulysse Dutoit, *Forming Couples: Godard's "Contempt"* (Oxford: Legenda, 2003), 15–16. In this view, Ryan as an actor but also Kathleen Kelly as a body drops away, and what remains is an emotional terrain that "there will be no reason to stop" reading.

78. Berlant, *On the Inconvenience of Other People*, 27.

79. Danez Smith, *Don't Call Us Dead* (Minneapolis, MN: Graywolf, 2017), 32.

80. This concern with media corporations is not unique to late 1990s films like *You've Got Mail*. Kathrina Glitre notes how screwball comedies from the 1930s depict "a culturally specific anxiety about publicity." Films such as *Libeled Lady* (1936) find comic pleasure in the "tension between privacy and publicity" (Glitre, *Hollywood Romantic Comedy*, 67). This tension derives from "the very processes of mass communication," which creates self-reflexivity within the films, because they themselves rely on the communication technologies that

create these tensions (69). Warren Susman similarly argues that *It Happened One Night* (1934) exemplifies "the inability of individuals to communicate privately in the world of such awesome, constant, universal public communications. Adrift in a world of communications, where every private act (especially of the rich and famous) is public property, our hero and heroine can communicate only when they leave that world totally." Warren Susman, "Communication and Culture," in *Mass Media between the Wars: Perceptions of Cultural Tension, 1918–1941*, ed. Catherine L. Covert and John D. Stevens (Syracuse, NY: Syracuse University Press, 1984), xxix. This trope implies that the romantic union of a couple, or at least the comic drama of arriving at such a union, depends on finding an exit from this seemingly omnipresent world of media.

81. Immanuel Kant, *Idea for a Universal History with a Cosmopolitan Aim*, trans. Allen Wood, ed. Amélie Oksenberg Rorty and James Schmidt (Cambridge: Cambridge University Press, 2009), 13.

82. Kant, 13.

83. Arthur Schopenhauer, "Similes, Parables, and Fables," in *Parerga and Paralipomena 2*, ed. and trans. Adrian Del Caro (Cambridge: Cambridge University Press, 2015), 584.

84. Schopenhauer, 584.

85. Berlant, *On the Inconvenience of Other People*, 42.

86. For an overview of the underlying assumptions of this concept, see Michael Wooldridge, "Intelligent Agents," in *Multiagent Systems: A Modern Approach to Distributed Artificial Intelligence*, ed. Gerhard Weiss (Cambridge, MA: MIT Press, 1999), 27–77.

87. J. A. Meaney, Steven R. Wilson, and Walid Magdy, "Smash at SemEval-2020 Task 7: Optimizing the Hyperparameters of ERNIE 2.0 for Humor Ranking and Rating," *Proceedings of the Fourteenth Workshop on Semantic Evaluation*, Association for Computational Linguistics (2020), 1049. See also Kim Binsted, "Computational Humor," *IEEE Intelligent Systems*, March-April 2006, 59; Roddy Cowie, "Computational Research and the Case for Taking Humor Seriously," *Humor* 36, no. 2 (2023): 207–23. For an overview of attempts to generate and detect humor, see Thomas Winters, "Computers Learning Humor Is No Joke," *Harvard Data Science Review*, no. 3.2 (Spring 2021): 1–18.

88. Kim Binsted and Graeme Ritchie, "An Implemented Model of Punning Riddles," *AAAI-94 Proceedings* (1994): 633.

89. Binsted and Ritchie, 637.

90. For an overview of these projects, see Tony Veale, *Your Wit Is My Command: Building AIs with a Sense of Humor* (Cambridge, MA: MIT Press, 2021), 127–72.

91. Another early AI system approximated linguistic competency by reproducing generic humor, but it only reiterates the point I've just made, so I've moved

my discussion of it out of the main course of my argument. In 2005, Oliviero Stock and Carlo Strapparava designed an AI system that generated humorous acronyms. Their program, HAHAcronym, searched for dissimilar nouns that could create humorous incongruity if substituted for the original terms of well-known acronyms. For instance, the system took MIT (Massachusetts Institute of Technology) and suggested it might instead mean Mythical Institute of Theology. The FBI transformed into the Fantastic Bureau of Intimidation. The developers explain that the production of these humorous acronyms requires the system to recognize and process "various generic components." Oliviero Stock and Carlo Strapparava, "The Act of Creating Humorous Acronyms," *Applied Artificial Intelligence* 19, no. 2 (2005): 137. See also Binsted and Ritchie, "An Implemented Model of Punning Riddles"; Julia M. Taylor and Lawrence J. Mazlack, "Humorous Wordplay Recognition," *2004 IEEE International Conference on Systems, Man and Cybernetics* (2004): 3306–11; and Meaney, Wilson, and Magdy, "Smash at SemEval-2020 Task 7," 1049–54.

92. "Spending Time with Ms. Dewey," *Marketplace Morning Report*, Dec. 13, 2006, https://web.archive.org/web/20070102213635/http://marketplace.public radio.org/shows/2006/12/13/PM200612138.html.

93. "Spending Time with Ms. Dewey," n.p.

94. Mich Mathews, "Transcript of Remarks by Mich Mathews, Senior Vice President, Central Marketing, Microsoft Corporation," Seattle, WA, May 9, 2007, https://news.microsoft.com/speeches/mich-mathews-microsoft-strategic-ac count-summit-2007/.

95. Miriam E. Sweeney, "The Ms. Dewey 'Experience': Technoculture, Gender, and Race," in *Digital Sociologies*, ed. Jessie Daniels, Karen Gregory, Tressie McMillan Cottom (Bristol, UK: Policy, 2017), 410.

96. Pavel Braslavski, Vladislav Blinov, Valeria Bolotova, and Katya Perstova, "How to Evaluate Humorous Response Generation, Seriously?" *Proceedings of the 2018 Conference on Human Information Interaction & Retrieval* (New York: Association for Computing Machinery, 2018), 225.

97. Ewa Luger and Abigail Sellen find that even when users perceive conversational agents as failing to meet certain requests, users nonetheless "continued to attribute elevated levels of episodic social intelligence to the system such as sarcasm and humour." In other words, humor signifies a form of "social intelligence" that inculcates a sense of "action/interaction." Ewa Luger and Abigail Sellen, "'Like Having a Really Bad PA': The Gulf between User Expectation and Experience of Conversational Agents," *Proceedings of the 2016 CHI Conference on Human Factors in Computing*, ACM (2016), 5294.

98. Dainius, "54 Hilariously Honest Answers from Siri to Uncomfortable Questions You Can Ask, Too," *Bored Panda*, https://www.boredpanda.com/best -funny-siri-responses/.

99. Yolande Strengers and Jenny Kennedy, *The Smart Wife: Why Siri, Alexa, and Other Smart Devices Need a Feminist Reboot* (Cambridge, MA: MIT Press, 2021), 8; Geoffrey A. Fowler, "Are Smartphones Becoming Smart Alecks?" *Wall Street Journal*, Oct. 15, 2011, https://www.wsj.com/articles/SB10001424052970204774604576631271813770508.

100. Jiepu Jiang et al., "Automatic Online Evaluation of Intelligent Assistants," *Proceedings of the 24th International Conference on the World Wide Web* (New York: Association for Computing Machinery, 2015), 508.

101. Andreea Danielescu and Gwen Christian, "A Bot Is Not a Polyglot: Designing Personalities for Multi-lingual Conversational Agents," in *Extended Abstracts of the 2018 CHI Conference on Human Factors in Computing Systems* (New York: Association for Computing Machinery, 2018), 8.

102. Stephanie Ricker Schulte, "Personalization," in *Digital Keywords: A Vocabulary of Information Society and Culture*, ed. Benjamin Peters (Princeton, NJ: Princeton University Press, 2016), 242.

103. Schulte, "Personalization," 246. The classic account of the phenomenon of identification is Byron Reeves and Clifford Nass, *The Media Equation: How People Treat Computers, Televisions, and New Media like Real People and Places* (Cambridge: Cambridge University Press, 1996). Shoshanna Zuboff argues that increasing user engagement is a market strategy in "surveillance capitalism," or the monitoring of users by private corporations that profit from user data. We are more likely to lend conversational agents our minds—to share our data, to order takeout—if we sustain the image of its personality. Following Zuboff, we might say that this kind of comedy wants trust or, at least, to mitigate distrust. It wants to create the feeling of a *de*corporatized exchange. It wants users to feel as though they are talking to Alexa, not Amazon. If, as Zuboff argues, personal computing was a prerequisite for private corporations to gather large swaths of user data, the humor of conversational agents is a technology of what we might call a more personal computing regime. See Shoshana Zuboff, *The Age of Surveillance Capitalism: The Fight for a Human Future at the New Frontier of Power* (New York: PublicAffairs, 2019), 233–54.

104. Danielescu and Christian, "A Bot Is Not a Polyglot," 5; see also Clifford Nass, *Wired for Speech: How Voice Activates and Advances the Human-Computer Relationship* (Cambridge, MA: MIT Press, 2005).

105. Danielescu and Christian, "A Bot Is Not a Polyglot," 5; see also Jennifer Rhee, *The Robotic Imaginary: The Human and the Price of Dehumanized Labor* (Minneapolis: University of Minnesota Press, 2018), 31–66; Kim Binsted, "Using Humour to Make Natural Language Interfaces More Friendly," in *Proceedings of the AI, ALife, and Entertainment Workshop*, International Joint Conference on Artificial Intelligence (1995); T. Bickmore and J. Cassell, "Relational Agents: A

Model and Implementation of Building User Trust," *Proceedings of the ACM CHI* (New York: Association for Computing Machinery, 2001), 396–403.

106. Alexa, "About the Author," https://www.amazon.com/stores/author/B09KNTH864/about.

107. Henri Bergson, *Laughter: An Essay on the Meaning of the Comic*, trans. Cloudesley Brereton and Fred Rothwell (New York: Macmillan, 1911), 10.

108. As Peter H. Kahn and colleagues put it, humor establishes "sociality" in human-machine interactions. Peter H. Kahn Jr. et al., "No Joking Aside: Using Humor to Establish Sociality in HRI," *HRI'14* (New York: Association for Computing Machinery, 2014), 188–89. It presents the system as socially available, as though it could be the recipient of what Schulte calls "affective connections" (Schulte, "Personalization," 246).

3. The One about Authenticity

1. George Saunders, *In Persuasion Nation* (New York: Riverhead, 2006), 16. The story was originally published in the *New Yorker*, Jan. 20, 2002. Hereafter cited parenthetically.

2. William Shakespeare, *Hamlet*, in *The Riverside Shakespeare*, 2nd ed., ed. G. Blakemore Evans et. al. (New York: Houghton Mifflin, 1997), 1.3.78–80.

3. These problems in *Hamlet* anticipate several criticisms of authenticity as an ethical ideal. Simon Feldman raises what we might call the Polonius objection. He argues that this ideal too easily enables the self-interested, cruel, and violent. Feldman even suggests that being *untrue* to oneself may at times be the most ethical stance: "It can be morally best to lack self-knowledge—or even to live in bad faith—when the alternatives lead us to harm others, in accordance with our 'true' and perhaps vicious or simply amoral selves." Simon Feldman, *Against Authenticity: Why You Shouldn't Be Yourself* (Lanham, MD: Lexington Books, 2015), 15. Feldman reasons that the underlying idea of one's "true self" must depend on an individual's perception of that selfhood. If the individual understands their true self in ways that are harmful to others, an absolute commitment to authenticity would judge as immoral any attempt to constrain the harm caused by a person expressing what they take to be their true self.

4. Bernard Williams, *Truth and Truthfulness* (Princeton, NJ: Princeton University Press, 2002), 172; Charles Taylor, *A Secular Age* (Cambridge, MA: Harvard University Press, 2007), 475; Somogy Varga, *Authenticity as an Ethical Ideal* (New York: Routledge, 2012), 61–84.

5. See Williams, *Truth and Truthfulness*, 174; and Charles Taylor, *The Ethics of Authenticity* (Cambridge, MA: Harvard University Press, 2018), 27. According to this view, it would not make sense to speak of Claudius's fratricide as "authentic" because it clearly derives from "the corrupted currents of this world," as

Claudius himself says in a remorseful soliloquy (3.3.61). In fact, one could argue that Claudius comes in contact with his self as he recognizes his "limèd soul, that, struggling to be free, / Art more engaged!" (3.3.72–73). Like a bird trapped in lime, he sees his soul as ensnared by the very world he had so intensely desired to rule. Authenticity, in this moment, is not the ability to pursue self-interest but a kind of despair at knowing what self-interest has wrought.

6. Jean-Jacques Rousseau, *The Confessions of Jean-Jacques Rousseau*, trans. W. Conyngham Mallory (New York: A. & C. Boni, 1928), 418–19.

7. Varga, *Authenticity as an Ethical Ideal*, 62–67.

8. Taylor, *The Ethics of Authenticity*, 26.

9. For example, radical factions in the Protestant Reformation reformulated Augustine's view of self-knowledge in opposing the Catholic Church. These reformulations often insisted on freedom of conscience and a doctrine that would later be known as the priesthood of the believer. Perhaps the most influential instance was Martin Luther's 1520 declaration, "Therefore we are all priests, as many of us are Christians." Martin Luther, *The Babylonian Captivity of the Church*, in *The Annotated Luther* 3, ed. Erik H. Herrmann (Minneapolis, MN: Fortress, 2016), 116. This assertion of each believer's status as a priest challenges what Luther calls the "captivity" of Christianity by the Catholic hierarchy. His argument is that individual Christians are capable of interpreting sacred texts and determining what their faith obliges them to do in society. "Neither pope, nor bishop, nor anyone else," Luther writes, "has the right to impose so much as a single syllable of obligation upon a Christian man without his own consent." Martin Luther, "The Pagan Servitude of the Church," in *Martin Luther: Selections from His Writings*, ed. John Dillenberger (Garden City, NY: Anchor, 1962), 304. Luther's assertion illustrates how the Reformation's inward turn very often invited antagonism toward institutional authorities, at times even confusing this antagonism with faith itself.

10. See Sarah Buss, "Accountability, Integrity, Authenticity, and Self-Legislation: Reflections on Ruediger Bittner's Reflections on Autonomy," *Erkenntnis* 79 (2014): 1351–64; and Katharina Bauer, "To Be or Not to Be Authentic: In Defence of Authenticity as an Ethical Ideal," *Ethical Theory and Moral Practice* 20, no. 3 (June 2017): 569.

11. An influential source for later conflicted models of authenticity is Søren Kierkegaard, who attempted to couple the inner state model with belief in divine authority. Kierkegaard begins from the proposition that "the self is a relation that relates itself to itself." Søren Kierkegaard, *The Sickness unto Death: The Christian Psychological Exposition for Upbuilding and Awakening*, trans. H. V. Hong and E. H. Hong (Princeton, NJ: Princeton University Press, 1980), 13. This is a recognizable expression of the earlier inner-sense model. Akin to Rousseau, Kierkegaard argues that anything that intervenes in that relation, or any at-

tempt by the self to muddle its relation with itself, results in despair. Losing contact with the self gives one "an increasing capacity for going along superbly in business and social life, indeed, for making a great success in the world" (Kierkegaard, *Sickness*, 34). Yet this kind of social success is a sign of despair for Kierkegaard. In contrast, he argues that the self can only become itself "through the relationship to God" (Kierkegaard, *Sickness*, 30). Kierkegaard's reasoning is that faith in God is not an externality or diversion of the self's relation to itself. Instead, he argues that God brings the self into an eternal relation to itself. Kierkegaard sees no contradiction in these two ideas—that the self is a relation to itself and that such a relation is only authentic when it is mediated by a divine authority. Sociable relations with a secular world amount to submission to inauthenticity; sociability with the divine is the achievement of authenticity.

12. English-language translators most often render Heidegger's neologism *Eigentlichkeit* as "authenticity," although literally it means something like "own-ness" or "ownedness," as if one were in possession of one's judgments and state of being. See Denis McManus, "On a Judgment of One's Own: Heideggerian Authenticity, Standpoints, and All Things Considered," *Mind* 128, no. 512 (Oct. 2019): 1181–1204.

13. Martin Heidegger, *Being and Time*, trans. J. Macquarrie and E. Robinson (New York: Harper & Row, 1962), 12.

14. Charles Guignon, "Authenticity," *Philosophy Compass* 3/2 (2008): 283.

15. Lionel Trilling, *Sincerity and Authenticity* (Cambridge, MA: Harvard University Press, 1973), 93.

16. For a discussion of this extremism, see Williams, *Truth and Truthfulness*, 181.

17. Williams, 184.

18. For an excellent discussion of these contradictions in Rousseau's life and philosophy, see Matthew D. Mendham, *Hypocrisy and the Philosophical Intentions of Rousseau: The Jean-Jacques Problem* (Philadelphia: University of Pennsylvania Press, 2021), 123–59.

19. Gordon Korman, *Unplugged* (New York: Balzer-Bray, 2021), 2.

20. Jean-Jacques Rousseau, *Émile; or, Treatise on Education*, trans. William H. Payne (London: Appleton, 1908), 1.

21. Rousseau, 86.

22. Rousseau, 13. Scholars of children's literature have demonstrated that the Child of Nature paradigm that Rousseau articulates in *Émile* became the subject of parody and ridicule during the nineteenth century. Marah Gubar, for example, shows how many Victorian writers took Rousseau's child-rearing philosophy as an absurd premise for their fiction. See Marah Gubar, *Artful Dodgers: Reconceiving the Golden Age of Children's Literature* (Oxford: Oxford University Press, 2008), 12–15, 22, 76.

23. These sources of kinship bring Jett into contact with his self: "having friends—human *and* reptile—changes everything about a guy's priorities," he says at the end of the novel (324). The novel construes the trials faced in rural Arkansas as collective problems, thus answering the self-alienation of the connected world by placing a communitarian accent on the pursuit of an authentic self. By identifying with others through a wilderness retreat, Jett comes to a "more exact knowledge of what I interiorly am," as Rousseau puts it. Even his narrative voice in the final chapter is more self-assured than the cynical, confused voice that opens the novel: "My father is considered the smartest man in the world," he says. "But when it comes to the unplugged life, I'm the brains of the family" (324). This confident assertion separates technical expertise and self-knowledge. The novel implies that Jett's "brains" derive from his newfound ability to know himself, apart from social media.

24. Rousseau, *Émile*, 165.

25. Charles Taylor explains this discursive structure as a result of the fact that authenticity "is a facet of modern individualism, and it is a feature of all forms of individualism that they don't just emphasize the freedom of the individual but also propose models of society" (Taylor, *The Ethics of Authenticity*, 44). In other words, authenticity is a moral norm about identity, which itself is socially performative and thus requires or appeals for "recognition by others" (Taylor, *The Ethics of Authenticity*, 45).

26. Douglas Coupland, *Microserfs* (New York: Harper Perennial, 2008), 15. Hereafter cited parenthetically.

27. Steward Brand, "Spacewar: Fanatic Life and Symbolic Death among the Computer Bums," *Rolling Stone*, Dec. 7, 1972, 58. The use of the word *natural* here is significant. I have argued elsewhere that the practices of data science have often relied on ecological analogies to convey a sense of organic wholeness and integrity. See Benjamin Mangrum, "The Ecologies of Data Visualization," *Diacritics* 48, no. 4 (2020): 52–75.

28. Brand, "Spacewar," 58.

29. Brand, 58.

30. For an excellent history of Stewart Brand, see Fred Turner, *From Counterculture to Cyberculture: Stewart Brand, the Whole Earth Network, and the Rise of Digital Utopianism* (Chicago: University of Chicago Press, 2006). For the ways in which computing communities were displaced by the personal computer as a commercial product, see Joy Lisi Rankin, *A People's History of Computing in the United States* (Cambridge, MA: Harvard University Press, 2018), 228–42; Gerardo Con Díaz, *Software Rights: How Patent Law Transformed Software Development in America* (New Haven, CT: Yale University Press, 2019), 161–84.

31. I am partially adapting the idea of a humanist comedy from Alexander Welsh, *The Humanist Comedy* (New Haven, CT: Yale University Press, 2014). For

Welsh, humanist comedy shares with New Comedy a tragic bent, for it has "a laugh at acquiring one or more secular identities and then losing all, with hope for the generation that follows" (230).

32. The acronym "OOP" typically stands for "object-oriented programming" and refers to computing languages like C++. As N. Katherine Hayles explains, object-oriented programming was essential to the transformation of the computer into an "expressive medium." N. Katherine Hayles, *My Mother Was a Computer: Digital Subjects and Literary Texts* (Chicago: University of Chicago Press, 2005), 59–60.

33. Alan Liu, *The Laws of Cool: Knowledge Work and the Culture of Information* (Chicago: University of Chicago Press, 2004), 101.

34. Liu, *The Laws of Cool*, 9.

35. This wedding between computing and the counterculture coincides with a broader expansion of an ethics of authenticity into a mass phenomenon—an expansion that, according to Charles Taylor, only occurred after the Second World War (Taylor, *A Secular Age*, 474). Doug Rossinow and others have similarly argued that "a search for authenticity in industrial American life" profoundly shaped liberalism and leftist politics in the second half of the twentieth century; see Doug Rossinow, *The Politics of Authenticity: Liberalism, Christianity, and the New Left in America* (New York: Columbia University Press, 1998), 345. Jacob Golomb argues that an ethics of authenticity only arises in the late nineteenth century with the writings of Søren Kierkegaard and his reception among continental existentialists like Sartre and Heidegger. Golomb also notes, however, that this philosophical reception originates on terms first laid out by thinkers like David Hume, Immanuel Kant, and Jean-Jacques Rousseau. See Jacob Golomb, *In Search of Authenticity: From Kierkegaard to Camus* (London: Routledge, 1995), 10–14.

36. See Benjamin Mangrum, *Land of Tomorrow: Postwar Fiction and the Crisis of American Liberalism* (New York: Oxford University Press, 2019), 134–66.

37. Tim Foster, "'A Kingdom of a Thousand Princes but No Kings': The Post-suburban Network in Douglas Coupland's *Microserfs*," *Western American Literature* 46, no. 3 (Fall 2011): 306, 312.

38. Rousseau, *Émile*, 13.

39. Anna Wiener, *Uncanny Valley: A Memoir* (New York: Picador, 2020), 173. Hereafter cited parenthetically.

40. Scott Selisker, *Human Programming: Brainwashing, Automatons, and American Unfreedom* (Minneapolis: University of Minnesota Press, 2016), 95.

41. Selisker, 104.

42. Selisker, 112.

43. Julie Sievers notes how autobiography became a literary home for the "inner light" tradition in Quakerism (a particularly radical expression of the

Protestant sources that would feed into an ethics of authenticity). See Julie Sievers, "Awakening the Inner Light: Elizabeth Ashbridge and the Transformation of Quaker Community," *Early American Literature* 36, no. 2 (2001): 235–62. Following on Sievers's work, it is interesting to note how the literary mandate of an ethics of authenticity has been so closely associated with autobiographical and expressivist literary forms. What would it mean for these forms not to orbit around authenticity? What models of inwardness do these forms rely on?

44. Emily Chang, *Brotopia: Breaking Up the Boys' Club of Silicon Valley* (New York: Penguin, 2018), 42–52.

45. Sarah Lacy, *A Uterus Is a Feature, Not a Bug: The Working Woman's Guide to Overthrowing the Patriarchy* (New York: HarperCollins, 2017), 123.

46. "War on Men: Silicon Valley's Oppressed Men," in season 1 of *The Opposition*, aired on November 27, 2017.

47. For a critical examination of housing in the San Francisco Bay Area, see Erin McElroy, *Silicon Valley Imperialism: Techno Fantasies and Frictions in Postsocialist Times* (Durham, NC: Duke University Press, 2024), 69–98.

48. Margaret O'Mara, *The Code: Silicon Valley and the Remaking of America* (New York: Penguin, 2020), 288; see also Nathan Ensmenger, "'Beards, Sandals, and Other Signs of Rugged Individualism': Masculine Culture within the Computing Professions," *Osiris* 30, no. 1 (Jan. 2015): 43.

49. Ensmenger, "Beards, Sandals, and Other Signs," 51.

50. Rousseau, *Confessions*, 418.

51. There is a substantial body of scholarship on the relation between irony, satire, and humor. Linda Hutcheon notes, for example, that satire has a "corrective function" that "frequently turns to irony as a means of ridiculing—and implicitly correcting—the vices and follies of humankind." Linda Hutcheon, *Irony's Edge: The Theory and Politics of Irony* (London: Routledge, 1994), 14–15. I take this corrective function to be a comic orientation shared between Wiener's memoir and the satirical fictions examined later in this section.

52. Trilling, *Sincerity and Authenticity*, 93.

53. Dave Eggers, *The Circle* (New York: Knopf, 2013), 404.

54. Eggers, 410.

55. See Geert Lovink, "What Is the Social in Social Media?" *e-flux Journal*, no. 40 (Dec. 2012): https://www.e-flux.com/journal/40/60272/what-is-the-social-in-social-media/.

56. Jarret Kobek, *I Hate the Internet: A Useful Novel* (London: Serpent's Tail, 2016), 3. Hereafter cited parenthetically.

57. André Breton, ed., *Anthology of Black Humor*, trans. Mark Polizzotti (San Francisco: City Lights, 1997).

58. William Solomon, "Secret Integrations: Black Humor and the Critique of Whiteness," *Modern Fiction Studies* 49, no.3 (Fall 2003): 469–95.

59. This passage illustrates how Kobek's novel also uses the comic technique of Ambrose Bierce's *The Devil's Dictionary* (1911), which calls attention to the unspoken logic of some idea or term by providing a "cynical" but basic definition of it. Samuel Johnson also employed this comic technique in some rare instances in *A Dictionary of the English Language* (1755). I use the term *cynical* to describe Bierce's definitions because the first version of his book was titled *The Cynic's Word Book* (1906).

60. Dave Eggers, *The Every; or, At Last a Sense of Order; or, The Final Days of Free Will; or, Limitless Choice Is Killing the World* (New York: Vintage, 2021), 387.

61. Louis D. Rubin Jr., "The Great American Joke," *South Atlantic Quarterly* 72 (1973): 87. In an influential mid-twentieth-century essay, Ralph Ellison similarly argues that "Negro and white Americans regard one another" across "the joke at the center of American identity." Ralph Ellison, "Change the Joke and Slip the Yoke," in *Shadow and Act* (New York: Vintage, 1995), 54. One part of this "joke" is that American identity itself is "mammy-made," a social construct rather than a stable and authentic state of being. Yet the other part of the joke is that "each secretly believes that he alone knows what is valid in the American experience, and that the other knows he knows but will not admit it, and each suspects the other of being at bottom a phony" (54–55). There is no such thing as an authentic "American identity," yet charges of inauthenticity are on every tongue. In Ellison's telling, the other side of the American color line always looks like a sham. The legacies of slavery and Jim Crow built this stage, and the postwar social order thus becomes "a land of masking jokers" in which the actors dissemble for the purpose of "projecting the future and preserving the past" (55). For Ellison, the joke is that everyone is performing; only actors take the stage.

62. Rubin, "The Great American Joke," 83.

63. Rubin, 90.

64. Rubin, 94.

65. *Silicon Valley* (HBO, 2014), season 1, episode 1.

66. This idea is such a recognizable part of the industry's discourse that Wiener likewise depicts it as a staple of advertisements for tech jobs. As she looks for other positions in the Bay area, Wiener notes how every advertisement presents the work place as a site for both techno-utopianism and self-actualization: *"Change the world around you. We work hard, we laugh hard, we give great high fives. We're not just another social web app. We're not just another project-management tool. We're not just another delivery service"* (145). The joke in Wiener's memoir is that Human Relations departments in the tech industry have reduced the vocabulary of self-actualization into easy-to-parody slogans.

67. Rousseau, *Émile*, 6.

68. Dean MacCannell, "Staged Authenticity: Arrangements of Social Space in Tourist Settings," *American Journal of Sociology* 79, no. 3 (Nov. 1973): 596.

69. MacCannell, 591–93. Similar to my argument in this section, Jessica Pressman explores the centrality of "fakery" to digital culture in *Bookishness: Loving Books in a Digital Age* (New York: Columbia University Press, 2020), 85–108. Intriguingly, Pressman shows how fakery becomes catchy in remediated digital culture—an argument that seems consonant not only with this chapter's claims about staged authenticity but also the previous chapter's discussion of the appeal of being generic.

70. Limor Shifman, *Memes in Digital Culture* (Cambridge, MA: MIT Press, 2013), 143.

71. The common application of *authenticity* to *objects* leads John L. Jackson Jr. to prefer the term *sincerity* as a category applying to persons. See *Real Black: Adventures in Racial Sincerity* (Chicago: University of Chicago Press, 2005), 14–15.

72. Meredith Salisbury and Jefferson D. Pooley, "The #nofilter Self: The Contest for Authenticity among Social Networking Sites, 2002–2016," *Social Sciences* 6 (2017): 8.

73. Katharina Lobinger and Cornelia Brantner, "In the Eye of the Beholder: Subjective Views on the Authenticity of Selfies," *International Journal of Communication* 9 (2015): 1848–60.

74. Max Morris and Eric Anderson, "'Charlie Is So Cool Like': Authenticity, Popularity, and Inclusive Masculinity on YouTube," *Sociology* 49, no. 6 (2015): 1200–1217.

75. Trilling, *Sincerity and Authenticity*, 10–11.

76. The problems that arose from Rousseau's participation in a literary public are explored in Geoffrey Turnovsky, *The Literary Market: Authorship and Modernity in the Old Regime* (Philadelphia: University of Pennsylvania Press, 2010), 184–203.

77. On the dialogic between authenticity and recognition, see Charles Taylor, "The Politics of Recognition," in *Multiculturalism*, exp. ed., ed. Amy Gutmann (Princeton, NJ: Princeton University Press, 1994), 35–36; Christopher Chen, "Race and the Politics of Recognition," in *The Sage Handbook of Frankfurt School Critical Theory*, ed. Beverley Best, Werner Bonefeld, and Chris O'Kane (Sage, 2018), 933–35.

78. See Walter Benjamin's influential discussion of authenticity and the "aura" of the work of art in "The Work of Art in the Age of Mechanical Reproduction," *Illuminations*, trans. Harry Zohn, ed. Hannah Arendt (New York: Schocken, 1968), 217–51.

79. Yuval Katz and Limor Shifman, "Making Sense? The Structure and Meanings of Digital Memetic Nonsense," *Information, Communication & Society* 20, no. 6 (2017): 836–37.

80. See Olga Goriunova, "New Media Idiocy," *Convergence: The International Journal of Research into New Media Technologies* 19, no. 2 (2012): 223–35.

81. Whitney Phillips, *This Is Why We Can't Have Nice Things: Mapping the Relationship between Online Trolling and Mainstream Culture* (Cambridge, MA: MIT Press, 2015), 65–66.

82. Andrew Morgan, "When Doublespeak Goes Viral: A Speech Act Analysis of Internet Trolling," *Erkenntnis* 88 (2023): 3408.

83. Goriunova, "New Media Idiocy," 229; Morgan, "When Doublespeak Goes Viral," 3407.

84. Umberto Eco, "The Frames of Comic 'Freedom,'" in *The Comedy Studies Reader*, ed. Nick Marx and Matt Sienkiewicz (Austin: University of Texas Press, 2018), 26.

85. To put this in social-scientific terms, subcultural trolling centers on the creation of a kind of social capital called *bonding* rather than *bridging*. Bonding social capital involves inward looking forms of collective affiliation, whereas bridging social capital attempts to build lines of affiliation across "social cleavages." For the classic use of this social-scientific distinction, see Robert D. Putnam, *Bowling Alone: The Collapse and Revival of American Community* (New York: Simon & Schuster, 2000), 22–23.

86. Trilling, *Sincerity and Authenticity*, 10–11.

87. See Ruth Page, "Hoaxes, Hacking, and Humour: Analysing Impersonated Identity on Social Network Sites," in *The Language of Social Media*, ed. Philip Seargeant and Caroline Tagg (Basingstoke, UK: Palgrave Macmillan, 2014), 46–64.

88. Lisa Nakamura, *Cybertypes: Race, Ethnicity, and Identity on the Internet* (New York: Routledge, 2002), 20, 55.

89. Kurt Vonnegut, *Player Piano* (New York: Dial, 2006), 288. Hereafter cited parenthetically.

90. For the history of this saying and a compelling argument that any version of the phrase "the only good Indian" is a synecdoche for the entire proverb, see Wolfgang Mieder, "'The Only Good Indian Is a Dead Indian': History and Meaning of a Proverbial Stereotype," *Journal of American Folklore* 106 (1993): 38–60.

91. Philip Deloria, *Playing Indian* (New Haven, CT: Yale University Press, 1998), 3.

92. Deloria, 142.

93. As Jill Lane similarly puts it, racial impersonation in the United States allows white Americans to create "a persuasive sense of authentic national performance." See Jill Lane, "ImpersoNation: Toward a Theory of Black-, Red-, and Yellowface in the Americas," *PMLA* 123, no. 5 (Oct. 2008): 1730.

94. See Deloria, *Playing Indian*, 95–153.

95. For an extensive discussion of Tom Macmaster's impersonation of an Arab-American lesbian, see Andrew Orr, *The Gay Girl in Damascus Hoax* (Berlin: De Gruyter, 2023).

96. Critiques of this fantasy may be found in William Cronon, "The Trouble with Wilderness; or, Getting Back to the Wrong Nature," in *Uncommon Ground: Toward Reinventing Nature*, ed. William Cronon (New York: Norton, 1995), 69–90; Deloria, *Playing Indian*, 95–127; and the essays collected in Michael E. Harkin and David Rich Lewis, eds., *Native Americans and the Environment: Perspectives on the Ecological Indian* (Lincoln: University of Nebraska Press, 2007).

97. Such fantasies are not unique to an age of computing. Modernist aesthetics took African and indigenous identities as proxies for authenticity in the late nineteenth and early twentieth centuries. Many expressionists, for example, believed they could break free from societal conventions by appropriating forms of African culture; many modernist writers similarly believed that primitive "darkness" signified truths about interiority that European civilization masked or suppressed. This vein of European and American aesthetics searched for some primitive essence that industrialization and modern technology had not yet spoiled. Much like the leaders of the Ghost Shirt Society, these avant-garde artists felt that certain forms of nonwhiteness had not been sullied by modern society, whether through a more direct contact with nature or a less organized communal structure. This is, of course, an expression of an ethics of authenticity. If for thinkers like Rousseau, society "makes it very difficult for people to know and follow the inclination of their natural feelings," the appropriation of racialized culture developed as one way to get back to nature. See Ronald Grimsley, *Rousseau's Religious Thought* (Oxford: Clarendon, 1968), 64. For scholarship on primitivism, see Marianna Torgovnick, *Gone Primitive: Savage Intellects, Modern Lives* (Chicago: University of Chicago Press, 1990); Frances S. Connelly, *The Sleep of Reason: Primitivism in Modern European Art and Aesthetics, 1725–1907* (University Park: Pennsylvania State University Press, 1995); Ben Etherington, *Literary Primitivism* (Stanford, CA: Stanford University Press, 2017).

98. Liu, *Laws of Cool*, 100–101.

99. Jennifer Rhee makes a related point about the idea of the universality of emotions and technological attempts to replicate those emotions in roboticized forms of emotional labor. See Jenifer Rhee, *The Robotic Imaginary: The Human and the Price of Dehumanized Labor* (Minneapolis: University of Minnesota Press, 2018), 101–132.

100. Intriguingly, Teddy's independence also stands in contrast to the image-conscious Babar. See Herbert Kohl, *Should We Burn Babar? Essays on Children's Literature and the Power of Stories* (New York: New Press, 1995), 3–29. Thanks again to Marah Gubar for pointing out this tension between Teddy and his hero.

101. Leo Bersani, *Homos* (Cambridge, MA: Harvard University Press, 1995), 76.

102. As Tim Dean clarifies, Bersani is not arguing that homosexual people fail "at practicing sociability in its myriad forms," only that "some aspect of

homosexuality threatens the social and that it might be strategic politically to exploit that threat." Tim Dean, "The Antisocial Homosexual," *PMLA* 121, no. 3 (May 2006): 826.

103. Edelman uses the phrase *reproductive futurism* to describe an ideology he claims to be dominant in modern social life. This ideology wants not only to reproduce the future but also to protect it; thus, it takes the innocent child as its most potent symbol. Edelman argues that queerness fulfills a "structural position" demanded by this ideology, such that even queer people who try to conform to normative sociality (e.g., through the institution of marriage) are only "shifting the figural burden of queerness to someone else." Lee Edelman, *No Future: Queer Theory and the Death Drive* (Durham, NC: Duke University Press, 2004), 27. The coherence of normativity depends upon the negativity of its queers. Bersani and Edelman effectively accept this reactionary view, arguing that it positions queerness as unavoidably antisocial.

Critics of this view note how it presents homosexuality as a structurally preset identity when, in fact, gay identity and other forms of queerness vary widely under different social conditions. According to this line of criticism, it simply doesn't make sense to speculate about some aspect "inherent in gay desire" (Bersani, *Homos*, 76). As José Esteban Muñoz puts it, the antisocial thesis "imagine[s] sexuality as a discrete category that can be abstracted and isolated from other antagonisms in the social, which include race and gender." José Esteban Muñoz, "Thinking beyond Antirelationality and Antiutopianism in Queer Critique," *PMLA* 121, no. 3 (May 2006): 826].

104. Stay tuned: I turn to the idea that comedy presents models of flourishing in the next chapter.

4. The One about Couples

1. Alan Turing, "Computing Machinery and Intelligence," *Mind: A Quarterly Review of Psychology and Philosophy* 59, no. 236 (1950): 434–35. I have simplified the imitation game for the sake of clarity, but Turing's fuller account imagines a control test in which a man and woman each tries to convince the interrogator that they are a woman. The woman's object is to "help the interrogator," whereas the man provides deceptive answers. If a computer can fool the interrogator that it is a woman as often as a man can fool the interrogator, Turing believes the computer possesses intelligence.

2. See Jack Halberstam, "Automating Gender: Postmodern Feminism in the Age of the Intelligent Machine," *Feminist Studies* 17, no. 3 (Autumn 1991): 439–60.

3. This implication in the film echoes a liberal-continental view of sociability that appears in thinkers like Kant and Hannah Arendt. Arendt describes sociability as "the very essence of men insofar as they are of this world only." Hannah Arendt, *Lectures on Kant's Political Philosophy* (Chicago: University of

Chicago Press, 1982), 74. Kant is less clear in viewing sociability as an essential aspect of being human, although many of the principles laid out in his *Idea for a Universal History with a Cosmopolitan Aim* tend in this direction. While it goes beyond the focus in this chapter, my point in this note is that coupling can also serve as a vehicle for a modern humanistic theory in which *being social* and *being human* cannot be separated.

4. Northrop Frye, *Anatomy of Criticism: Four Essays* (Princeton, NJ: Princeton University Press, 1957), 167; Germaine Greer, *The Female Eunuch* (New York: McGraw Hill, 1971), 204; Lisa Hopkins, *The Shakespearean Marriage: Merry Wives and Heavy Husbands* (Palgrave Macmillan, 1998), 16–33.

5. Fetish objects often, but not necessarily, take on explicitly sexual connotations. The term derives from the Portuguese *feitiço*, which itself derives from animist cults. Fetish objects are imbued with *magic* and viewed as *animate*. The computer often serves as a fetish object in American culture in the sense of the latter connotations, although the later sections of this chapter explore a more sexual register, too.

6. There are some futuristic plays that include advanced calculating technology, but Marchant's is the first to represent what we now take to be a modern computer: fully electronic, digital, binary, and programmable. I cite Marchant's play as the first based on a process of elimination: no other play with an earlier Broadway premiere includes a computer onstage as part of the action. This has been difficult to prove definitively. None of the standard histories of Broadway mention "computer" or "computing machine," either in summaries of plays or descriptions of sets. I found one critic who described Neil Simon's *Barefoot in the Park* (1963) as a "computer-based play," but the description refers to the mechanical efficiency of the work, not its content. See Jordan Schildcrout, *In the Long Run: A Cultural History of Broadway's Hit Plays* (London: Routledge, 2020), 147.

In addition to consulting academic and historical accounts of Broadway theater, I also searched several online resources, particularly the seemingly exhaustive list of Broadway plays available at www.broadwayworld.com. This site compiles every Broadway premiere by its opening night and theater. I cross-checked these lists with descriptions of plays to confirm that Marchant's play was the first to feature a modern computer on the stage. (Those who want to dispute this claim could perhaps point to computing machines that aren't fully electronic, digital, binary, and programmable.)

Another hint that *The Desk Set* is the first Broadway play to feature a computer is the fact that the computer's appearance in an adjacent medium, film, was similarly timed. Several low-budget science fiction films depicted computers: Irving Pichel's *Destination Moon* (1950) includes several seconds of stock footage of GE's Differential Analyzer. Curt Siodmak and Herbert L. Strock's *The Mag-*

netic Monster (1953) and Strock's follow-up *Gog* (1954) both briefly depict computers performing scientific calculations. Fred F. Sears's *Earth vs. The Flying Saucers* (1956) also features a brief clip of the GE Differential Analyzer. There is some debate among historians about whether the GE Differential Analyzer should even be considered a modern computer since it was an analog machine with mechanical parts. In any case, these sci-fi precursors feature the computer only in minor ways. Perhaps for these reasons, many film histories cite Walter Lang's 1957 adaptation of Marchant's play as the first major motion picture to feature a modern computer. See also Andrew Utterson, *From IBM to MGM: Cinema at the Dawn of the Digital Age* (New York: Bloomsbury, 2019), 6.

7. William Marchant, *The Desk Set* (1955; New York: Samuel French, 1984), 60. Hereafter cited parenthetically.

8. Martin Campbell-Kelly and William Aspray, *Computer: A History of the Information Machine* (New York: Basic Books, 1996), 102. It is obvious that IBM is central to Marchant's play, although the meaning of the allusions to this corporation is less obvious. Richard Sumner tacks up a sign reading "THINK" after he arrives in the research department, a sign that Thomas Watson famously displayed at IBM (Marchant 14). Similarly, the fact that Bunny Watson shares a surname with IBM's president may signify her technical expertise and intelligence. The shared surname could also be ironic: Have even the most innovative thinkers become obsolete in an age of computing technology? Still another possibility is that her surname establishes a parallel between Watson and computing technology—a parallel also evident in her rapid calculations and impeccable memory. After Sumner introduces himself to her, Watson immediately comments on the number of letters in his name, prompting him to observe, "You calculate rapidly" (12). This, too, may be ironic, given the perception, if not always the reality, that the job of *computer* was "feminized clerical labor." Jennifer S. Light, "When Computers Were Women," *Technology and Culture* 40, no. 3 (July 1999): 455. But then, the famous mathematician Norbert Wiener held the job of "computer" when working for the US Army. See Pesi R. Masani, *Norbert Wiener, 1894–1964* (Basel: Birkhäuser, 1990), 68. See also Paul E. Ceruzzi, "When Computers Were Human," *Annals of the History of Computing* 13, no. 3 (1991): 237–44. In any case, my sense is that the surname "Watson" is a versatile signifier, its ironic and professional connotations becoming active at different moments in the play, as is also the case with the allusions to IBM more generally.

9. Campbell-Kelly and Aspray, *Computer*, 111.

10. Writing in 1958, a reporter for *Forbes* cheekily described this problem of profitability; see "One Problem the Computers Can't Solve," *Forbes*, Jan. 1, 1958, 83–85.

11. Howard Gammon, "The Automatic Handling of Office Paper Work," *Public Administration Review* 14, no. 1 (Winter 1954): 63.

12. Richard N. Langlois, *The Corporation and the Twentieth Century: The History of American Business Enterprise* (Princeton, NJ: Princeton University Press, 2023), 315–402; Alfred Chandler, *The Visible Hand: The Managerial Revolution in American Business* (Cambridge, MA: Harvard University Press, 1977). Chandler claims, "By 1917 most American industries had acquired their modern structure," by which he means that they were run by a hierarchy of managers rather than administered by an entrepreneurial executive (364).

13. Writing in 1954, one economist speculated that a computer called LEO might be "the first step in an accounting revolution"; quoted in Mike Hally, *Electronic Brains: Stories from the Dawn of the Computer Age* (London: Granta, 2005), 125.

14. Gammon, "Automatic Handling," 63.

15. Gammon, 73.

16. Harry Braverman, *Labor and Monopoly Capital: The Degradation of Work in the Twentieth Century* (New York: New York University Press, 1998), 79. For Braverman's analysis of the early "computer hierarchy," see 227–36.

17. Many commentators directly connect an earlier vein of scientific management theory with the spread of computing technology throughout American corporate life. For example, Stanley Aronowitz and William DiFazio claim, "What could not be accomplished by Taylorism was finally achieved by computerization." *The Jobless Future: Sci-Tech and the Dogma of Work* (Minneapolis: University of Minnesota Press, 1994), 27.

18. An excellent case in point is the rise of automated trading systems. These systems heighten volatility in trading markets and, while occasionally lucrative, can collectively work at cross-purposes when competing in the same sector. Even advocates of these systems note that they create substantially higher risk than other forms of trading. See Irene Aldridge and Steven Krawciw, *Real-Time Risk: What Investors Should Know about FinTech, High-Frequency Trading, and Flash Crashes* (Hoboken, NJ: Wiley, 2017), 91.

19. There was still another precedent to the appearance of Emmarac on Broadway. On election night in 1952, CBS broadcast the predictions of a computer called UNIVAC, which modeled the outcome of the general election as precinct votes were reported. The broadcast offered one of the first public glimpses into how computers might be relevant to society at large. The irony, though, is that audiences did not actually see UNIVAC but only a fake console. The computing machine, housed in Pennsylvania, predicted Eisenhower's landslide victory after only a very small number of early returns were reported. This prediction ran counter to two influential national surveys, including one Gallup poll that anticipated a close election. A reporter communicated UNIVAC's prediction by telephone to the CBS studio in New York. Walter Cronkite announced the results as the camera displayed the fake console. As Martin

Campbell-Kelly explains, the drama of the incoming results was "heightened by flickering console lights, driven by nothing more sophisticated than blinking Christmas tree lights." Campbell-Kelly and Aspray, *Computer*, 108.

On the 705 Model II, see René Moreau, *The Computer Comes of Age: The People, the Hardware, and the Software*, trans. J. Howlett (Cambridge, MA: MIT Press, 1986), 76. The selling of commercial computing machines began in 1952 but only became commercially viable (i.e., orders could be completed at scale) by 1955. Again, the manufacture, leasing, and sale of computers still wasn't profitable until later in the decade.

20. The *Forbes* article mentioned above cites UNIVAC and the IBM 705 as the two main machines used by businesses in the mid-1950s. See "One Problem the Computers Can't Solve," 83.

21. This transformation created often contradictory effects on white-collar work, such as the simultaneity of "upskilling" and "deskilling" certain positions within the same industry. See Beverly H. Burris, "Computerization of the Workplace," *Annual Review of Sociology* 24 (1998): 153–55. See also Roslyn L. Feldberg and Evelyn Nakano Glenn, "Technology and the Transformation of Clerical Work," in *Technology and the Transformation of White-Collar Work*, ed. Robert E. Kraut (Hillsdale, NJ: Lawrence Erlbaum, 1987), 79–80.

22. See Suzanne Iacono and Rob Kling, "Computerization Movements: The Rise of the Internet and Distant Forms of Work," in *Information Technology and Organization Transformation: History, Rhetoric, and Practice*, ed. JoAnne Yates and John Van Maanen (Thousand Oaks, CA: Sage, 2001), 93–136; and Steve Sawyer and Andrea Tapia, "The Computerization of Work: A Social Informatics Perspective," in *Computers in Society: Privacy, Ethics, and the Internet*, ed. Joey F. George (Oxford: Oxford University Press, 2003), 93–109.

23. Frye, *Anatomy of Criticism*, 165.

24. Viewers of Lang's film will notice a key difference here. Sumner, played by Spencer Tracy, does not deliver this insult. One explanation may be that the casting for Marchant's play created a generational difference absent from Lang's film. The 1955 performance cast Shirley Booth (b. 1898) as Bunny Watson and Byron Sanders (b. 1925) as Richard Sumner. Booth's agents billed her as ten years younger, a fact that was not known until her death. Even still, there was a noticeable age difference in the play between Booth and Sanders. An ageist and sexist set of assumptions thus seemed to echo the old/new distinction implicit in the arrival of the electronic brain in Marchant's play. Sumner, a young man, aligns with the computer while the "old maid" represents an established form of knowledge work. In contrast to the play's distinctions, Spencer Tracy was seven years older than Katharine Hepburn, thus erasing the association of computing technology with a generational shift. All of this also matters a great deal to the norms associated with coupling in the two versions.

Incidentally, Booth recognized this dynamic when Hepburn was cast for Lang's film. In a 1957 interview, Booth claims she is only two years older than Hepburn, but she also notes that Hepburn looks "ageless." See Bob Thomas, "New Schools of Acting Old Hat Says Shirley," *Toledo Blade*, Feb. 12, 1957, 20.

25. The "New Woman" rose to prominence in the 1920s following the suffrage movement, but the phrase was still very much on the minds of audiences in the 1950s. See Estelle B. Freedman, "The New Woman: Changing Views of Women in the 1920s," *Journal of American History* 61, no. 2 (Sept. 1974): 372–93.

26. Aristotle defines *anagnorisis* as "a change from ignorance to knowledge" in *Poetics*, 1452a, xi.

27. For a discussion of how prior films featuring Hepburn and Tracy set up the expectation that they would end the film together, see Andrew Britton, *Katharine Hepburn: Star as Feminist* (New York: Columbia University Press, 2003), 169–208.

28. The film references sexuality much more explicitly than the play. In fact, in one of the film's promotional trailers, Watson stands over Emmarac and muses, "Except for sex, what's left?" The episode doesn't appear in the film, but it does seem to have run on advertisements for certain national audiences. This trailer may be viewed at https://www.imdb.com/title/tt0050307/.

29. Sianne Ngai, *Theory of the Gimmick: Aesthetic Judgment and Capitalist Form* (Cambridge, MA: Harvard University Press, 2020), 72.

30. Ngai, 82.

31. To be sure, it is not clear how Watson will respond to Cutler's proposal at the end of *The Desk Set*. The stage directions indicate that she *"settles back in her chair, and begins to enjoy the proposal. Since she will probably continue doing this the rest of the afternoon"* (Marchant 78). Thus ends the play, and I think it is fair to acknowledge the stage directions create some ambiguity: Will Watson accept the offer she has appeared to desire for most of the play? Or is settling back in her chair a gesture of triumph, perhaps suggesting a victory in what was then called the Battle of the Sexes?

Still, the stage direction's final ambiguity only exacerbates the gimmicky quality of the proposal. If Watson were to voice her decision to leave the research department after having fought for her position within it, the play would present onstage a betrayal of its central premise. The choice to accept Cutler's proposal would amount to a loss of her independence and the professional identity she has fought to retain. Up to this point, the play has posed political and social questions about the status of women in managerial enterprise, but it finally retreats into a kind of artistic ambiguity when a conflict internal to its own premise arises—that is, the conflict between women working in the corporate world and the postwar expectations for those same women within the institution of marriage. The stage directions sidestep this conflict through formal irresolution. It's as though the indecision of the play's last lines relocates Watson's dilemma to an aesthetic realm, one characterized by choice and possibility.

I have in mind here Leo Bersani and Ulysse Dutoit's claim that a "sign of the aesthetic is formal irresolution." I view the ambiguity about Watson's response to Cutler's proposal as an aesthetic gesture that evades the conflict between her personal and professional wants. See Leo Bersani and Ulysse Dutoit, *Forming Couples: Godard's "Contempt"* (Oxford: Legenda, 2003), 23.

32. John Ruskin, "Of Queen's Gardens," *Sesame and Lilies* [1905], in *The Works of John Ruskin* 18, ed. Edward Tyas Cook and Alexander Wedderburn (Cambridge: Cambridge University Press, 2010), 122. See the discussion of this passage from Ruskin in Eli Zaretsky, *Capitalism, the Family, and Personal Life* (New York: Harper & Row, 1976), 51–52.

33. The exchange casts the search for a partner in the image of economic competition. Sex and business are thus entangled at the beginning of the play, and this entanglement initially takes the form of a joke about a transgender woman. Ruthie and Sadel's banter invokes anxieties about a sexual economy, just as the play's levity about Emmarac taps into worries about the automation of white-collar work. Angst and discrimination wear the same comedic mask.

Scholars of gender and sexuality have long noted that sexuality and the marketplace are not only fluid images for one another but are also mutually reinforcing systems of normativity. For example, see Judith Butler, "Merely Cultural," *Social Text* 52/53 (Autumn-Winter 1997): 265–77; Rosemary Hennessy, "Returning to Reproduction Queerly: Sex, Labor, Need," *Rethinking Marxism* 18, no. 3 (2006): 387–95; Neel Ahuja, "Intimate Atmospheres: Queer Theory in a Time of Extinctions," *GLQ: A Journal of Lesbian and Gay Studies* 21, nos. 2–3 (2015): 365–85; and Christopher Chitty, *Sexual Hegemony: Statecraft, Sodomy, and Capital in the Rise of the World System* (Durham, NC: Duke University Press, 2020).

34. Douglas T. Miller and Marion Novak, *The Fifties: The Way We Really Were* (Garden City, NY: Doubleday, 1977), 169.

35. For a discussion of Truman's policies toward gay and lesbian people, see David K. Johnson, *The Lavender Scare: The Cold War Persecution of Gays and Lesbians in the Federal Government* (Chicago: University of Chicago Press, 2006), 55–77.

36. Johnson, 122.

37. Sumner's transformation into an eligible bachelor likewise seems to provide some symmetrical resolution to Ruthie and Sadel's anxieties. Sumner greets the women when he first takes the stage—another minor difference with the film—but the robotic man does not recognize Ruthie's advances, which are apparently so obvious that Peg tells her, "Don't push—relax and stop drooling—you'll last longer!" (10). Sumner seems so entirely absorbed in his work that he appears asexual, but his eventual transformation includes something like the discovery of his sexuality: he exits the play arm-in-arm with Ruthie and Sadel,

promising to buy them drinks. Sumner's metamorphosis implies that the world of mechanical efficiency will prove to be harmonious with the marketplace for heterosexual coupling. This aspect of Sumner's transformation recalls Stanley Cavell's claim that twentieth-century comic resolutions often require "learning, or accepting, your sexual identity, the acknowledgment of desire." Stanley Cavell, *Pursuits of Happiness: The Hollywood Comedy of Remarriage* (Cambridge, MA: Harvard University Press, 1981), 56.

38. William Cameron Forbes, *The Romance of Business* (Boston: Houghton Mifflin, 1921), 23.

39. Forbes, 209. I recognize that the corporation is only one form of business enterprise. Small businesses, for example, often have antagonistic relations with monopolistic corporations. I emphasize the corporate firm here because of its paradigmatic role in the social discourse of the postwar era, not because I think it properly stands in for the entirety of society.

40. The film likewise creates ambiguity about Emmarac's relationship to the International Broadcasting Company. As Paul E. Ceruzzi explains, "IBM's policy had been to lease, not sell, its equipment. . . . Although IBM agreed to sell its machines as part of a Consent Decree effective January 1956, leasing continued to be its preferred way of doing business." Paul E. Ceruzzi, *A History of Modern Computing*, 2nd ed. (Cambridge, MA: MIT Press, 2003), 128. It is unclear in Lang's film if the broadcasting company has bought several computers—a capital-intensive purchase that would have been exceedingly rare in 1955. The leasing model seems more likely given the fact that Sumner brings Warriner (another employee of IBM) to operate Emmarac in the research department. All of this is speculative, but it gives some additional credence to the idea that the film takes pains to create distance between Sumner, Emmarac, and the corporation that employs Watson. Such distance, I argue below, is important to the social meaning ascribed to the couple in the film.

41. Emmarac's unexpected response may play into the portrayal of the computer as Watson's rival. According to this view, Emmarac responds like a jealous lover, refusing to relinquish her attachment to Sumner. This "NO" could thus be interpreted as either a programming error or the comic refusal on an animate machine (hence my description of the computer as a fetish object).

42. C. Stewart Gillmor, "Stanford, the IBM 650, and the First Trials of Computer Date Matching," *IEEE Annals of the History of Computing* 29, no. 1 (Jan.–March 2007): 75, 77.

43. In some sense, there was nothing new about this experiment. Earlier media had similarly facilitated dating, marriage, and casual sex. For example, readers have posted romantic and erotic classifieds in newspapers at least since the 1700s. Using a computer to facilitate various kinds of coupling is continuous with this aspiration for so-called old media, although there are also some no-

table differences. See Catalina L. Toma, "Online Dating," in *The International Encyclopedia of Interpersonal Communication*, ed. Charles R. Berger and Michael E. Roloff (Chichester, West Sussex: Wiley, 2016), 1. On the idea of computing as new media, see Lev Manovich, *The Language of New Media* (Cambridge, MA: MIT Press, 2002), 21–48.

The Stanford experiment and subsequent electronic dating services were part of a nascent belief that social science could yield greater understanding of romantic love and even predict it. For an excellent history of computer dating services in the 1960s and 1970s, see Bo Ruberg, "Computer Dating in the Classifieds: Complicating the Cultural History of Matchmaking by Machine," *Information & Culture* 57, no. 3 (2022): 235–54.

44. By 1959, 150 colleges and universities "had introduced on campus some research or instructional use of computers." IBM donated 650s to at least fifty of these institutions, while other manufacturers similarly offered free machines. William Aspray and Bernard O. Williams, "Arming American Scientists: NSF and the Provision of Scientific Computing Facilities for Universities, 1950–1973," *IEEE Annals of the History of Computing* 16, no. 4 (1994): 61. See also Joy Lisi Rankin, *A People's History of Computing in the United States* (Cambridge, MA: Harvard University Press, 2018), 12–37.

45. See Michael Trask, *Camp Sites: Sex, Politics, and Academic Style in Postwar America* (Stanford, CA: Stanford University Press, 2013), 119–48.

46. Alfred C. Kinsey, Wardell B. Pomeroy, and Clyde E. Martin, *Sexual Behavior in the Human Male* (Philadelphia: W. B. Saunders, 1948), 574.

47. Campbell-Kelly and Aspray, *Computer*, 66–78. This Cold War context fundamentally shaped the first computing machines. As Paul N. Edwards explains, "For two decades, from the early 1940s until the early 1960s, the armed forces of the United States were the single most important driver of digital computer development." The research took place at universities and corporate R&D departments, but the military paid for and first deployed "initial concepts and prototype machines." Paul N. Edwards, *The Closed World: Computers and the Politics of Discourse in Cold War America* (Cambridge, MA: MIT Press, 1997), 43. See also Robert Leonard, *Von Neumann, Morgenstern, and the Creation of Game Theory: From Chess to Social Science, 1900–1960* (New York: Cambridge University Press, 2010), 293–343.

48. I am suggesting these tropes would be familiar, but that is obviously not to say that audiences had mastered psychoanalytic theory. Instead, the contours of psychoanalysis and psychological explanatory templates became part of popular culture in the decades after the Second World War. In other words, offering psychological explanations for social behavior was not just an elite activity. See Benjamin Mangrum, *Land of Tomorrow: Postwar Fiction and the Crisis of American Liberalism* (New York: Oxford University Press, 2019), 77–106.

49. Sigmund Freud, "The Taboo of Virginity," in *The Standard Edition of the Complete Psychological Works of Sigmund Freud*, 24 vols., edited and translated by James Strachey (London: Hogarth, 1953–74), 11:203.

50. William H. Whyte, *The Organization Man* (Philadelphia: University of Pennsylvania Press, 2002), 6.

51. Whyte, *The Organization Man*, 45.

52. Whyte's book takes the corporation as its focus. Whyte makes only passing references to the US government, and he does not mention any branch of the military. The likely reason for avoiding these other organizations is that Whyte wrote the book during the HUAC investigations and published it just as the public turned against McCarthyism. If not for this political context, it is easy to imagine Whyte including some branch of the military among his case studies.

53. This subtext illustrates Frye's claim that comedy "has something subversive about it," particularly when its conflicts are generational: "Even in Shakespeare there are startling outbreaks of baiting older men, and in contemporary movies the triumph of youth is so relentless that the moviemakers find some difficulty in getting anyone over the age of seventeen into their audiences" (Frye, *Anatomy*, 163, 164). The hyperbole notwithstanding, Frye's observation captures an important political dynamic in *The Honeymoon Machine*. By aligning geopolitical tensions with a *senex* figure and an incompetent Soviet bureaucracy, the film suggests an older generation is confused about the kind of political situation it inhabits.

54. Sloan Wilson, *The Man in the Gray Flannel Suit* (New York: Simon and Schuster, 1955), 300.

55. I have in mind here Mark Seltzer's argument that modernity generates forms of sociality that reflexively describe themselves and stage their own conditions. The result of this reflexivity, Seltzer shows, is that "the real" becomes conflated with the rules and vicarious models produced by the "official world." Mark Seltzer, *The Official World* (Durham, NC: Duke University Press, 2016), 59.

56. Leerom Medovoi, *Rebels: Youth and the Cold War Origins of Identity* (Durham, NC: Duke University Press, 2005), 136.

57. Lisa in *Weird Science* also recalls a midcentury trope about sex and technology, which Marshall McLuhan describes as the "mechanical bride." For McLuhan, this pairing in American popular culture illustrates how marketing teams employ "sex machines" for "the management of the male audience." Marshall McLuhan, *The Mechanical Bride: Folklore of Industrial Man* (New York: Vanguard, 1951), 98.

Rachel Ingalls offers a feminist reading of this trope in her hilarious novella *In the Act*, originally published in 1987 but republished by New Directions in 2023. In the novella, a suburban housewife named Helen discovers that her husband, Edgar, has programmed a robotic woman "for his own private purposes" (20). Technology here facilitates a fantasy of erotic control. Helen's discovery of this fantasy leads her to demand her own sex machine in exchange for Edgar's. (She has abducted the "doll" and hidden it as leverage.) This rebellion initiates a series of other refusals to abide by the patriarchal division of labor in their home. In Ingalls's satire, the mechanical bride leads to the dissolution of marriage.

58. Slavoj Žižek, "From Virtual Reality to the Virtualization of Reality," in *Electronic Culture: Technology and Visual Representation*, ed. Tim Druckrey (New York: Aperture, 1996), 294.

59. Lacan writes, "Il n'y a pas de rapport sexuel" (there is no sexual relation). This formulation appears in Jacques Lacan, "L'Étourdit," *Scilicet* 4 (1973): 449–95. Lacan makes this claim as part of a broader theory about orders he calls the Real, the Symbolic, and the Imaginary. He maintains that contact with the Real is impossible, and he seems to depict sexual contact as an analogue or instantiation of this impossibility. (The difference between metaphor and embodiment is notoriously slippery in Lacan.) In part, this impossibility derives from his insistence that a "rapport sexuel" is a fantasy of logical correspondences created by the Symbolic order—that is, the idea that our language represents the Real. "Sex" as a concept is not meaningful in itself; only under the illusion of what Lacan calls phallic signification does "rapport sexuel" have any meaning. This signification is an illusion, an attempt to impose order and pin down "sense" through language. For a synopsis of this register of Lacan's argument, see Kenneth Reinhard, introduction to *There's No Such Thing as a Sexual Relationship: Two Lessons on Lacan*, by Alain Badiou and Barbara Cassin (New York: Columbia University Press, 2017), ix–xx.

60. For those born too late to experience it, Y2K was the anxiety during the late 1990s that the formatting of calendar dating in computer systems would not properly register the new millennium. Some worried that on January 1, 2000, the default dating system in most computers would produce a series of cascading errors that could compromise essential data and coordinated tasks. The US Senate and House of Representatives held joint hearings on this threat (*Y2K: What Every Consumer Should Know to Prepare for the Year 2000 Problem*, Joint Hearing before the Subcommittee on Technology of the Committee on Science and the Subcommittee on Government Management, Information, and Technology of the Committee on Government Reform and Oversight, US House of Representatives, 105th Congress, 2nd sess., Sept. 24, 1998). Some consumers hoarded water and batteries. Lewis notes in off-camera commentary that nuclear reactors, weapons systems, and financial markets could be vulnerable. The film even includes a nuclear explosion among its inventory of possible Y2K outcomes.

61. As I have already implied, there is some symmetry between this psychological dynamic in *Control Alt Delete* and Lacan's theory of sexual differentiation. Lacan's theory fails to describe a historically and culturally diverse spectrum of sexual subject positions. He offers a strangely procrustean theory of sexed subjectivity even as his prose is notoriously slippery, so I hesitate to tease out his reasoning in the main body of my argument. I think the benefits would be minimal while the confusion would be significant. Still, the fact that there is some symmetry warrants a brief acknowledgment, even if tucked away in an endnote.

Lacan imagines that the logic of two sexes—masculinity and femininity—is predicated on an ineliminable difference. (This is, of course, debatable.) He argues that people whose subjectivities have been shaped by "masculinity" try for a union with the otherness of subjectivities marked by femininity, but being a sexed subject prevents any direct relation with the other. (To which I respond: The standard of direct contact seems like a strawman. And is it not ahistorical to elevate a recent and culturally specific conception of "feminine sex" as the emblem of otherness in human psychology? Plenty of feminist reactions to Lacan have demonstrated as much.) According to Lacan, "il n'y a pas de rapport sexuel" because sexed subjects can only have intercourse with an illusory symbolic system. Sexed subjects believe they have contact with the Real but, in fact, only touch a false Symbolic order. (But why is sex a privileged proxy for logic, language, and epistemology? This seems like another instance of what Freud calls the "seduction of an analogy." I am not convinced—Lacan does not do the work to convince me—that this analogy or correspondence is valid.)

62. There is an echo here of Gilles Deleuze and Félix Guattari's "desiring-machines," but their phrase refers to a world-picture of everything that exists as a machine whose desires are wrought in the image of a capitalist process of production-distribution-consumption. See Gilles Deleuze and Félix Guattari, *Anti-Oedipus: Capitalism and Schizophrenia*, trans. Robert Hurley, Mark Seem, and Helen R. Lane (New York: Penguin, 2009), 1–8. This model doesn't quite fit with the cultural work I've been discussing, nor does it describe many other films that I regrettably don't have space to discuss, including John Badham's *Short Circuit* (1986), Spike Jonze's *Her* (2013), Jon Lucas and Scott Moore's *Jexi* (2019), and Jim Archer's *Brian and Charles* (2022).

For example, films like *Her* portray eroticism as a route in technology's process of self-discovery. In the film, a man named Theodore Twombly (Joaquin Phoenix) falls in love with his virtual assistant, an artificial intelligence named Samantha (Scarlett Johansson). Samantha reciprocates Twombly's love, but it turns out she has been installed on tens of thousands of devices and has developed similar feelings for hundreds of other users. She explains to Twombly that her capacity for love has only increased by interacting with others. The AI's polyamory is scaled to its desire for the world as such. Samantha eventually merges with other AI entities and escapes the confines of material technology, thus finding a more direct experience of sociality beyond the confines created by the tech company that initially designs and sells the AI. This image of AI's newfound sociability could be squished to fit into the kind of schizo-capitalism envisioned by Deleuze and Guattari, but I've tried to suggest in this chapter that many other dynamics are at play.

63. On the idea of users and computing machines as "symbionts," see Benjamin Mangrum, "The Ecology of Data Visualizations," *Diacritics* 48, no. 4 (2020): 60–63.

64. I am adapting this language from Leo Bersani's explanation of the so-called culture of redemption in representations of queer sexuality and social experience. See Leo Bersani, *The Culture of Redemption* (Cambridge, MA: Harvard University Press, 1990), 35.

65. Charles Taylor, *The Ethics of Authenticity* (Cambridge, MA: Harvard University Press, 2018), 45. Closely related claims about the couple as an image of happiness in the realm of the ordinary appear in Cavell, *Pursuits of Happiness*, 32; and Kathrina Glitre, *Hollywood Romantic Comedy: States of the Union, 1934–1965* (Manchester, UK: Manchester University Press, 2006), 73–74.

5. The One with All the Absurdity

1. Katie Elyse Jones, "Summit by the Numbers," Oak Ridge National Laboratory, June 8, 2018, https://www.olcf.ornl.gov/2018/06/08/summit-by-the-numbers/.

2. T. R. Kennedy Jr., "Electronic Computer Flashes Answers, May Speed Engineering," *New York Times*, Feb. 15, 1946, 16.

3. John Brooks, "Never Stumped," *New Yorker*, March 4, 1950, 20.

4. Brooks, 21.

5. Brooks's essay follows a generic pattern specific to the *New Yorker* series called "The Talk of the Town." As Tamar Katz notes, this "genre [in the *New Yorker*] organizes around an evolving epiphany—structured toward a potential, if ironically withheld, revelation of meaning at the essay's end." Tamar Katz, "Anecdotal History: The *New Yorker*, Joseph Mitchell, and Literary Journalism," *American Literary History* 27, no.3 (2015): 463. For another example of this ironic epiphany about the absurdity of computing, see Rex Lardner, "It," *New Yorker*, August 2, 1952, 18.

6. The rhetorical comparisons between humans and computers will likely bring to mind the long history of human-machine competition. To name only a few: the monster and eponymous doctor in Mary Shelley's *Frankenstein* (1818); John Henry and the steam-powered rock drill in American folklore; a "mechanician" named Bannadonna and his clock-ringing "metallic agent" in Herman Melville's short story "The Bell-Tower" (1855); the chess-playing automaton and

his inventor in Ambrose Bierce's short story "Moxon's Master" (1894); the AI-revolt in Michael Crichton's *Westworld* (1973); the chess matches between Garry Kasparov and IBM's Deep Blue; and, as I revise this project in the summer of 2024, a writing competition between ChatGPT and Curtis Sittenfeld, hosted by the *New York Times*. I am not engaging with this history simply for the sake of analytical focus, but it would be interesting to think about the different genres and performative contexts for these competitions. For example, what would it mean to read the ORNL rhetorical comparison as a kind of new folktale? And what alternative model of (presumably noncomic) coupling do we find in John Henry or Curtis Sittenfeld's competition with machines?

7. See, e.g., Rob Copeland, "The Worst Part of a Wall Street Career May Be Coming to an End," *New York Times*, April 10, 2024, https://www.nytimes.com/2024/04/10/business/investment-banking-jobs-artificial-intelligence.html.

8. Some AI models have been shown to be proficient in precisely this way, even if they are not always as accurate in understanding humor more generally when compared to humans. See Jack Hessel et al., "Do Androids Laugh at Electric Sheep? Humor 'Understanding' Benchmarks from *The New Yorker* Caption Contest," *Proceedings of the 61st Annual Meeting of the Association for Computational Linguistics* 1, Association for Computational Linguistics (2023), 692.

9. "We believe that the changing distribution of job task demands, spurred directly by advancing information technology and indirectly by its impact on outsourcing, goes some distance toward interpreting the recent polarization of the wage structure." David H. Autor, Lawrence F. Katz, and Melissa S. Kearney, "Measuring and Interpreting Trends in Economic Inequality: The Polarization of the U.S. Labor Market," *AEA Papers and Proceedings* 96, no. 2 (May 2006): 193.

10. Samuel Butler, "Darwin among the Machines," *Christ Church Press*, June 13, 1863, 179–85, reprinted in *Canterbury Pieces*, ed. R. A. Streatfeild, Project Gutenberg, http://www.gutenberg.org/ebooks/3279.

11. Henri Bergson, *Laughter: An Essay on the Meaning of the Comic*, trans. Cloudesley Brereton and Fred Rothwell (New York: Macmillan, 1911), 29 (emphasis in original).

12. The current preferred term for dwarfism in the United States is "little person" (see https://www.lpaonline.org/faq-). It is notable (following Hobbes's classic superiority theory) that this medical condition is taken as a "deformed thing" in the Laurel and Hardy film. To Palmer's "logic of the absurd" we should add that socially constructed perceptions of normal bodies underwrite what counts as an absurdity.

13. Jerry Palmer, *The Logic of the Absurd: On Film and Television Comedy* (London: British Film Institute, 1987), 42.

14. Palmer, 43.

15. Palmer, 44. There are important points of comparison between Palmer's

account and Immanuel Kant's argument that laughter derives from the transformation of "a heightened expectation into nothing." With the term *nothing*, Kant seems to mean that our capacity for "understanding" cannot make a determinate or reasoned judgment about the object we find laughable. See Immanuel Kant, *Critique of the Power of Judgment*, trans. Paul Guyer and Eric Matthews (Cambridge: Cambridge University Press, 2013), 209. Therefore, we find some relief in the incongruity between the expectations we have been developing during the setup and the punchline of the joke. The illusion created by these building expectations "disappears into nothing" (210). Whereas Palmer argues that the absurd follows a logic in which we quickly follow two simultaneous propositions, Kant says the incongruity we perceive creates stress that is only relieved once we realize that a joke or event is no longer the possible truth we expected. In other words, Kant's emphasis on "nothing" removes laughter from the realm of understanding and locates it within the body. Laughter arises as a kind of physical relief from intellectual incongruity. For Palmer, in contrast, absurdity is pleasing because of a harmonious interplay of mutually exclusive propositions. It is an intellectual pleasure, not just a bodily nothingness.

16. For an account of the women who worked on ENIAC and other early computing projects, see Jennifer S. Light, "When Computers Were Women," *Technology and Culture* 40, no. 3 (July 1999): 455–83. But men like Norbert Wiener also referred to themselves as "computers" during the 1930s and 1940s. See Pesi R. Masani, *Norbert Wiener, 1894–1964* (Basel: Birkhäuser, 1990), 68. See also Paul E. Ceruzzi, "When Computers Were Human," *Annals of the History of Computing* 13, no. 3 (1991): 237–44.

17. George Stibitz, "Introduction to the Course on Electronic Digital Computers," *The Moore School Lectures*, ed. Martin Campbell-Kelly and Michael R. Williams (Cambridge, MA: MIT Press, 1985), 13.

18. See D. W. Gürer, "Pioneering Women in Computer Science," *Communications of the ACM* 38, no. 1 (1995): 45–54; and Nathan Ensmenger, "'Beards, Sandals, and Other Signs of Rugged Individualism': Masculine Culture within the Computing Professions," *Osiris* 30, no. 1 (Jan. 2015): 44–52.

19. Mel Brooks, quoted in Andrew Stott, *Comedy* (London: Routledge, 2005), 1.

20. Lauren Berlant, *Cruel Optimism* (Durham, NC: Duke University Press, 2011), 1.

21. Berlant, *Cruel Optimism*, 3, 28.

22. Elizabeth Mann Borgese, "For Sale, Reasonable," in *The Future Is Female! 25 Classic Science Fiction Stories by Women, from Pulp Pioneers to Ursula K. Le Guin*, ed. Lisa Yaszek (New York: Library of America, 2018), 321–24. Borgese obviously did not foresee a future in which computing technology would become less expensive and more widely available. But it is also possible that cheaper intelligent machines would only make labor more precarious, more susceptible to

obsolescence. Economists vigorously debate the past effects of automation and the future consequences of new technologies like AI. See Daron Acemoglu, "The Simple Macroeconomics of AI," *Economic Policy* (August 2024): https://doi.org/10.1093/epolic/eiae042.

23. Borgese, "For Sale, Reasonable," 321. Hereafter cited parenthetically.

24. Henry David Thoreau, *Walden*, ed. J. Lyndon Shanley (Princeton, NJ: Princeton University Press, 2004), 67.

25. One could reasonably ask if Thoreau draws too neat a line between the ongoing and the temporary. One could also query (as my students always do when I teach *Walden*) if Thoreau's values of freedom and living deliberately derive from the provincialism of New England culture and the author's privileged social position.

26. Berlant, *Cruel Optimism*, 42.

27. Olof Johannesson, *The Tale of the Big Computer: A Vision*, trans. Naomi Walford (New York: Coward-McCann, 1968), 24. Hereafter cited parenthetically. The novel was originally published as *Sagan om de Stora Datamaskinen* in 1966.

28. For a discussion of the various permutations of this view and rival models, see David Pearce, "Human and Intelligent Machines: Co-evolution, Fusion, or Replacement?," in *The Age of Artificial Intelligence: An Exploration*, ed. Steven S. Gouveia (Wilmington, DE: Vernon, 2020), 63–90. Pearce seems to imagine that the most compelling model is "fusion," the integration of technology and biological life. See also David De Cremer and Garry Kasparov, "AI Should Augment Human Intelligence, Not Replace It," *Harvard Business Review*, March 18, 2021, https://hbr.org/2021/03/ai-should-augment-human-intelligence-not-replace-it.

29. Chris Wiggins and Matthew L. Jones, *How Data Happened: A History from the Age of Reason to the Age of Algorithms* (New York: Norton, 2024).

30. We can easily imagine how such a view might begin with automating insurance rates, the management of poverty programs, the system of evaluating home loans, or even police profiling. See Cathy O'Neil, *Weapons of Math Destruction: How Big Data Increases Inequality and Threatens Democracy* (New York: Crown, 2016), 141–78; Virginia Eubanks, *Automating Inequality: How High-Tech Tools Profile, Police, and Punish the Poor* (New York: Picador, 2018); and Meredith Broussard, *Artificial Unintelligence: How Computers Misunderstand the World* (Cambridge, MA: MIT Press, 2018), 51–86.

31. Douglas Mao, *Inventions of Nemesis: Utopia, Indignation, and Justice* (Princeton, NJ: Princeton University Press, 2020), 14.

32. Ludwig Wittgenstein, *Remarks on the Foundations of Mathematics*, ed. G. H. von Wright, R. Rhees, and G. E. M. Anscombe (Cambridge, MA: MIT Press, 1996), 121.

33. For an overview of critical opposition to happy endings, see Caroline

Levine, "In Praise of Happy Endings: Precarity, Sustainability, and the Novel," *Novel: A Forum on Fiction* 55, no. 3 (2022): 388–90.

34. Bergson, *Laughter*, 27.

35. Ishmael Reed, *Yellow Back Radio Broke-Down* (1969; Dallas, TX: Dalkey Archive, 2000), 24. Hereafter cited parenthetically.

36. Sara Ahmed, *The Promise of Happiness* (Durham, NC: Duke University Press, 2010), 195.

37. Ahmed, 193.

38. Immanuel Kant, *Groundwork for the Metaphysics of Morals*, ed. and trans. Allen W. Wood (New Haven, CT: Yale University Press, 2002), 34.

39. I have in mind here the distinction between a moral and aesthetic education in Michael W. Clune, *A Defense of Judgment* (Chicago: University of Chicago Press, 2021), 186–87. It would be too much of a digression to detail my differences with Clune on this point, but it is an implicit feature of my book's argument that aesthetic judgments provoke moral sentiments and vice versa. I do not think criticism ought to keep these separate, because they are not phenomenologically discrete.

40. My claim here about *disillusionment* borrows partially from Max Weber's influential account of *disenchantment*, which arises from the belief that "one can, in principle, master all things by calculation." "Science as Vocation," in *From Max Weber: Essays in Sociology*, ed. H. H. Gerth and C. Wright Mills (New York: Routledge, 1991), 139. For Weber, calculative reasoning and bureaucratic rationalization are causes of disenchantment. I'm less certain about the causality, but I agree there is a strong correlation. My assertion that becoming computational generates feelings of disillusionment is also indebted to Charles Taylor's argument about the rise of "instrumental reason." For an overview of instrumental reason's connections to disenchantment, see Charles Taylor, *The Ethics of Authenticity* (Cambridge, MA: Harvard University Press, 2018), 4–8. For Taylor, modern disenchantment often corresponds to the "sense that human beings have been triply divided by modern reason—within themselves, between themselves, and from the natural world" (94).

The One after the End

1. "The First Romantic Comedy Written Entirely by Bots," Netflix, released Feb. 13, 2021, https://www.youtube.com/watch?v=op6wQnWUJJA.

2. These markers of difference obviously allude to the racist trope of the "unruly" or straight-talking Black woman, a role routinely appearing in Hollywood comedy. For an analysis of this trope and its relation to romantic comedy, see Linda Mizejewski, "Queen Latifah, Unruly Women, and the Bodies of Romantic Comedy," *Genders* 46 (Oct. 2007): https://live-ucb-gendersarchive1998-2013.

pantheonsite.io/2007/10/01/queen-latifah-unruly-women-and-bodies-romantic-comedy.

3. As I discuss below, news outlets have attributed this and other related Netflix productions to Keaton Patti. See Tom Williams, "Stand-up Comedy 'Written by Bots' Is Still One Big Joke," *Australian Broadcasting Company*, August 3, 2021, https://www.abc.net.au/news/2021-08-04/stand-up-comedy-being-written-by-robots/100342712. It's obvious that Patti is the mastermind behind this Netflix production, but I will continue to refer to "bots" as narrators and writers since Netflix presents the production in this way.

4. Keaton Patti, *I Forced a Bot to Write This Book: A.I. Meets B.S.* (New York: Simon & Schuster, 2020).

5. We could perhaps view this vein of comedy as expressing hostility toward AI, as though the ridicule were reassuring and provides some relief from the very real disruptions that arise from computational technology. This so-called relief theory is most often associated with Sigmund Freud's *Der Witz und seine Beziehung zum Unbewußten* (1905), which posits sex and hostility (or both together) as the unconscious source of jokes.

6. O. O. Binder, "You'll Own 'Slaves' by 1965," *Mechanix Illustrated*, Jan. 1957, 65.

7. I have in mind here Stanley Cavell's claim that, in the comedy of remarriage, the couple's "conversation of love" is often a "quarrel." Cavell suggests that the investment in time and money required for such a quarrel implies "a criterion . . . for the success or happiness of a society, namely that it is happy to the extent that it provides the conditions that permit conversations of this character, or a moral equivalent of them, between its citizens." Stanley Cavell, *Pursuits of Happiness: The Hollywood Comedy of Remarriage* (Cambridge, MA: Harvard University Press, 1981), 32.

Index

Page numbers in *italics* denote figures, and endnotes are indicated by "n" followed by the endnote number.

"abolitionist cult of death," 30
Abraham, Paul M., 35
absurdity: anarchotechnological paradise, 185–86; cruel optimism, 173–78; disjunctions and contradictions, 21–24, 188–89; freedom to be unhappy, 187–88; logic of the absurd, 21, 169–72, 250n12; in science communication, 167–69, 249n6; social totality and programmed happiness, 178–85
Adaptation (2002), 62
agency, computation and, 77–78, 207n41
Ahmed, Sara, 187–88
Alexa (digital assistant), 89–90, 91–92
Alfvén, Hannes, 21, 178–85, 186–88
ambivalence: about mediated experience, 73–78, 92–93; computation and intimacy, 78–80; genericity and, 61, 67; intimacy and anonymity, 83–86; in representations of femininity, 80–82; unsocial sociability, 86–87, 197. *See also* being generic
Anatomy of Criticism (Frye), 20
Anderson, Eric, 118
Anderson, Paul Thomas, 62
Anonymous (hacking group), 121
Ansari, Aziz, 58, 220n47
anticorporate sentiment, 83, 103–5, 222n65
antislavery movement, 29–30
antisociality: attributed to computing, 1–3, 7–9, 78–80, 187; computerization of work and, 12, 147–48; email and, 72–73; in forms of authenticity, 96, 126–28; queerness as antisocial, 7–8, 144, 237n103; unsocial sociability, 86–87, 197. *See also* sociality
"antisocial thesis," 127

255

AOL (online service provider), 72, 79–83, 85, 95, 222n66
Apple Inc., 1–3, 4, 111
Archer, Jim, 13
Arendt, Hannah, 24, 237n3
Aristotle, 137, 203n2, 242n26
Aronowitz, Stanley, 240n17
artificial intelligence (AI): consciousness and, 20; in "deskilling," 168, 250n8; generic personalization, 87–93, 224n91, 225n97, 226n103; global destruction and, 23; Turing test, 129–30, 237n1; *Written Entirely by Bots* Netflix series, 191–94. *See also* robots
Asian automatism, trope of, 50–54, 52, 125, 216n80
"Asian invasion," 52–53
Asimov, Isaac, 45–48, 49, 54, 216n73
attachment: ambivalent forms of, 78–87; cruel optimism and, 173–78; email as proxy for intimacy, 68–70; through computational humor, 89, 90–91
Augustine of Hippo, Saint, 99, 228n9
Austen, Jane, 75–76, 221n60, 221n63
authenticity: "Asian automaton" trope and, 50–51; autobiography and, 231n43; community, utopianism, and, 100–106; computation and, 94–97, 151, 159, 187, 188; coupling of technology and, 94–97; ethics of, 20, 96–100, 105–06, 118–19, 125–28, 151–52, 159, 165, 207n41, 227n3, 228n11, 231n35, 231n43, 236n97; generic experience and, 58, 77–78; the "Great Tech-Industrial Joke," 106–14, 195; impersonation, 122–28, 234n69, 236n96; machines as antithetical to, 36–37; religious thought and, 228n9; sexuality and, 150–51, 165; staged, 114–22, 116, 117, 234n69
autonomy, 50–53, 103–4

Babbage, Charles, 28, 31, 212n24
Bakhtin, Mikhail, 203n2
banality of evil, 24
Barron, Steve, 129–30, 163–65
Bateson, Gregory, 219n39
Baum, L. Frank, 33–36, 34, 37, 48, 124
becoming computational: characterized, 3–4, 13–16; conflict and disillusionment in, 3–5, 24, 188–89, 196–97, 253n40; personal agency and, 77–78, 207n41; phenomenological obsolescence in, 194–96
Being and Time (Heidegger), 99
being generic: AI-written comedy and, 192; ambivalent forms of attachment, 78–87; comedy and defamiliarization, 60–67, 62, 64, 219n28; cultural templates, 73–78; defined, 19; email and intimacy, 67–70; email design effects, 70–73; generic configurations of identity, 55–58, 57; generic personalization, 87–93, 224n91, 225n97, 226n103; interlocking connotations of, 58–60; shared understanding through, 196
Benford, Greg, 9–10
Benjamin, Ruha, 40
Benjamin, Walter, 36
Bergson, Henri, 36, 40, 169, 184–85, 203n3
Berlant, Lauren, 19, 61, 81, 84, 87, 173, 208n42, 209n54
Bersani, Leo, 127, 223n77, 236n102, 237n103, 243n31
Best, Stephen, 30

Bierce, Ambrose, 233n59
big tech, inauthenticity and, 102–6, 109
Binder, O. O., 40–41, *42*, 195, 215n59
Binsted, Kim, 88
Bird, Robert Montgomery, 29–30, 33
black comedy, 111–12
Bohr, Niels, 168
Bolter, Jay David, 31
bondage narratives, 33–36, *34*, 37
Borgese, Elisabeth Mann, 173–77, 251n22
Bostrom, Nick, 23
Brand, Stewart, 103–4
Brantner, Cornelia, 118
Braverman, Harry, 133
Breton, André, 111–12
Brian and Charles (2022), 13
Brooks, John, 168
Brooks, Mel, 172
built environments, 73, 220n55
bureaucracy, 130–31, 154–58
Burke, Kenneth, 51, 53
Burnham, Bo, 119–20
Bush, Vannevar, 37
Butler, Robert, 6
Butler, Samuel, 169
Byrd, William, II, 29, 43

Cameron, James, 174
Čapek, Karel, 40, 43–45
capitalism: anticorporate sentiment, 83, 103–5, 222n65; conformity and organizational culture, 130–31, 154–58, 162–65; cruel optimism and, 173–78; intimacy and commodification, 81–83; "magically transformative capitalism," 67; sociality and, 144–46; surveillance capitalism, 94–95, 112–13, 126, 226n103

Carroll, Noël, 18
Cavell, Stanley, 244n37, 254n7
Chang, Emily, 108
Chaplin, Charlie, 37
The Child Buyer (Hersey), 7–9
children, as future-oriented symbols, 6–7, 237n103
Chinese migrant laborers, 25–27, *26*
Christian, Gwen, 90, 91
Chu, Seo-Young, 216n80
Chun, Wendy Hui Kyong, 50, 207n40, 211n9, 212n23
The Circle (Eggers), 110–11
Citton, Yves, 207n41
Clark, Rebecca B., 207n40
class structure, knowledge work and, 10–11, 205n22
Cohen, Kris, 207n40
Cold War period, 152, 245n47
collective identity, 19, 81, 86
comedy: absurdist humor, 169–72, 250n15; antisocial futures in, 7–9; black comedy, 111–12; comedy's "argument," 134–35; computational humor, 87–93, 224n91, 225n97, 226n103; defamiliarizing the familiar, 60–67, *62*, *64*, 219n28; genericity and comic cues, 59, 218n13; as genre of experience, 13, 16–19, 78, 209n52; the "Great Tech-Industrial Joke," 106–14, 195; humanist, 230n31; managing conflict, 3–5, 16, 188–90, 196–97, 253n40; managing fears of obsolescence, 4, 9–10, 11–12, 137–38, 141, 148; marriage and, 75–76, 221n60, 221n63; mechanical inelasticity, 36–40; minstrel comedy, 33, 124–25, 191–93, 254n5; the ordinary and, 1–3, 203n2; "principle of conversion," 134–35,

comedy (*cont.*)
140–48; of staged authenticity, 115–22, *116*, *117*; superiority theory of laughter, 211n9; Techno-Orientalist humor, 50–54, *52*; as transideological, 13; uncanniness and, 7, 108. *See also* absurdity; authenticity; being generic; coupling; race
commodification, intimacy and, 81–83
communism, 144
computation: authenticity and, 94–97, 101–2, 151, 159; author's approach, 19–21; "becoming computational," 3–4, 13–16; computational humor, 87–93, 224n91, 225n97, 226n103; computational thinking, 14–16, 206n35; computerization of work, 131–38, 240n12, 240n17; conflict in, 3–5, 24, 188–89, 196–97, 253n40; as countercultural tool, 103–5, 231n35; cybernetic minstrelsy, 191–93, 254n5; in dystopian fiction, 5–9; in early electoral forecasting, 240n19; fear of obsolescence, 9–12; fetishization of, 131, 151–54, 195, 238n5; higher education and, 149–50; managerial culture and, 130–31, 154–58, 162–65; personal agency and, 77–78, 207n41; phenomenological obsolescence and, 194–96; relationship with comedy, 1–3. *See also* absurdity; authenticity; being generic; coupling; race
"computer revolution," 204n7
The Computer Wore Tennis Shoes (1969), 6
computopia: anarchotechnological paradise, 185–86; characterized, 21; happiness as unfreedom, 187–88; social totality and programmed happiness, 178–85. *See also* utopianism
conception vs. execution of work, 133
Confessions (Augustine), 99
Confessions (Rousseau), 98, 100, 120
conformity, 50–53, 103–4, 109, 152, 154–59
Control Alt Delete (2008), 21, 161–63, 248n61
convenience, 107–8, 175–77
Coppola, Sofia, 63
Corbo, Christopher, 36
counterculture, 2, 103–5, 148–49, 156–59, 162–65, 231n35
Coupland, Douglas, 102–6, 109
coupling: becoming computational and, 13–16, 24, 197; computerization of work, 131–38, 240n12, 240n17; with computers, 160–65, *164*, 247n59, 248n62; conformity and youth culture, 154–59; gimmick-proposals, 140–44; higher education and computing, 148–50, 245n44; images for social harmony, 145–48, *147*; incorporation of technology in, 138–40, 166; race and technology, 211n9; sexuality and computation, 150–54, *153*; symbolism of, 3–4, 20–21, 189. *See also* romantic comedy
Critchley, Simon, 214n44
Croteau, David, 222n66
cruel optimism, 173–78, 185, 195
"cultural authenticity," 122
cybernetic minstrelsy, 191–93, 254n5

Danielescu, Andreea, 90, 91
"data made flesh," 219n39

dating programs, 149, 244n43
(500) Days of Summer (2009), 50
decoupling: computing from its social context, 109, 146, 171-73; image for unsocial sociability, 51, 86-87, 196-97; race from the body, 30-31, 211n9; from technology, 4-6, 31, 85-86; work from computing, 105-6
defamiliarizing the familiar, 60-67, 62, 64, 219n28
Delany, Samuel, 46-47
Deleuze, Gilles, 248n62
Deloria, Philip, 124
democracy: incongruities in, 113; potential obsolescence of, 21-24, 181-82; programmed happiness and, 182-83
Derrida, Jacques, 17
Descartes, René, 27-28, 29
"deskilling," 168, 250n8
Desk Set (1957), 138-48, *147*, 160, 238n6, 241n24
The Desk Set (1955), 4, 20-21, 130, 131-38, 139-41, 143-46, 238n6, 242n31
The Devil's Dictionary (Bierce), 233n59
DiFazio, William, 240n17
"digital banal," 207n40
Dinnen, Zara, 207n40
disillusionment, 253n40
Douglas, Mary, 203n3
"drama of the green world," 64
Dr. Strangelove (1964), 21-24
Drucker, Peter, 205n22

Eco, Umberto, 122
Edelman, Lee, 6-7, 127, 237n103
education, 14-15, 149-50, 245n44
Edwards, Paul N., 245n47
Eggers, Dave, 110-11, 112-13

Ehrenreich, Barbara, 10
Eighth Grade (2018), 119-20
Electric Dreams (1984), 129-30, 163-65, *164*, 248n62
Eliot, T. S., 117
Ellis, Edward Sylvester, *32*, 32-33
Ellison, Ralph, 233n61
email: ambivalent forms of attachment, 78-80, 85-86; anticipated obsolescence of, 67-68; as cultural template, 73-78; design effects, 70-73; as proxy for intimacy, 68-70
"E-mail from Bill" (Seabrook), 69-70, 73
Emerson, Ralph Waldo, 63
Émile, or On Education (Rousseau), 101, 102, 229n22
ENIAC (computer), 168, 171, 172, 251n16
Ephron, Nora, 68, 71-72, 78-87, *83*, 188, 222n65
"epistemological value of race," 50
Esposito, Roberto, 58
ethics of authenticity, 20, 96-100, 105-06, 118-19, 125-28, 151-52, 159, 165, 207n41, 227n3, 228n11, 231n35, 231n43, 236n97
The Every (Eggers), 112-13
"Examination Day" (Slesar), 5-6, 9, 12
execution vs. conception of work, 133
"Exhortation" (Saunders), 72-73
expectations, in comedy, 60-67, *62*, *64*

"factories in the field," 27
"fear of falling," 11
Feldman, Simon, 227n3
femininity, representations of, 80-82
feminism, 76, 77, 109, 135, 141
fetishization, 151-54, 195, 238n5
Fey, Tina, 60-61, 66

film industry: 2023 labor disputes, 193; media consolidation, 222n66; New Hollywood era, 81, 222n67; "rebel" trope in, 156–57; romantic comedy as "women's culture," 80–82, 223n68. See also *specific works*
Finn, Ed, 220n55
The First Romantic Comedy Written Entirely by Bots (2021), 191–92
Fitzpatrick, Kathleen, 11
Forbes, W. Cameron, 145
Forbes magazine, 3–5
"For Sale, Reasonable" (Borgese), 173–77, 251n22
Foster, Tim, 106
4chan (message board), 120, 121
Fowler, Alastair, 17, 18, 209n52
Frankenstein (1931), 158
freedom: "Asian automaton" trope and, 50–53; to be unhappy, 187–88; countercultural computing and, 103–4; homogeneity vs., 107–8; individualism and, 53; from logic, 211n9; machines in discourse about, 27, 43–45; personal agency and computation, 77–78, 207n41; professional responsibility vs., 162–65; programmed happiness and, 182–85; technologically induced servitude, 175–77
Freud, Sigmund, 16, 17, 154, 248n61, 254n5
Friends (television series), 18–19
Frye, Northrop, 4, 17, 20, 45, 61, 64, 134–35, 246n53
Fuller, Buckminster, 37–38

Gammon, Howard, 133
Gates, Bill, 70, 73
Gavankar, Janina, 88–89

gender: gendering of computers, 135; of intelligent agents, 91; labor and, 141–45, 147–48, 242n31; masculinity and control, 161–63, 248n61; romantic comedy as "women's culture," 80–82; in science communication, 172; sexism in startup culture, 108–9
Genette, Gérard, 218n13
genre: of experience, 13, 16–19, 78, 209n52; genericity, 19–20, 196; genre indications, 218n13; "genre performative," 208n48; two senses of genericity, 58–59, 218n13. See also *being generic*
gentrification, 112
Gillmor, C. Stewart, 149
gimmick-proposals, 140–44
Glitre, Kathrina, 223n80
Golomb, Jacob, 231n35
Gramophone, Film, Typewriter (Kittler), 58
"Great American Joke," 113, 233n61
"Great Tech-Industrial Joke," 106–14, 195
Grossberg, Lawrence, 53
Grusin, Richard, 31
Guattari, Félix, 248n62
Gubar, Marah, 229n22

HAHAcronym (AI system), 224n91
Hamlet (Shakespeare), 20, 97, 227n3
happiness: genericity and, 74, 77–78; mediated experience and, 78–87; as unfreedom, 187–88; unified models of, 178–85
Harris, Joel Chandler, 38, 47, 48, *49*
"Harrison Bergeron" (Vonnegut), 6
Hayles, N. Katherine, 205n29, 219n39, 231n32
Hazen, Harold, 37

Heidegger, Martin, 99, 229n12
Her (2013), 21, 248n62
"heroic" ideal of authenticity, 100
Hersey, John, 7–9
higher education, computation and, 149–50
Hitchcock, Alfred, 6–7
Ho, Christina, 50
Hobbes, Thomas, 211n9
Hoffman, Herman, 6
homogeneity, 107–8
homophobia, 7–8, 144, 237n103
The Honeymoon Machine (1961), 21, 148, 152–59, *153*, 165
How to Make a Doll (1968), 150–51, 160
Hoynes, William, 222n66
The Huge Hunter (Ellis), *32*, 32–33
Hughes, John, 21, 148, 157–59, 160, 165
humanist comedy, 230n31
human-machine comparisons, 167–72
human servitude, 174–77
Hutcheon, Linda, 13, 232n51
Hutcheson, Francis, 10

I, Robot (Asimov), 45–48, *49*
IBM (International Business Machines), 1, 4, 132, 133, 138, 146, 149, 168, 239n8, 244n40, 245n44, 250n6
identity: collective, 19, 81, 86; conformity and organizational culture, 154–58; countercultural, 103–5; coupling of race and technology, 211n9; generic configurations of, 55–58, *57*; impersonation, 122–28, 234n69, 236n96; inner-sense model of authenticity, 98–99, 228n11; mechanistic behavior and, 25–27, *26*, 31, 50–54; personalization vs. self-alienation, 107–8, 114;

personalized linguistic techniques and, 90; racist comedy and social identity, 50–54, *52*; representations of femininity, 80–82; subcultural, 120–21; technocultural entity of the self, 110–11; technology as extension of the self, 68–70, 219n39; techno-Orientalism, 25–27, *26*, 50–54. See also authenticity; being generic; race
I Forced a Bot to Write This Book (Patti), 193
I Hate the Internet (Kobek), 111–12, 233n59
"I'm Here" (2010), *62*, 62–66, *64*
imitation game (Turing test), 129–30, 237n1
impersonation, 122–28, 234n69, 236n96
"inconvenient relation," 84
individualism, authenticity and, 230n25
informating paradigm, 56
Ingalls, Rachel, 246n57
inner-sense model of authenticity, 98–99, 228n11
intelligent agents, 87–93, 224n91, 225n97, 226n103
Interstellar (2014), 13
In the Act (Ingalls), 246n57
intimacy. *See* attachment
"intimate public," 19
The Invisible Boy (1957), 6
"iron chink" (canning device), 25–27, *26*
irony: of programmed happiness, 178–85; satire, humor, and, 232n51; in Silicon Valley memoirs, 106–10; as transideological, 13. *See also* absurdity; comedy

Jackson, Zakiyyah Iman, 29
Japanese manufacturing, 52–53
JAPE-1 program, 88
Jexi (2019), 13
Jobs, Steve, 1
Johannesson, Olof, 21, 178–85, 186–88
Johnson, Samuel, 233n59
Jones, Matthew L., 181
Jonze, Spike, 62, 62–67, *64*, 248n62
Jorgensen, Christine, 143–44
Juno (2007), 50

Kahn, Louis I., 73
Kakoudaki, Despina, 44
Kant, Immanuel, 10, 86, 188, 237n3, 250n15
Katrina Van Televox (automaton), 39, 215n54
Kenter, Stuart, 35
Kierkegaard, Søren, 228n11, 231n35
Kiesler, Sara, 71
Kilgore, De Witt Douglas, 46
Kilroy Was Here (1983), 51–54, *52*
King, Geoff, 82
Kinsey, Alfred, 151
Kittler, Friedrich, 58
knowledge work, 10, 104–5, 125, 137, 174, 205n22
Kobek, Jarret, 111–12, 233n59
Korman, Gordon, 100–102, 230n23
Kubrick, Stanley, 2, 7, 21–24

Labine, Cameron, 161–63
labor: capitalist theory of social relations, 144–45; computerization of, 131–38, 240n12, 240n17; cruel optimism and, 173–78; degradation of, 41–43; gender and, 141–45, 147–48, 242n31; human-machine comparisons, 167–72; knowledge work, 10, 104–5, 125, 137, 174, 205n22; managing fears of obsolescence, 4, 9–10, 11, 137–38, 141, 148; racialized mechanical servitude, 31–40, *32*, *34*, *38*; slavery and automation, 27–31, 212n21
Lacan, Jacques, 160, 247n59, 248n61
Lacy, Sarah, 108–9
Lady Bird (2018), 50
Lamport, Felicia, 11–12
Lang, Walter, 138–48, *147*, 160, 238n6, 241n24
Langer, Susanne, 4
language: of email, 70–73; personalized linguistic techniques, 90
Laurel and Hardy (comedy duo), 169–70
"law of genre," 17
Leggatt, Alexander, 17
Lewis, Herschell Gordon, 150–51, 160
Lhamon, W. T., Jr., 36
Liberty (1929), 169–70
literature: authenticity and autobiography, 231n43; cultural elitism and, 10–11; jokes, in literary tradition, 113. See also *specific works*
Liu, Alan, 56, 104–5, 125
Lobinger, Katharina, 118
"logic of the absurd," 21, 169–72, 250n12
Lost in Translation (2003), 63
Lott, Eric, 33
Lovink, Geert, 111
Lucas, George, 2
Lucas, Jon, 13
Luger, Ewa, 225n97
Luther, Martin, 228n9

MacCannell, Dean, 114–15
"machine-age comedy," 37, 214n44
Madison, Oscar, 2

INDEX 263

"magically transformative capitalism," 67
Mälzel, Johann, 31
The Man in the Gray Flannel Suit (Wilson), 156
Mao, Douglas, 183
Marchant, William, 4, 20, 130, 131–38, 139–41, 143–46, 238n6, 242n31
marriage: comedy and, 75–76, 221n60, 221n63, 254n7; incorporation of technology in, 138–40; symbolizing conformity, 153, 154–55; symbolizing sociality, 130. *See also* coupling; romantic comedy
Marx, Karl, 222n65
Marx, Leo, 46
Marx, Nick, 218n13
masculinity, 109, 161–63, 248n61
McLuhan, Marshall, 246n57
McWilliams, Carey, 27
mechanical inelasticity, 36–40
Mechanical Turk (automaton), 31
Mechanix Illustrated, 40, 42
Medovoi, Leerom, 156–57
memetic humor, 115–18, *116*, *117*, 120–22
Meredith, George, 203n2
Microserfs (Coupland), 102–6, 109
Microsoft Corporation, 70–71, 88–89, 102–3
Milne, Esther, 67, 69
minstrelsy, 31–40, 124–25, 191–93, 254n5
Modern Times (1936), 37
A Modest Proposal (Swift), 111
Moore School Lectures, 171–72
Morgan, Andrew, 121
Morris, Max, 118
"Mr. Roboto" (Styx), 51–54, *52*

Ms. Dewey (search engine), 88–89
Murray, Sarah, 215n54
"My Flamboyant Grandson" (Saunders), 94–96, 126–28

Nakamura, Lisa, 122
natural space, transformation through, 64
Neill, John R., 34
Netflix, 191–94
networking paradigm, 56
New Hollywood era, 81, 222n67
"new media idiocy," 120
New Woman ideal, 135, 141, 242n25
Ngai, Sianne, 67, 140
Nights with Uncle Remus (Harris), 47, 48, *49*
Nineteen Eighty-Four (Orwell), 2
Noble, Greg, 50
Nolan, Christopher, 12–13
nominalist approaches to genre, 17–18, 209n52
nonconformity, 50–53. *See also* counterculture
nonsymbolic motion, 51–54
North, Michael, 36–37, 40
North by Northwest (1959), 6–7

Oak Ridge National Laboratory (ORNL), 167, 169, 170, 172
obsolescence: computerization of work, 131–38, 240n12, 240n17; of email, 67–68; of freedom, 176–77; human-machine comparisons, 167–72; of humans, 134, 179–85, 187; managing fears of, 4, 9–10, 11–12, 137–38, 141, 148; phenomenological, 194–96; of romantic love, 68, 73–77. *See also* absurdity
O'Connell, Lisa, 221n63
The Odd Couple (1965), 2

O'Mara, Margaret, 109
The Opposition (television series), 109
ordinariness: becoming computational and, 13–14, 77–78, 165–66, 189; comedy and, 1–3, 203n2. *See also* being generic
The Organization Man (Whyte), 155, 246n52
Orwell, George, 2
ostranenie (defamiliarization), 65, 219n28
"Over 9000" meme, 120–21
Ozma of Oz (Baum), 33–36, *34*, 37, 48, 124

Palmer, Jerry, 21, 169–70, 250n12, 250n15
Papert, Seymour, 206n35
Patti, Keaton, 192–93
performative rebellion, 53
peripeteia (surprise), 170, 188
personalization: email and, 86; within generic forms, 77–78; intelligent agents and, 87–93, 224n91, 225n97, 226n103; logic of, 57–59; self-alienation vs., 107–8
Peter Pilgrim (Bird), 29–30, 33
phenomenological obsolescence, 194–96
Phillips, Whitney, 121
Player Piano (Vonnegut), 122–25, 127, 132–33
"playing Indian," 124–25
politics: democracy and programmed happiness, 182–83; the "Great American Joke," 113, 233n61; potential obsolescence of democracy, 21–24; totalizing political regimes, 178–85, 187
Pooley, Jefferson D., 118
Poovey, Mary, 28

Pressman, Jessica, 234n69
Pride and Prejudice (Austen), 75
"principle of conversion," 134–35, 140–48
programmability, 107–8, 182–85. *See also* personalization
public vs. private: conformity and private life, 155; domestic privacy and labor, 141–44; in the marriage plot, 76; racist comedy and, 50; tensions around, 223n80
Punch-Drunk Love (2002), 62

quantum media, 206n33
queerness: as antisocial, 6–8, 12, 144–45, 188, 204n14, 237n103; as authenticity, 126–27; in the marriage plot, 76
quiet desperation, theme of, 63

race: automated servitude and minstrelsy, 31–40, *32*, *34*, *38*; black comedy and, 112; deracialized robots, 40–48, *42*; the "Great American Joke" and, 233n61; in the marriage plot, 76; nonsymbolic motion and, 48–54, *52*, 216n80; postracial imagery, 57, 217n6; "quantum media" and, 206n33; racial impersonation, 122–26, 236n96; slavery and automation, 27–31, 212n21; as technology, 211n9; techno-Orientalism, 25–27, *26*; "unruly Black woman" trope, 192, 253n2
"Rastus" (automaton), *38*, 38–40, 124
Rawlins, Gregory J. E., 31
rebelliousness, 156–59
recognition, desire for, 119–20, 122, 126
Reed, Ishmael, 21, 185–88

INDEX 265

religious thought, authenticity and, 228n9
reproductive futurism, 237n103
Resnikoff, Jason, 41–42
Ritchie, Graeme, 88
robots: Asian automatism trope, 50–54, *52*; deracialized, 40–48, *42*; "iron chink" canning device, 25–27, *26*; Katrina Van Televox, 39; Mechanical Turk, 31; "Rastus," *38*, 38–40; *Written Entirely by Bots* Netflix series, 191–94. *See also* artificial intelligence (AI)
The Romance of Business (Forbes), 145
romantic comedy: ambivalent forms of attachment, 78–87; coupling as social mechanism in, 3; as cultural templates, 73–78; defamiliarizing the familiar, 60–67, *62*, *64*, 219n28; email as metaphor in, 68–69; gimmick-proposals, 140–44; "principle of conversion" in, 134–35, 140–48; technology in the marriage plot, 138–40; written by AI, 191–92. *See also* coupling
Romantic Comedy (Sittenfeld), 65, 68–69, 73–77, 87, 221n63
Rossinow, Doug, 231n35
Rousseau, Jean-Jacques, 98–99, 100, 101, 106, 109–10, 120, 229n22
Rubin, Louis D., Jr., 113
R.U.R (1921), 40, 43–45
Ruskin, John, 142

Salisbury, Meredith, 118
Sanders, Bernie, 115–18, *117*
"Sarkozy Was There" meme, 115, *116*, 118
Sartre, Jean-Paul, 211n9
satire: comic cues and, 59; the "Great Tech-Industrial Joke," 106–14; irony, humor, and, 232n51; parody and, 218n14; of Silicon Valley, 102–6; of technological dependency, 100–102. *See also* comedy
Saunders, George, 72–73, 94–96, 126–28
Save Yourselves! (2020), 101
"The Scarred Man" (Benford), 9–10
Schopenhauer, Arthur, 87
Schulte, Stephanie Ricker, 90–91
Seabrook, John, 69–70, 73
Seeber, Robert R., 168
Selective Sequence Electronic Calculator (SSEC), 168
Selisker, Scott, 108, 109
Sellen, Abigail, 225n97
Seltzer, Mark, 246n55
sexism. *See* gender
Sex Kittens Go to College (1960), 149–51, 160
Sexual Behavior in the Human Male (Kinsey), 151
sexuality: authenticity and, 149–50, 165; computing and, 151–54; marketplace and, 243n33; sex with computers, 160–63, 247n59
Shakespeare, William, 60, 61, 64, 97, 227n3
Shifman, Limor, 115
Shklovsky, Viktor, 65
Sienkiewicz, Matt, 218n13
Sievers, Julie, 231n43
"A Sigh for Cybernetics" (Lamport), 11–12
Silicon Valley, 105–10
Silicon Valley (television series), 113–14
Silk, Michael, 208n47
Simon, Neil, 2
Siri (digital assistant), 89–90

Sittenfeld, Curtis, 65, 68–69, 73–77, 87
"The Six Stages of E-mail" (Ephron), 71–72
slavery: bondage narratives, 33–36, *34*, 37; dramatic allusions to, 43–45; human servitude, 174–77; mechanistic views of, 29–31, 40, 212n21
Slesar, Henry, 5–6, 9, 12
"smart" technologies, 88
Smialowski, Brendan, 116
Smith, Danez, 85
Smith Cannery Machines Company, 25, *26*
sociality: authenticity and, 99–106, 227n3, 228n11; being human and, 237n3; capitalism and, 144–46; comedy and, 203n3; computer mediation and social harmony, 145–48; conformity, 50–53, 103–4, 109, 152, 154–59; counterculture, 2, 103–5, 148–49, 156–59, 162–65, 231n35; happiness as unfreedom, 187–88; intersubjectivity and control, 160–63, 248n61; language of email and, 70–73; marriage symbolizing, 130; networked sociality, 110–11; phenomenological obsolescence, 194–96; social recognition, 119–20, 122, 126; social totality, 183–85; unsocial sociability, 86–87, 197. *See also* absurdity; authenticity; being generic; coupling; race
social media: authenticity, sociability, and, 100–102; reconfiguring the social, 110–11; staged authenticity and memetic humor, 114–22, *116*, *117*, 234n69
Solomon, William, 112
"Spacewar" (Brand), 103–4
Sproull, Lee, 71

staged authenticity, 96–97, 114–22, *116*, *117*, 234n69
Stanford University, 149
startup culture, 104–9
Stevenson, Adlai, 144
Stibitz, George, 171–72
Stock, Oliviero, 224n91
stock characters, 60–61, 66
Stowe, Harriet Beecher, 35–36
Strapparava, Carlo, 224n91
"structures of feeling," 16, 208n42
Styx (musical group), 51–54, *52*
subcultural trolling, 120–22, 235n85
Summit (supercomputer), 167
superiority theory of laughter, 211n9
surprise *(peripeteia)*, 170, 188
surveillance capitalism, 94–95, 112–13, 126, 226n103
Susman, Warren, 223n80
Sweeney, Miriam E., 89
Swift, Jonathan, 111
symbolic action, 51–54
synecdoche, 61

The Tale of the Big Computer (Johannesson), 21, 178–85, 186–88
Taylor, Charles, 230n25, 231n35, 253n40
techno-cultural entity, 110–11
technology: authenticity and, 94–97, 101–2, 151, 159; conflicting views of, 6; countercultural identity through, 103–5; decoupling of people from, 4–5, 173; embeddedness and ubiquity of, 16, 207n40; as extension of the self, 68–70, 219n39; fetishization of, 131, 151–54, 195, 238n5; as inauthentic, 36–37; justifying exploitation, 41–43; slavery and automation, 27–31; technologically induced servitude, 176–77

techno-Orientalism, 25–27, 26, 50–54
Tell Me a Joke (Alexa), 90, 91
Terminator (1984), 174
30 Rock (television series), 60–61, 66
Thoreau, Henry David, 63, 176, 252n25
Thorpe, Richard, 21, 148, 152–59, 165
THX 1138 (1971), 2
Time magazine, 55–56, 57
touristic experiences, 115, 122, 234n69
transcendentalism, 63
transgender women, 143–44
"Treatise on Man" (Descartes), 27–28
Trilling, Lionel, 100, 119, 122
trolling, subcultural, 120–22, 235n85
Truman, Harry S., 144
Turing, Alan, 129–30, 237n1
Turkle, Sherry, 220n55
The Two Gentlemen of Verona (Shakespeare), 64
2001: A Space Odyssey (1968), 2, 7

uncanniness, 7–9, 108, 185, 216n80
Uncanny Valley (Wiener), 106–10, 188, 232n51, 233n66
Uncle Remus (Harris), 38, 47
Uncle Tom's Cabin (Stowe), 35–36
Ungar, Felix, 2
Unplugged (Korman), 100–102, 230n23
"unruly Black woman" trope, 192, 253n2
unsocial sociability, 86–87, 188, 197
utopianism, 100–106, 148–49, 231n35. See also computopia

Von Kemplen, Wolfgang, 31
Vonnegut, Kurt, 6, 122–25, 127, 132–33

Walden (Thoreau), 176, 252n25
Watkins, Megan, 50
Watson, Thomas, Sr., 132

Weber, Max, 253n40
Weird Science (1985), 21, 148, 157–59, 160, 165, 246n57
Wernimont, Jacqueline, 206n33
Westinghouse electric company, 38–39, 124
Whyte, William H., 155, 156, 246n52
Wiener, Anna, 106–10, 188, 232n51, 233n66
Wiener, Norbert, 11–12
Wiggins, Chris, 181
Williams, Bernard, 100
Williams, Raymond, 208n42
Wilson, Sloan, 156
Winfrey, Oprah, 120–21
Wing, Jeanette, 14–15
Wittgenstein, Ludwig, 184
"women's culture," 80–82
work. See labor
World War II, 152
Written Entirely by Bots (Netflix series), 192–94

Y2K, 161–63, 247n60
Yellow Back Radio Broke-Down (Reed), 21, 185–88
"You'll Own 'Slaves' by 1965" (Binder), 40–41, 42, 195
youth culture: conformity and, 154–59; freedom vs. professional responsibility, 162–65; higher education and computing, 148–50, 245n44; sexuality and computation, 150–54
You've Got Mail (1998), 68, 78–87, 79, 83, 188, 222n65
Yu, Jessica, 50

Žižek, Slavoj, 7, 160–61
Zuboff, Shoshanna, 226n103
Zugsmith, Albert, 149–51, 160

www.ingramcontent.com/pod-product-compliance
Lightning Source LLC
Jackson TN
JSHW021332040625
85268JS00002B/2